THE GREAT
WRITERS
L I B R A R Y

ROBINSON CRUSOE

ROBINSON CRUSOE

DANIEL DEFOE

"I descended a little on the side of that delicious valley, surveying it with a secret kind of pleasure... to think that this was all my own; that I was king and lord of all this country indefeasibly, and had a right of possession; and, if I could convey it, I might have it in inheritance as completely as any lord of a manor in England."

Front cover: Crusoe's Island/Mansell Collection

This edition is the copyright © 1988 of Marshall Cavendish Ltd.

Published in 1988 for The Great Writers library by
Marshall Cavendish Ltd, 58 Old Compton Street, London W1V 5PA.
Printed and bound in Spain by Printer Industria Gráfica, Barcelona. D.L.B. 38917-1988
ISBN 0-86307-714-5

This is a facsimile reproduction of an edition published by
Associated Newspapers Ltd, London.

ROBINSON CRUSOE

CHAPTER I

I WAS born in the year 1632, in the city of York, of a good family, though not of that country, my father being a foreigner, of Bremen, who settled first at Hull; he got a good estate by merchandise, and leaving off his trade, lived afterward at York; from whence he had married my mother, whose relations were named Robinson, a very good family in that country, and from whom I was called Robinson Kreutznaer; but, by the usual corruption of words in England, we are now called, nay, we call ourselves, and write our name, Crusoe; and so my companions always called me.

I had two elder brothers, one of whom was lieutenant-colonel to an English regiment of foot in Flanders, formerly commanded by the famous Colonel Lockhart, and was killed at the battle near Dunkirk against the Spaniards. What became of my second brother I never knew, any more than my father or mother did know what was become of me.

Being the third son of the family, and not bred to any trade, my head began to be filled very early with rambling thoughts; my father, who was very ancient, had given me a competant share of learning, as far as house-education and a country free-school generally goes, and designed me for the law; but I would be satisfied with nothing but going to sea; and my inclination to this led me so strongly against the will, nay, the commands, of my father, and against all the entreaties and persuasions of my mother and other friends, that there seemed to be something fatal in that propension of nature, tending directly to the life of misery which was to befall me.

My father, a wise and grave man, gave me serious and excellent counsel against what he foresaw was my design. He called me one morning into his chamber, where he was confined by the gout, and expostulated very warmly with me upon this subject; he asked me what reasons, more than a mere wandering inclination, I had for leaving my father's house and my native country, where I might be well introduced, and had a prospect of raising my fortune by application and industry, with a life of ease and pleasure. He told me it was men of desperate fortunes on one hand, or of aspiring, superior fortunes on the other, who went abroad upon adventures, to rise by enterprise, and make themselves famous in undertakings of a nature out of the common road; that these things were all either too far above me or too far below me; that mine was the middle state, or what might be called the upper station of low life, which he had found by long experience was the best state in the world, the most suited to human happiness, not exposed to the miseries and hardships, the labour and sufferings of the mechanic part of mankind, and not embarrassed with the pride, luxury, ambition, and envy of the upper part of mankind. He told me, I might judge of the happiness of this state by this one thing, viz., that this was the state of life which all other people envied; that kings have frequently lamented the miserable consequence of being born to great things, and wished they had been placed in the middle of the two extremes, between the mean and the great; that the wise man gave his testimony to this, as the just standard of true felicity, when he prayed to have neither poverty nor riches.

He bade me observe it, and I should always find that the calamities of life were shared among the upper and lower part of mankind; but that the middle station had the fewest disasters, and was not exposed to so many vicissitudes as the higher or lower part of mankind; nay, they were not subjected to so many distempers and uneasinesses, either of body or mind, as those were who, by vicious living, luxury, and extravagances on one hand, or by hard labour, want of necessaries, and mean or insufficient diet on the other hand, bring distempers upon themselves by the natural consequences of their way of living; that the middle station of life was calculated for all kind of virtues and all kind of enjoyments; that peace and plenty were the handmaids of a middle fortune; that temperance, moderation, quietness, health, society, all agreeable diversions, and all desirable pleasures were the blessings attending the middle station of life; that this way men went silently and smoothly through the world, and comfortably out of it, not embarrassed with the labours of the hands or of the head, not sold to a life of slavery for daily bread, nor harassed with perplexed circumstances, which rob the soul of peace, and the body of rest; nor enraged with the passion of envy, nor the secret burning lust of ambition for great things; but, in easy circumstances, sliding gently through the world and sensibly tasting the sweets of living, without the bitter; feeling that they are happy and learning by every day's experience to know it more sensibly.

After this he pressed me earnestly, and in the most affectionate manner, not to play the young man, nor to precipitate myself into miseries which Nature, and the station of life I was born in, seemed to have provided against; that I was under no necessity of seeking my bread; that he would do well for me, and endeavour to enter me fairly into the station of life which he had just been recommending to me; and that if I was not very easy and happy in the world, it must be my mere fate or fault that must hinder it; and that he should have nothing to answer for, having thus discharged his duty in warning me against measures which he knew would be to my hurt; in a word, that as he would do very kind things for me, if I would stay and settle at home as he directed, so he would not have so much hand in my misfortunes as to give me any encouragement to go away; and to close all, he told me I had my elder brother for an example, to whom he had used the same earnest persuasions to keep him from going into the Low Country wars, but could not prevail, his young desires prompting him to run into the army, where he was killed; and though he said he would not cease to pray for me, yet he would venture to say to me, that if I did take this foolish step, God would not bless me, and I should have leisure hereafter to reflect upon having neglected his counsel, when there might be none to assist in my recovery.

I observed in this last part of his discourse, which was truly prophetic, though I suppose my father did not know it to be so himself—I say, I observed the tears run down his face very plentifully, especially when he spoke of my brother who was killed; and that when he spoke of my having leisure to repent, and none to assist me, he was so moved that he broke off the discourse, and told me his heart was so full he could say no more to me.

I was sincerely affected with this discourse, as indeed who could be otherwise? and I resolved not to think of going abroad any more, but to settle at home according to my father's desire. But, alas! a few days wore it all off; and, in short, to prevent any of my father's further importunities, in a few weeks after I resolved to run quite away from him. However, I did not act quite so hastily neither as the first heat of my resolution prompted, but I took my mother at a time when I thought her a little more pleasant than ordinary, and told her that my thoughts were so entirely bent upon seeing the world, that I should never settle to anything with resolution enough to go through with it, and my father had better give me his consent than force me to go without it; that I was now eighteen years old, which was too late to go apprentice to a trade, or clerk to an attorney; that I was sure, if I did, I should never serve out my time, but I should certainly run away from my master before my time was out, and go to sea; and if she would speak to my father to let me go one voyage abroad, if I came home again, and did not like it, I would go no more, and I would promise, by a double diligence, to recover the time that I had lost.

This put my mother into a great passion; she told me she knew it would be to no purpose to speak to my father upon any such subject; that he knew too well what was my interest to give his consent to anything so much for my hurt; and that she wondered how I could think of any such thing after the discourse I had had with my father, and such kind and tender expressions as she knew my father had used to me; and that, in short, if I would ruin myself, there was no help for me; but I might depend I should never have their consent to it; that for her part, she would not have so much hand in my destruction; and I should never have it to say that my mother was willing when my father was not.

Though my mother refused to move it to my father, yet I heard afterwards that she reported all the discourse to him, and that my father, after showing a great concern at it, said to her with a sigh: "That boy might be happy if he would stay at home, but if he goes abroad, he will be the most miserable wretch that ever was born; I can give no consent to it."

It was not till almost a year after this that I broke loose, though, in the mean time, I continued obstinately deaf to all proposals of settling to business, and frequently expostulated with my father and mother about their being so positively determined against what they knew my inclinations prompted me to. But being one day at Hull, whither I went casually, and without any purpose of making an elopement at that time; but I say, being there, and one of my companions being going by sea to London in his father's ship, and prompting me to go with them, with the common allurement of a seafaring man, that it should cost me nothing for my passage, I consulted neither father nor mother any more, nor so much as sent them word of it; but leaving them to hear of it as they might, without asking God's blessing, or my father's, without any consideration of circumstances or consequences, and in an ill hour, God knows, on the 1st of September, 1651, I went on board a ship bound for London. Never any young adventurer's misfortunes, I believe, began sooner or continued longer than mine. The ship was no sooner got out of the Humber than the wind began to blow, and the sea to rise in a most frightful manner; and, as I had never been at sea before, I was most inexpressibly sick in body and terrified in mind. I began now seriously to reflect upon what I had done, and how justly I was overtaken by the judgment of Heaven for my wicked leaving my father's house, and abandoning my duty. All the good counsels of my parents, my father's tears and my mother's entreaties, came now fresh into my mind; and my conscience, which was not yet come to the pitch of hardness to which it has come since, reproached me with the contempt of advice, and the breach of my duty to God and my father.

All this while the storm increased, and the sea went very high, though nothing like what I have seen many times since; no, nor what I saw a few days after; but it was enough to affect me then, who was but a young sailor, and had never known anything of the matter. I expected every wave would have swallowed us up, and that every time the ship fell down, as I thought it did, in the trough or hollow of the sea, we should never rise more: in this agony of mind I made many vows and resolutions, that if it would please God to spare my life in this one voyage, if ever I got once my foot upon dry land again, I would go directly home to my father, and never set it into a ship again while I lived; that I would take his advice, and never run myself into such miseries as these any more. Now I saw plainly the goodness of his observations about the middle station of life, how easy, how comfortable he had lived all his days, and never had been exposed to tempests at sea; or troubles on shore; and, in short, I resolved that I would, like a true, repenting prodigal, go home to my father.

These wise and sober thoughts continued all the while the storm lasted, and indeed some time after; but the next day the wind was abated and the sea calmer, and I began to be a little inured to it; however, I was very grave for all that day, being also a little seasick still; but towards night the weather cleared up, the wind was quite over, and a charming fine evening followed, the sun went down perfectly clear, and rose so the next morning; having little or no wind, and a smooth sea, the sun shining upon it, the sight was, as I thought, the most delightful that ever I saw.

I had slept well in the night, and was now no more sea-sick, but very cheerful, looking with wonder upon the sea that was so rough and terrible the day before, and could be so calm and so pleasant in so little a time after. And now, lest my good resolutions should continue, my companion, who had enticed me away, comes to me.

"Well, Bob," says he, clapping me upon the shoulder, "how do you do after it? I warrant you were frighted, wer'n't you, last night, when it blew but a capful of wind?"

"A capful, d'you call it?" said I; "'twas a terrible storm."

"A storm, you fool, you!" replies he; "do you call that a storm? why, it was nothing at all; give us but a good ship and sea-room, and we think nothing of such a squall of wind as that; but you're but a fresh-water sailor, Bob. Come, let us make a bowl of punch, and we'll forget all that; d'ye see what charming weather 'tis now?"

To make short this sad part of my story, we went the way of all sailors; the punch was made, and I was made half drunk with it; and in that one night's wickedness I drowned all my repentance, all my reflections upon my past conduct, all my resolutions for the future. In a word, as the sea was returned to its smoothness of surface and settled calmness by the abatement of that storm, so the hurry of my thoughts being over, my fears and apprehensions of being swallowed up by the sea being forgotten, and the current of my former desires returned, I entirely forgot the vows and promises that I made in my distress. I found, indeed, some intervals of reflection; and the serious thoughts did, as it were, endeavour to return again sometimes; but I shook them off, and roused myself from them as it were from a distemper, and applying myself to drinking and company, soon mastered the return of those fits, for so I called them; and I had, in five or six days, got as complete a victory over my conscience as any young fellow that resolved not to be troubled with it could desire. But I was to have another trial for it still; and Providence, as in such cases generally it does, resolved to leave me entirely without excuse; for if I would not take this for a deliverance, the next was to be such a one as the worst and most hardened wretch among us would confess both the danger and the mercy.

The sixth day of our being at sea we came into Yarmouth Roads; the wind having been contrary, and the weather calm, we had made but little way since the storm. Here we were obliged to come to an anchor, and here we lay, the wind continuing contrary, viz., at southwest, for seven or eight days, during which time a great many ships from Newcastle came into the same Roads, as the common harbour where the ships might wait for a wind for the river.

We had not, however, rid here so long, but we should have tided it up the river, but that the wind blew too fresh, and, after we had lain four or five days, blew very hard. However, the Roads being reckoned as good as an harbour, the anchorage good, and our ground-tackle very strong, our men were unconcerned, and not in the least apprehensive of danger, but spent the time in rest and mirth, after the manner of the sea; but the eighth day, in the morning, the wind increased, and we had all hands at work to strike our topmasts, and make everything snug and close, that the ship might ride as easy as possible. By noon the sea went very high indeed, and our ship rode forecastle in, shipped several seas, and we thought once or twice our anchor had come home; upon which our master ordered out the sheet-anchor so that we rode with two anchors ahead, and the cables veered out to the better end.

By this time it blew a terrible storm indeed; and now I began to see terror and amazement in the faces even of the seamen themselves. The master, though vigilant in the business of preserving the ship, yet as he went in and out of his cabin by me, I could hear him softly to himself say, several times, "Lord, be merciful to us! we shall all be lost! we shall be all undone!" and the like. During these first hurries I was stupid, lying still in my cabin, which was in the steerage, and cannot describe my temper. I could ill resume the first penitence which I had so apparently trampled upon, and hardened myself against: I thought the bitterness of death had been past, and that this would be nothing too, like the first; but when the master himself came by me, as I said just now, and said we should be all lost, I was dreadfully frightened. I got up out of my cabin, and looked out; but such a dismal sight I never saw; the sea ran mountains high, and broke upon us every three or four minutes. When I could look about, I could see nothing but distress round us; two ships that rode near us, we found, had cut their masts by the board, being deep laden; and our men cried out that a ship which rid about a mile ahead of us was foundered. Two more ships, being driven from their anchors, were run out of the Roads to sea, at all adventures, and that not with a mast standing. The light ships fared the best, as not so much labouring in the sea; but two or three of them drove, and came close by us, running away with only their spritsail out before the wind.

Toward evening the mate and boatswain begged the master of our ship to let them cut away the foremast, which he was very unwilling to do; but the boastwain protesting to him that if he did not, the ship would founder, he consented; and when they had cut away the foremast, the mainmast stood so loose, and shook the ship so much, they were obliged to cut that away also, and make a clear deck.

And one must judge what a condition I must be in at all this, who was but a young sailor, and who had been in such a fright before at but a little. But if I can express at this distance the thoughts I had about me at that time, I was in tenfold more horror of mind upon account of my former convictions, and the having returned from them to the resolutions I had wickedly taken at first, than I was at death itself; and these, added to the terror of the storm, put me into such a condition that I can by no words describe it. But the worst was not come yet; the storm continued with such fury, that the seamen themselves acknowledged they had never seen a worse. We had a good ship, but she was deep laden, and wallowed in the sea, so that the seamen every now and then cried out she would founder. It was my advantage in one respect, that I did not know what they meant by *founder*, till I inquired. However, the storm was so violent that I saw, what is not often seen, the master, the boatswain, and some others more sensible than the rest, at their prayers, and expecting every moment that the ship would go to the bottom. In the middle of the night, and under all the rest of our distresses, one of the men, that had been down to see, cried out we had sprung a leak; another said, there was four feet water in the hold. Then all hands were called to the pump. At that word, my heart, as I thought, died within me; and I fell backwards upon the side of my bed, where I sat, into the cabin. However, the men roused me, and told me that I, that was able to do nothing before, was as well able to pump as another; at which I stirred up, and went to the pump, and worked very heartily. While this was doing, the master seeing some light colliers, who, not able to ride out the storm, were obliged to slip, and run away to the sea, and would come near us, ordered to fire a gun as a signal of distress. I, who knew nothing what they meant, thought the ship had broken, or some dreadful thing happened. In a word, I was so surprised that I fell down in a swoon. As this was a time when everybody had his own life to think of, nobody minded me or what was become of me; but another man stepped up to the pump, and thrusting me aside with his foot, let me lie, thinking I had been dead; and it was a great while before I came to myself.

We worked on; but the water increasing in the hold, it was apparent that the ship would founder; and though the storm began to abate a little, yet as it was not possible she could swim till we might run into any port, so the master continued firing guns for help; and a light ship, who had rid it out just ahead of us, ventured a boat out to help us. It was with the utmost hazard the boat came near us; but it was impossible for us to get on board, or for the boat to lie as near the ship's side, till at last the men rowing very heartily, and venturing their lives to save ours, our men cast them a rope over the stern with a buoy to it, and then veered it out a great length, which they after much labour and hazard took hold of, and we hauled them close under our stern, and got all into their boat. It was to no purpose for them or us, after we were in the boat, to think of reaching to their own ship; so all agreed to let her drive, and only to pull her in towards shore as much as we could; and our master promised them, that if the boat was staved upon shore, he would make it good to their master: so partly rowing, and partly driving, our boat went away to the northward, sloping towards the shore almost as far as Winterton Ness.

We were not much more than a quarter of an hour out of our ship till we saw her sink, and then I understood for the first time what was meant by a ship foundering in the sea. I must acknowledge I had hardly eyes to look up when the seamen told me she was sinking; for from the moment that they rather put me into the boat, than that I might be said to go in, my heart was, as it were, dead within me, partly with fright, partly with horror of mind and the thoughts of what was yet before me.

While we were in this condition, the men yet labouring at the oar to bring the boat near the shore, we could see (when, our boat mounting the waves, we were able to see the shore) a great many people running along the strand, to assist us when we should come near; but we made but slow way towards the shore; nor were we able to reach the shore till, being past the lighthouse at Winterton, the shore falls off to the westward, towards Cromer, and so the land broke off a little the violence of the wind. Here we got in, and, though not without much difficulty, got all safe on shore, and walked afterwards on foot to Yarmouth, where, as unfortunate men, we were used with great humanity, as well by the magistrates of the town, who assigned us good quarters, as by particular merchants and owners of ships, and had money given us sufficient to carry us either to London or back to Hull, as we thought fit.

Had I now had the sense to have gone back to Hull, and have gone home, I had been happy, and my father, an emblem of our blessed Saviour's parable, had even killed the fatted calf for me; for hearing the ship I went away in was cast away at Yarmouth Roads, it was a great while before he had any assurances that I was not drowned.

But my ill fate pushed me on now with an obstinacy that nothing could resist; and though I had several times loud calls from my reason, and my more composed judgment, to go home, yet I had no power to do it. I know not what to call this, nor will I urge that it is a secret, overruling decree that hurries us on to be the instruments of our own destruction, even though it be before us, and that we rush upon it with our eyes open. Certainly, nothing but some such decreed unavoidable misery attending, and which it was impossible for me to escape, could have pushed me forward against the calm reasonings and persuasions of my most retired thoughts, and against two such visible obstructions as I had met with in my first attempt.

My comrade, who had helped to harden me before, and who was the master's son, was now less forward than I. The first time he spoke to me after we were at Yarmouth, which was not till two or three days, for we were separated in the town to several quarters; I say, the first time he saw me, it appeared his tone was altered; and looking very melancholy, and shaking his head, he asked me how I did, and telling his father who I was, and how I had come on this voyage only for a trial, in order to go farther abroad: his father turning to me with a very grave and concerned tone, "Young man," says he, "you ought never to go to sea any more; you ought to take this for a plain and visible token that you are not to be a seafaring man." "Why, sir," said I, "will you go to sea no more?" "That is another case," said he; "it is my calling, and therefore my duty; but as you made this voyage for a trial, you see what a taste Heaven has given you of what you are to expect if you persist. Perhaps this has all befallen us on your account, like Jonah in the ship of Tarshish. Pray," continues he, "what are you; and on what account did you go to sea?" Upon that I told him some of my story; at the end of which he burst out into a strange kind of passion: "What had I done," says he, "that such an unhappy wretch should come into my ship? I would not set my foot in the same ship with thee again for a thousand pounds." This indeed was, as I said, an excursion of his spirits, which were yet agitated by the sense of his loss, and was farther than he could have authority to go. However, he afterwards talked very gravely to me, exhorting me to go back to my father, and not tempt Providence to my ruin; telling me I might see a visible hand of Heaven against me. "And, young man," said he, "depend upon it, if you do not go back, wherever you go, you will meet with nothing but disasters and disappointments, till your father's words are fulfilled upon you."

We parted soon after, for I made him little answer, and I saw him no more; which way he went I know not. As for me, having some money in my pocket, I travelled to London by land; and there, as well as on the road, had many struggles with myself what course of life I should take, and whether I should go home or go to sea.

As to going home, shame opposed the best motions that offered to my thoughts; and it immediately occured to me how I should be laughed at among the neighbours, and should be ashamed to see, not my father and mother only, but even everybody else; from whence I have often since observed, how incongruous and irrational the common temper of mankind is, especially of youth, to that reason which ought to guide them in such cases, viz., that they are not ashamed to sin, and yet are ashamed to repent; not ashamed of the action for which they ought justly to be esteemed fools, but are ashamed of the returning, which only can make them be esteemed wise men.

In this state of life, however, I remained some time, uncertain what measures to take, and what course of life to lead. An irresistible reluctance to going home continued; and as I stayed a while, the remembrance of the distress I had been in wore off; and as that abated, the little motion I had in my desires to a return wore off with it, till at last I quite laid aside the thoughts of it, and looked out for a voyage.

That evil influence which carried me first away from my father's house, which hurried me into the wild and indigested notion of raising my fortune; and that impressed those conceits so forcibly upon me, as to make me deaf to all good advice, and to the entreaties and even the commands of my father: I say, the same influence, whatever it was, presented the most unfortunate of all enterprises to my view; and I went on board a vessel bound to the coast of Africa; or, as our sailors vulgarly call it, a voyage to Guinea.

It was my great misfortune that in all these adventures I did not ship myself as a sailor; when, though I might indeed have worked a little harder than ordinary, yet at the same time I should have learnt the duty and office of a foremast man, and in time might have qualified myself for a mate or lieutenant, if not for a master. But as it was always my fate to choose for the worse, so I did here; for having money in my pocket, and good clothes upon my back, I would always go on board in the habit of a gentleman; and so I neither had any business in the ship nor learnt to do any.

It was my lot first of all to fall into pretty good company in London, which does not always happen to such loose and misguided young fellows as I then was; the devil generally not omitting to lay some snare for them very early; but it was not so with me. I first got acquainted with the master of a ship who had been on the coast of Guinea; and who, having had very good success there, was resolved to go again; this captain taking a fancy to my conversation, which was not at all disagreeable at that time, hearing me say I had a mind to see the world, told me if I would go the voyage with him, I should be at no expense; I should be his messmate and his companion; and if I could carry anything with me, I should have all the advantage of it that the trade would admit; and perhaps I might meet with some encouragement.

I embraced the offer; and entering into a strict friendship with this captain, who was an honest, plain-dealing man, I went the voyage with him, and carried a small adventure with me, which, by the disinterested honesty of my friend the captain, I increased very considerably; for I carried about £40 in such toys and trifles as the captain directed me to buy. This £40 I had mustered together by the assistance of some of my relations whom I corresponded with, and who, I believe got my father, or at least my mother, to contribute so much as that to my first adventure.

This was the only voyage which I may say was successful

ROBINSON CRUSOE

in all my adventures, and which I owe to the integrity and
honesty of my friend the captain; under whom also I got
a competent knowledge of the mathematics and the rules
of navigation, learned how to keep an account of the ship's
course, take an observation, and in short, to understand
some things that were needful to be understood by a sailor;
for, as he took delight to instruct me, I took delight to learn;
and, in a word, this voyage made me both a sailor and a
merchant; for I brought home five pounds nine ounces
of gold-dust for my adventure, which yielded me in London,
at my return, almost £300; and this filled me with those
aspiring thoughts which have since so completed my ruin.

Yet even in this voyage I had my misfortunes too;
particularly, that I was continually sick, being thrown
into a violent calenture by the excessive heat of the climate;
our principal trading being on the coast, from the latitude
of fifteen degrees north, even to the line itself.

CHAPTER II

I WAS now set up for a Guinea trader; and my friend, to my great misfortune, dying soon after his arrival, I resolved to go the same voyage again, and I embarked in the same vessel with one who was his mate in the former voyage, and had now got the command of the ship. This was the unhappiest voyage that ever man made; for though I did not carry quite £100 of my new-gained wealth, so that I had £200 left which I had lodged with my friend's widow, who was very just to me, yet I fell into terrible misfortunes in this voyage; and the first was this, viz., our ship making her course towards the Canary Islands, or rather between those Islands and the African shore, was surprised in the gray of the morning by a Moorish rover of Sallee, who gave chase to us with all the sail she could make. We crowded also as much canvas as our yards would spread, or our masts carry, to have got clear; but finding the pirate gained upon us, and would certainly come up with us in a few hours, we prepared to fight; our ship having twelve guns, and the rogue eighteen. About three in the afternoon he came up with us, and bringing to, by mistake, just athwart our quarter, instead of athwart our stern, as he intended, we brought eight of our guns to bear on that side, and poured in a broadside upon him, which made him sheer off again, after returning our fire, and pouring in also his small shot from near two hundred men which he had on board. However, we had not a man touched, all our men keeping close. He prepared to attack us again, and we to defend ourselves; but laying us on board the next time upon our other quarter, he entered sixty men upon our decks, who immediately fell to cutting and hacking the sails and rigging. We plied them with small-shot, half-pikes, powder-chests, and such like, and cleared our deck of them twice. However, to cut short this melancholy part of my story, our ship being disabled, and three of our men killed, and eight wounded, we were obliged to yield, and were carried all prisoners into Sallee, a port belonging to the Moors.

The usage I had there was not so dreadful as at first I apprehended; nor was I carried up the country to the emperor's court, as the rest of our men were, but was kept by the captain of the rover as his proper prize, and made his slave, being young and nimble, and fit for his business. At this surprising change of my circumstances, from a merchant to a miserable slave, I was perfectly overwhelmed; and now I looked back upon my father's prophetic discourse to me, that I should be miserable and have none to relieve me; which I thought was now so effectually brought to pass that I could not be worse; for now the hand of Heaven had overtaken me, and I was undone without redemption. But, alas! this was but a taste of the misery I was to go through, as will appear in the sequel of this story.

As my new patron, or master, had taken me home to his house, so I was in hopes that he would take me with him when he went to sea again, believing that it would some time or other be his fate to be taken by a Spanish or Portuguese man-of-war; and that then I should be set at liberty. But this hope of mine was soon taken away; for when he went to sea, he left me on the shore to look after his little garden, and do the common drudgery of slaves about his house; and when he came home again from his cruise, he ordered me to lie in the cabin to look after the ship.

Here I meditated nothing but my escape, and what method I might take to effect it; but found no way that had the least probability in it; nothing presented to make the supposition of it rational; for I had nobody to communicate it to that would embark with me; no fellow-slave, no Englishman, Irishman, or Scotsman there but myself;

so that for two years, though I often pleased myself with the imagination, yet I never had the least encouraging prospect of putting it in practice.

After about two years, an odd circumstance presented itself, which put the old thought of making some attempt for my liberty again in my head. My patron lying at home longer than usual without fitting out his ship, which, as I heard, was for want of money, he used, constantly, once or twice a week, sometimes oftener, if the weather was fair, to take the ship's pinnace, and go out into the road a-fishing; and as he always took me and a young Moresco with him to row the boat, we made him very merry, and I proved very dexterous in catching fish; insomuch that sometimes he would send me with a Moor, one of his kinsmen, and the youth the Moresco, as they called him, to catch a dish of fish for him.

It happened one time, that going a-fishing with him in a calm morning, a fog rose so thick, that though we were not half a league from the shore, we lost sight of it; and rowing we knew not whither or which way, we laboured all day, and all the next night; and when the morning came, we found we had pulled out to sea instead of pulling in for the shore; and that we were at least two leagues from the land. However, we got well in again, though with a great deal of labour, and some danger; for the wind began to blow pretty fresh in the morning; but particularly we were all very hungry.

But our patron, warned by this disaster, resolved to take more care of himself for the future; and having lying by him the long-boat of our English ship which he had taken, he resolved he would not go a-fishing any more without a compass and some provision; so he ordered the carpenter of his ship, who also was an English slave, to build a little state-room, or cabin, in the middle of the long-boat, like that of a barge, with a place to stand behind it to steer and haul home the main-sheet; and room before for a hand or two to stand and work the sails.

She sailed with what we called a shoulder-of-mutton sail; and the boom jibbed over the top of the cabin, which lay very snug and low, and had in it room for him to lie, with a slave or two, and a table to eat on, with some small lockers to put in some bottles of such liquor as he thought fit to drink; and particularly his bread, rice, and coffee.

We went frequently out with this boat a-fishing; and as I was most dexterous to catch fish for him, he never went without me. It happened that he had appointed to go out in this boat, either for pleasure or for fish, with two or three Moors of some distinction in that place, and for whom he had provided extraordinarily, and had therefore sent on board the boat overnight a larger store of provisions than usual; and had ordered me to get ready three fusils with powder and shot, which were on board his ship, for that they designed some sport of fowling as well as fishing.

I got all things ready as he had directed; and waited the next morning with the boat washed clean, her ancient and pendants out, and everything to accommodate his guests; when by and by my patron came on board alone, and told me his guests had put off going, from some business that fell out, and ordered me, with the man and boy, as usual, to go out with the boat and catch them some fish, and that his friends were to sup at his house; he commanded me too, that as soon as I had got some fish, I should bring it home to his house: all which I prepared to do.

This moment my former notions of deliverance darted into my thoughts, for now I found I was likely to have a little ship at my command; and my master being gone, I prepared to furnish myself, not for fishing business, but for a voyage; though I knew not, neither did I so much as consider, whither I would steer; for anywhere to get out of that place was my desire.

My first contrivance was to make a pretence to speak to this Moor, to get something for our subsistence on board;

for I told him we must not presume to eat of our patron's bread.

He said that was true; so he brought a large basket of rusk or biscuit of their kind, and three jars with fresh water, into the boat. I knew where my patron's case of bottles stood, which it was evident, by the make, were taken out of some English prize, and I conveyed them into the boat while the Moor was on shore, as if they had been there before for our master. I conveyed also a great lump of beeswax into the boat, which weighed about half an hundred-weight, with a parcel of twine or thread, a hatchet, a saw, and a hammer, all of which were of great use to us afterwards, especially the wax to make candles. Another trick I tried upon him, which he innocently came into also; his name was Ismael, which they call Muley, or Moely; so I called to him: "Moely," said I, "our patron's guns are all on board the boat; can you not get a little powder and shot? It may be we may kill some alcamies (a fowl like our curlews) for ourselves, for I know he keeps the gunner's stores in the ship." "Yes," says he, "I'll bring some"; accordingly, he brought a great leather pouch, which held about a pound and a half of powder, or rather more; and another with shot, that had five or six pounds, with some bullets, and put all into the boat. At the same time, I had found some powder of my master's in the great cabin, with which I filled one of the large bottles in the case, which was almost empty, pouring what was in it into another; and thus furnished with everything needful, we sailed out of the port to fish. The castle, which is at the entrance of the port, knew who we were, and took no notice of us; and we were not above a mile out of the port before we hauled in our sail, and sat us down to fish. The wind blew from the N.N.E., which was contrary to my desire; for had it blown southerly, I had been sure to have made the coast of Spain, and at least reached to the bay of Cadiz; but my resolutions were, blow which way it would, I would be gone from that horrid place where I was, and leave the rest to fate.

After we had fished some time and caught nothing, for when I had fish on my hook I would not pull them up, that he might not see them, I said to the Moor, "This will not do; our master will not be thus served; we must stand farther off." He, thinking no harm, agreed, and, being in the head of the boat, set the sails; and, as I had the helm, I ran the boat out near a league farther, and then brought her to as if I would fish; when, giving the boy the helm, I stepped forward to where the Moor was, and making as if I stooped for something behind him, I took him by surprise with my arm under his waist, and tossed him clear overboard into the sea.

He rose immediately, for he swam like a cork, and called to me, begged to be taken in, telling me he would go all over the world with me. He swam so strong after the boat, that he would have reached me very quickly, there being but little wind; upon which I stepped into the cabin, and fetching one of the fowling-pieces, I presented it at him and told him I had done him no hurt, and if he would be quiet I would do him none. "But," said I, "you swim well enough to reach the shore, and the sea is calm; make the best of your way to shore, and I will do you no harm; but if you come near the boat, I'll shoot you through the head, for I am resolved to have my liberty." So he turned himself about, and swam for the shore, and I make no doubt but he reached it with ease, for he was an excellent swimmer.

I could have been content to have taken this Moor with me, and have drowned the boy, but there was no venturing to trust him. When he was gone, I turned to the boy, whom they called Xury, and said to him, "Xury, if you will be faithful to me, I'll make you a great man; but if you will not stroke your face to be true to me," that is, swear by Mahomet and his father's beard, I must throw you into the sea too." The boy smiled in my face, and spoke so innocently that I could not mistrust him, and swore to be faithful to me and go all over the world with me.

While I was in the view of the Moor that was swimming, I stood out directly to sea, with the boat rather stretching to windward, that they might think me gone towards the Strait's mouth (as indeed any one that had been in their wits must have been supposed to do); for who would have supposed we were sailing on to the southward to the truly barbarian coast, where whole nations of negroes were sure to surround us with their canoes, and destroy us; where we could never once go on shore but we should be devoured by savage beasts, or more merciless savages of human kind?

But as soon as it grew dusk in the evening, I changed my course, and steered directly south and by east, bending my course a little towards the east, that I might keep in with the shore; and, having a fair fresh gale of wind, and a smooth, quiet sea, I made such sail that I believe by the next day at three o'clock in the afternoon, when I first made the land, I could not be less than one hundred and fifty miles south of Sallee; quite beyond the Emperor of Morocco's dominions, or indeed of any other king thereabouts, for we saw no people.

Yet such was the fright I had taken at the Moors, and the dreadful apprehensions I had of falling into their hands, that I would not stop, or go on shore, or come to an anchor, the wind continuing fair, till I had sailed in that manner five days; and then, the wind shifting to the southward, I concluded also that if any of our vessels were in chase of me, they also would now give over; so I ventured to make to the coast, and came to an anchor in the mouth of a little river, I knew not what nor where; neither what latitude, what country, what nation, or what river. I neither saw, nor desired to see any people; the principal thing I wanted was fresh water. We came into this creek in the evening, resolving to swim on shore as soon as it was dark, and discover the country; but as soon as it was quite dark, we heard such dreadful noises of the barking, roaring, and howling of wild creatures, of which we knew not what kinds, that the poor boy was ready to die with fear, and begged of me not to go on shore till day. "Well, Xury," said I, "then I won't; but it may be we may see men by day, who will be as bad to us as those lions." "Then we give them the shoot gun," says Xury, laughing, "make them run wey." Such English Xury spoke by conversing among us slaves. However, I was glad to see the boy so cheerful, and I gave him a dram (out of our patron's case of bottles) to cheer him up. After all, Xury's advice was good, and I took it: we dropped our little anchor, and lay still all night; I say still, for we slept none; for in two or three hours we saw vast great creatures (we knew not what to call them), of many sorts, come down to the seashore, and run into the water, wallowing and washing themselves for the pleasure of cooling themselves; and they made such hideous howlings and yellings that I never indeed heard the like.

Xury was dreadfully frighted, and indeed so was I too; but we were both more frighted when we heard one mighty creature come swimming toward out boat: we could not see him, but we might hear him by his blowing to be a monstrous, huge, and furious beast. Xury said it was a lion, and it might be so for aught I know; but poor Xury cried to me to weigh the anchor and row away. "No," says I, "Xury; we can slip our cable, with the buoy to it, and go to sea; they cannot follow us far." I had no sooner said so, but I perceived the creature, whatever it was, within two oars' length, which something surprised me; however, I immediately stepped to the cabin-door, and taking up my gun, fired at him; upon which he immediately turned about, and swam towards the shore again.

But it is impossible to describe the horrid noises, and hideous cries and howlings that were raised, as well upon the edge of the shore as higher within the country, upon the noise or report of a gun, a thing I have some reason to believe those creatures had never heard before. This convinced me that there was no going on shore for us in the night upon that coast; and how to venture on shore in the day was another question too; for to have fallen into the hands of any of the savages had been as bad as to have fallen into the paws of lions and tigers; at least we were equally apprehensive of the danger of it.

Be that as it would, we were obliged to go on shore somewhere or other for water, for we had not a pint left in the boat; when or where to get it was the point. Xury said, if I would let him go on shore with one of the jars, he would find if there was any water, and bring some to me. I asked him why he would go? why I should not go, and he stay in the boat? The boy answered with such affection that it made me love him ever after. Says he, "If wild mans come, they eat me, you go wey." "Well, Xury," said I, "we will both go, and if the wild mans come, we will kill them, they shall eat neither of us." So I gave Xury a piece of rusk-bread to eat, and a dram out of our patron's case of bottles which I mentioned before; and we hauled the boat in as near the shore as we thought was proper, and waded on shore, carrying nothing but our arms and two jars for water.

I did not care to go out of sight of the boat, fearing the coming of canoes with savages down the river; but the boy, seeing a low place about a mile up the country, rambled to it, and by and by I saw him come running towards me. I thought he was pursued by some savage, or frighted with some wild beast, and I ran forward towards him to help him; but when I came nearer to him I saw something hanging over his shoulders, which was a creature that he had shot, like a hare, but different in colour, and longer legs; however, we were very glad of it, and it was very good meat; but the great joy poor Xury came with, was to tell me he had found good water, and seen no wild mans.

But we found afterwards that we need not take such pains for water, for a little higher up the creek where we were we found the water fresh when the tide was out, which flows but a little way up; so we filled our jars, and feasted on the hare we had killed, and prepared to go on our way, having seen no footsteps of any human creature in that part of the country.

As I had been one voyage to this coast before, I knew very well that the islands of the Canaries, and the Cape de Verde Islands also, lay not far off from the coast. But as I had no instruments to take an observation to know what latitude we were in, and did not exactly know, or at least not remember, what latitude they were in, I knew not where to look for them, or when to stand off to sea towards them; otherwise I might now easily have found some of these islands. But my hope was, that if I stood along this coast till I came to that part where the English traded, I should find some of their vessels upon their usual design of trade, that would relieve and take us in.

By the best of my calculation, that place where I now was must be that country which, lying between the Emperor of Morocco's dominions and the negroes, lies waste and uninhabited, except by wild beasts; the negroes having abandoned it, and gone farther south, for fear of the Moors; and the Moors not thinking it worth inhabiting, by reason of its barrenness; and indeed both forsaking it because of the prodigious numbers of tigers, lions, leopards, and other furious creatures which harbour there; so that the Moors use it for their hunting only, where they go like an army, two or three thousand men at a time: and indeed, for near a hundred miles together upon this coast, we saw nothing but a waste uninhabited country by day, and heard nothing but howlings and roarings of wild beasts by night.

Once or twice in the day-time, I thought I saw the Pico of Teneriffe, being the high top of the mountain Teneriffe in the Canaries; and had a great mind to venture out, in hopes of reaching thither; but having tried twice, I was forced in again by contrary winds, the sea also going too high for my little vessel; so I resolved to pursue my first design, and keep along the shore.

Several times I was obliged to land for fresh water, after we had left this place; and once in particular, being early in the morning, we came to an anchor under a little point of land, which was pretty high; and the tide beginning to flow, we lay still to go farther in. Xury, whose eyes were more about him than it seems mine were, calls softly to me, and tells me that we had best go farther off the shore; "for," says he, "look, yonder lies a dreadful monster on the side of that hillock, fast asleep." I looked where he pointed, and saw a dreadful monster indeed, for it was a terrible great lion that lay on the side of the shore, under the shade of a piece of a hill that hung as it were a little over him. "Xury," says I, "you shall go on shore and kill him." Xury looked frighted and said, "Me kill? he eat me at one mouth"—one mouthful he meant. However, I said no more to the boy, but bade him be still, and took our biggest gun, which was almost musket-bore, and loaded it with a good charge of powder, and with two slugs, and laid it down; then I loaded another gun with two bullets; and the third (for we had three pieces) I loaded with five smaller bullets. I took the best aim I could with the first piece to have shot him in the head, but he lay so, with his leg raised a little above his nose, that the slugs hit his leg about the knee, and broke the bone. He started up, growling at first, but finding his leg broke, fell down again; and then got up upon three legs, and gave the most hideous roar that ever I heard. I was a little surprised that I had not hit him on the head; however, I took up the second piece immediately, and though he began to move off, fired again, and shot him in the head, and had the pleasure to see him drop; and making but little noise, he lay struggling for life. Then Xury took heart, and would have me let him go on shore.

"Well, go," said I; so the boy jumped into the water, and taking the little gun in one hand, swam to shore with the other hand, and coming close to the creature, put the muzzle of the piece to his ear, and shot him in the head again, which dispatched him quite.

This was game indeed to us, but this was no food; and I was very sorry to lose three charges of powder and shot upon a creature that was good for nothing to us. However, Xury said he would have some of him; so he came on board, and asked me to give him the hatchet. "For what, Xury?" said I. "Me cut off his head," said he. However, Xury could not cut off his head, but he cut off a foot, and brought it with him, and it was a monstrous great one.

I bethought myself, however, that perhaps the skin of him might, one way or other, be of some value to us; and I resolved to take off his skin if I could. So Xury and I went to work with him; but Xury was much the better workman at it, for I knew very ill how to do it. Indeed, it took us both the whole day, but at last we got off the hide of him, and spreading it on the top of our cabin, the sun effectually dried it in two days' time, and it afterwards served me to lie upon.

After this stop, we made on to the southward continually for ten or twelve days, living very sparingly on our provisions, which began to abate very much, and going no oftener into the shore than we were obliged to for fresh water. My design in this was to make the River Gambia or Senegal; that is to say, anywhere about the Cape de Verde, where I was in hopes to meet with some European ship; and if I did not, I knew not what course I had to take, but to seek for the islands, or perish there among the negroes. I knew that all the ships from Europe which sailed either to the coast of Guinea or to Brazil, or to the East Indies, made this cape, or those islands; and, in a word, I put the whole of my fortune upon this single point, either that I must meet with some ship, or must perish.

When I had pursued this resolution about ten days longer, as I have said, I began to see that the land was inhabited; and in two or three places, as we sailed by, we saw people stand upon the shore to look at us; we could also perceive they were quite black, and stark naked. I was once inclined to have gone on shore to them; but Xury was my better counsellor, and said to me, "No go, no go." However, I hauled in nearer the shore that I might talk to them, and I found they ran along the shore by me a good way: I observed they had no weapons in their hands, except one, who had a long slender stick, which Xury said was a lance, and that they could throw them a great way with good aim; so I kept at a distance, but talked with them by signs as well as I could; and particularly made signs for something to eat: they beckoned to me to stop my boat, and they would fetch me some meat. Upon this, I lowered the top of my sail, and lay by, and two of them ran up into the country, and in less than half an hour came back, and brought with them two pieces of dried flesh and some corn, such as is the produce of their country; but we neither knew what the one nor the other was: however, we were willing to accept it, but how to come at it was our next dispute, for I would not venture on shore to them, and they were as much afraid of us: but they took a safe way for us all, for they brought it to the shore and laid it down, and went and stood a great way off till we fetched it on board, and then came close to us again.

We made signs of thanks to them, for we had nothing to make them amends; but an opportunity offered that very instant to oblige them wonderfully; for while we were lying on the shore, came two mighty creatures, one pursuing the other (as we took it) with great fury from the mountains towards the sea; whether it was the male pursuing the female, or whether they were in sport or in rage, we could not tell, any more than we could tell whether it was usual or strange: but I believe it was the latter; because, in the first place, these ravenous creatures seldom appear but in the night; and, in the second place, we found the people terribly frighted, especially the women. The man that had the lance or dart did not fly from them, as the rest did; however, as the two creatures ran directly into the water, they did not offer to fall upon any of the negroes, but plunged themselves into the sea, and swam about, as if they had come for their diversion: at last one of them began to come nearer our boat than at first I expected; but I lay ready for him, for I had loaded my gun with all possible expedition, and bade Xury load both the others. As soon as he came fairly within my reach, I fired, and shot him directly in the head; immediately he sank down into the water, but rose instantly, and plunged up and down, as if he was struggling for life, and so indeed he was; he immediately made to the shore; but between the wound, which was his mortal hurt, and the strangling of the water, he died just before he reached the shore.

It is impossible to express the astonishment of these poor creatures at the noise and fire of my gun; some of them were ready even to die for fear, and fell down as dead with the very terror. But when they saw the creature dead, and sunk into the water, and that I made signs to them to come to the shore, they took heart and began to search for the creature. I found him by his blood staining the water: and by the help of a rope, which I slung round him, and gave the negroes to haul, they dragged him on shore, and found that it was a most curious leopard, spotted, and fine to an admirable degree; and the negroes held up their hands with admiration, to think what it was I killed him with.

The other creature, frighted with the flash of fire and the noise of the gun, swam to the shore, and ran up directly to the mountains from whence they came; nor could I at that distance know what it was. I found quickly the negroes were for eating the flesh of this creature, so I was willing to have them take it as a favour from me; which, when I made signs to them that they might take it, they were very thankful for. Immediately they fell to work with him; and though they had no knife, yet, with a sharpened piece of wood, they took off his shin as readily, and much more readily, than we would have done with a knife. They offered me some of the flesh, which I declined, making as if I would give it them; but made signs for the skin, which they gave me very freely, and brought me a great deal more of their provision, which, though I did not understand, yet I accepted. Then I made signs to them for some water, and held out one of my jars to them, turning its bottom upward, to show that it was empty, and that I wanted to have it filled. They called immediately to some of their friends, and there came two women, and brought a great vessel made of earth, and burnt as I suppose in the sun; this they set down for me, as before, and I sent Xury on shore with my jars, and filled them all three. The women were as stark naked as the men.

I was now furnished with roots and corn, such as it was, and water; and leaving my friendly negroes, I made forward for about eleven days more, without offering to go near the shore, till I saw the land run out a great length into the sea, at about the distance of four or five leagues before me; and the sea being very calm, I kept a large offing to make this point. At length, doubling the point at about two leagues from the land, I saw plainly land on the other side, to seaward; then I concluded, as it was most certain indeed, that this was the Cape de Verde, and those the islands called, from thence, Cape de Verde Islands. However, they were at a great distance, and I could not well tell what I had best do; for if I should be taken with a fresh gale of wind, I might neither reach one nor other.

In this dilemma, as I was very pensive, I stepped into the cabin, and sat me down, Xury having the helm; when, on a sudden, the boy cried out, "Master, master, a ship with a sail!" and the foolish boy was frighted out of his wits, thinking it must needs be some of his master's ships sent to pursue us, when I knew we were gotten far enough out of their reach. I jumped out of the cabin, and immediately saw, not only the ship, but that it was a Portuguese ship; and, as I thought, was bound to the coast of Guinea, for negroes. But, when I observed the course she steered, I was soon convinced they were bound some other way, and did not design to go any nearer the shore: upon which I stretched out to the sea as much as I could, resolving to speak with them if possible.

With all the sail I could make, I found I should not be able to come in their way, but that they would be gone by before I could make any signal to them: but after I had crowded to the utmost, and began to despair, they, it seems, saw me by the help of their perspective glasses, and that it was some European boat, which they supposed must belong to some ship that was lost; so they shortened sail to let me come up. I was encouraged with this, and as I had my patron's ancient on board, I made a waft of it to them for a signal of distress, and fired a gun, both which they saw; or they told me they saw the smoke, though they did not hear the gun. Upon these signals they very kindly brought to, and lay by for me; and in about three hours' time I came up with them.

They asked me what I was, in Portuguese, and in Spanish, and in French, but I understood none of them; but at last a Scotch sailor, who was on board, called to me: and I answered him, and told him I was an Englishman, that had made my escape out of slavery from the Moors at Sallee; they then bade me come on board, and very kindly took me in, and all my goods.

It was an inexpressible joy to me, which any one will believe, that I was thus delivered, as I esteemed it, from such a miserable and almost hopeless condition as I was in; and I immediately offered all I had to the captain of the ship, as a return for my deliverance; but he generously told me he would take nothing from me, but that all I had should be delivered safe to me, when I came to the

Brazils. "For," says he, "I have saved your life on no other terms than as I would be glad to be saved myself; and it may, one time or other, be my lot to be taken up in the same condition. Besides," says he, "when I carry you to the Brazils, so great a way from your own country, if I should take from you what you have, you will be starved there, and then I only take away that life I have given. No, no," says he; "Seignor Inglese (Mr. Englishman), I will carry you thither in charity, and these things will help you to buy your subsistence there, and your passage home again."

CHAPTER III

AS he was charitable in this proposal, so he was just in the performance to a tittle; for he ordered the seamen that none should offer to touch anything I had: then he took everything into his own possession, and gave me back an exact inventory of them, that I might have them, even to my three earthen jars.

As to my boat, it was a very good one; and that he saw, and told me he would buy it of me for the ship's use; and asked me what I would have for it. I told him, he had been so generous to me in everything, that I could not offer to make any price of the boat, but left it entirely to him: upon which, he told me he would give me a note of his hand to pay me eighty pieces of eight for it at Brazil; and when it came there, if any one offered to give more, he would make it up. He offered me also sixty pieces of eight for my boy Xury, which I was loath to take; not that I was unwilling to let the captain have him, but I was very loath to sell the poor boy's liberty, who had assisted me so faithfully in procuring my own. However, when I let him know my reason, he owned it to be just, and offered me this medium, that he would give the boy an obligation to set him free in ten years, if he turned Christian: upon this, and Xury saying he was willing to go to him, I let the captain have him.

We had a very good voyage to the Brazils, and I arrived in the Bay de Todos los Santos, or All Saints Bay, in about twenty-two days after. And now I was once more delivered from the most miserable of all conditions of life; and what to do next with myself I was to consider.

The generous treatment the captain gave me, I can never enough remember: he would take nothing of me for my passage, gave me twenty ducats for the leopard's skin, and forty for the lion's skin, which I had in my boat, and caused everything I had in the ship to be punctually delivered to me; and what I was willing to sell, he bought of me: such as the case of bottles, two of my guns, and a piece of the lump of beeswax, for I had made candles of the rest; in a word, I made about two hundred and twenty pieces of eight of all my cargo; and with this stock I went on shore in the Brazils.

I had not been long here, but being recommended to the house of a good, honest man, like himself, who had an *ingenio*, as they call it (that is, a plantation and a sugar-house), I lived with him some time, and acquainted myself, by that means, with the manner of their planting and making of sugar; and seeing how well the planters lived, and how they got rich suddenly, I resolved, if I could get a licence to settle there, I would turn planter among them; resolving in the meantime, to find out some way to get my money, which I had left in London, remitted to me. To this purpose, getting a kind of letter of naturalisation, I purchased as much land that was uncured as my money would reach, and formed a plan for my plantation and settlement; such a one as might be suitable to the stock which I proposed to myself to receive from England.

I had a neighbour, a Portuguese, of Lisbon, but born of English parents, whose name was Wells, and in much such circumstances as I was. I call him neighbour, because his plantation lay next to mine, and we went on very sociably together. My stock was but low, as well as his; and we rather planted for food than anything else, for about two years. However, we began to increase, and our land began to come into order; so that the third year we planted some tobacco, and made each of us a large piece of ground ready for planting canes in the year to come; but we both wanted help; and now I found, more than before, I had done wrong in parting with my boy Xury.

But, alas! for me to do wrong that never did right, was no great wonder. I had no remedy but to go on; I had got into an employment quite remote to my genius and directly contrary to the life I delighted in, and for which I forsook my father's house, and broke through all his good advice; nay, I was coming into the very middle station, or upper degree of low life, which my father advised me to before, and which, if I resolved to go on with, I might as well have stayed at home, and never fatigued myself in the world, as I have done; and I used often to say to myself, "I could have done this as well in England, among my friends, as have gone five thousand miles off to do it among strangers and savages, in a wilderness, and at such a distance as never to hear from any part of the world that had the least knowledge of me."

In this manner I used to look upon my condition with the utmost regret. I had nobody to converse with, but now and then this neighbour; no work to be done, but by the labour of my hands; and I used to say, I lived just like a man cast away upon some desolate island, that had nobody there but himself. But how just has it been! and how should all men reflect, that when they compare their present conditions with others that are worse, Heaven may oblige them to make the exchange, and be convinced of their former felicity by their experience: I say, how just has it been, that the truly solitary life I reflected on, in an island, or mere desolation, should be my lot, who had so often unjustly compared it with the life which I then led, in which, had I continued, I had, in all probability, been exceeding prosperous and rich.

I was, in some degree, settled in my measures for carrying on the plantation, before my kind friend, the captain of the ship that took me up at sea, went back; for the ship remained there, in providing her lading, and preparing for the voyage, near three months; when, telling him what little stock I had left behind me in London, he gave me this friendly and sincere advice: "Seignor Inglese," says he (for so he always called me), "if you will give me letters, and a procuration in form to me, with orders to the person who has your money in London, to send your effects to Lisbon, to such persons as I shall direct, and in such goods as are proper for this country, I will bring you the produce of them, God willing, at my return; but, since human affairs are all subject to changes and disasters, I would have you give orders but for one hundred pounds sterling, which, you say, is half your stock, and let the hazard be run for the first; so that, if it come safe, you may order the rest the same way; and if it miscarry, you may have the other half to have recourse to for your supply."

This was so wholesome advice, and looked so friendly, that I could not but be convinced it was the best course I could take; so I accordingly prepared letters to the person with whom I had left my money, and a procuration to the Portuguese captain, as he desired.

I wrote the English captain's widow a full account of all my adventures, my slavery, escape and how I had met with the Portuguese captain at sea, the humanity of his behaviour, and what condition I was now in, with all other necessary directions for my supply; and when this honest captain came to Lisbon, he found means, by some of the English merchants there, to send over not the order only, but a full account of my story, to a merchant in London, who represented it effectually to her; whereupon she not only delivered the money, but out of her own pocket sent the Portugal captain a very handsome present for his humanity and charity to me.

The merchant in London vested this hundred pounds in English goods, such as the captain had written for, sent them directly to him at Lisbon, and he brought them all safe to me to the Brazils; among which, without my direction (for I was too young in my business to think of them), he had taken care to have all sorts of tools, iron work, and utensils necessary for my plantation, and which were of great use to me.

When this cargo arrived, I thought my fortune made; for I was surprised with the joy of it; and my good steward the captain had laid out the five pounds, which my friend had sent him for a present for himself, to purchase and bring me over a servant, under bond for six years' service, and would not accept of any consideration, except a little tobacco, which I would have him accept, being of my own produce.

Neither was this all; for my goods being all English manufacture, such as cloth, stuffs, baize, and things particularly valuable and desirable in the country, I found means to sell them at a very great advantage; so that I may say I had more than four times the value of my first cargo, and was now infinitely beyond my poor neighbour—I mean in the advancement of my plantation; for the first thing I did, I bought me a negro slave, and an European servant also: I mean another besides that which the captain brought me from Lisbon.

But as abused prosperity is oftentimes made the very means of our greatest adversity, so was it with me. I went on the next year with great success in my plantation: I raised fifty great rolls of tobacco on my own ground, more than I had disposed of for necessaries among my neighbours; and these fifty rolls, being each of above a hundred weight, were well cured, and laid by against the return of the fleet from Lisbon. And now increasing business and wealth, my head began to be full of projects and undertakings beyond my reach; such as are indeed often the ruin of the best heads in business. Had I continued in the station I was now in, I had room for all the happy things to have yet befallen me for which my father so earnestly recommended a quiet, retired life, and which he had so sensibly described the middle station of life to be full of; but other things attended me, and I was still to be the wilful agent of all my own miseries; and particularly to increase my fault, and double the reflections upon myself, which in my future sorrows I should have leisure to make;

all these miscarriages were procured by my apparent obstinate adhering to my foolish inclination of wandering abroad, and pursuing that inclination in contradiction to the clearest views of doing myself good in a fair and plain pursuit of those prospects and those measures of life, which nature and Providence concurred to present me with, and to make my duty.

As I had once done thus in breaking away from my parents, so I could not be content now, but I must go and leave the happy view I had of being a rich and thriving man in my new plantation, only to pursue a rash and immoderate desire of rising faster than the nature of the thing admitted; and thus I cast myself down again into the deepest gulf of human misery that ever man fell into, or perhaps could be consistent with life and a state of health in the world.

To come, then, by just degrees to the particulars of this part of my story: You may suppose, that having now lived almost four years in the Brazils, and beginning to thrive and prosper very well upon my plantation, I had not only learned the language, but had contracted acquaintance and friendship among my fellow-planters, as well as among the merchants at St. Salvadore, which was our port; and that, in my discourse among them, I had frequently given them an account of my two voyages to the coast of Guinea, the manner of trading with the negroes there, and how easy it was to purchase upon the coast for trifles—such as beads, toys, knives, scissors, hatchets, bits of glass, and the like—not only gold-dust, Guinea grains, elephants' teeth, etc., but negroes, for the serving of the Brazils, in great numbers.

They listened always very attentively to my discourses on these heads, but especially to that part which related to the buying of negroes; which was a trade, at that time, not only not far entered into, but, as far as it was, had been carried on by the Assiento, or permission of the King of Spain and Portugal, and engrossed in the public stock; so that few negroes were brought, and those excessively dear.

It happened, being in company one day with some merchants and planters of my acquaintance, and talking of
those things very earnestly, three of them came to me the
next morning, and told me they had been musing very
much upon what I had discoursed of with them the last
night, and they came to make a secret proposal to me;
and after enjoining me to secrecy, they told me that they
had a mind to fit out a ship to go to Guinea; that they had
all plantations as well as I, and were straightened for nothing
so much as servants; that as it was a trade that could not
be carried on, because they could not publicly sell the negroes
when they came home, so they desired to make but one
voyage, to bring the negroes on shore privately, and divide
them among their own plantations; and, in a word, the
question was, whether I would go their supercargo in the
ship, to manage the trading part upon the coast of Guinea;
and they offered me that I should have my equal share of
the negroes, without providing any part of the stock.

This was a fair proposal, it must be confessed, had it
been made to any one that had not had a settlement and
plantation of his own to look after, which was in a fair way
of coming to be very considerable, and with a good stock
upon it. But for me, that was thus entered and established,
and had nothing to do but go on as I had begun, for three
or four years more, and to have sent for the other hundred
pounds from England; and who in that time, and with that
little addition, could scarce have failed of being worth
three or four thousand pounds sterling, and that increasing
too—for me to think of such a voyage was the most preposterous thing that ever man in such circumstances could
be guilty of.

But I, that was born to be my own destroyer, could no
more resist the offer than I could restrain my first rambling
designs when my father's good counsel was lost upon me.
In a word, I told them I would go with all my heart, if they
would undertake to look after my plantation in my absence,
and would dispose of it as I should direct, if I miscarried.

This they all engaged to do, and entered into writings, or covenants, to do so; and I made a formal will, disposing of my plantation and effects in case of my death, making the captain of the ship that had saved my life, as before, my universal heir, but obliging him to dispose of my effects as I had directed in my will; one-half of the produce being to himself, and the other to be shipped to England.

In short, I took all possible caution to preserve my effects, and to keep up my plantation. Had I used half as much prudence to have looked into my own interest, and have made a judgment of what I ought to have done, and not to have done, I had certainly never gone away from so prosperous an undertaking, leaving all the probable views of a thriving circumstance, and gone upon a voyage to sea, attended with all its common hazards, to say nothing of the reasons I had to expect particular misfortunes to myself.

But I was hurried on, and obeyed blindly the dictates of my fancy rather than my reason; and accordingly, the ship being fitted out, and the cargo finished, and all things done as by agreement by my partners in the voyage, I went on board in an evil hour again, the 1st of September, 1659, being the same day eight years that I went from my father and mother at Hull, in order to act the rebel to their authority, and the fool to my own interests.

Our ship was about one hundred and twenty tons burden, carried six guns, and fourteen men, besides the master, his boy, and myself; we had on board no large cargo of goods, except of such toys as were fit for our trade with the negroes, such as beads, bits of glass, shells, and odd trifles, especially little looking-glasses, knives, scissors, hatchets, and the like.

The same day I went on board we set sail, standing away to the northward upon our own coasts, with design to stretch over for the African coast, when they came into about ten or twelve degrees of northern latitude; which, it seems, was the manner of their course in those days.

We had very good weather, only excessively hot, all the way upon our own coast, till we came to the height of Cape St. Augustino; from whence, creeping farther off at sea, we lost sight of land, and steered as if we were bound for the Isle Fernando de Noronha, holding our course N.E. by N., and leaving those isles on the east. In this course we passed the line in about twelve days' time, and were, by our last observation, in seven degrees twenty-two minutes northern latitude, when a violent tornado, or hurricane, took us quite out of our knowledge. It began from the southeast, came about to the northwest, and then settled into the northeast; from whence it blew in such a terrible manner, that for twelve days together we could do nothing but drive, and, scudding away before it, let it carry us wherever fate and the fury of the winds directed; and during these twelve days, I need not say that I expected every day to be swallowed up; nor did any in the ship expect to save their lives.

In this distress we had, besides the terror of the storm, one of our men to die of the calenture, and a man and a boy to be washed overboard. About the twelfth day, the weather abating a little, the master made an observation as well as he could, and found that he was in about eleven degrees of north latitude, but that he was twenty-two degrees of longitude difference west from Cape St. Augustino; so that he found he was gotten upon the coast of Guiana, or the north part of Brazil, beyond the river Amazon, towards that of the river Orinoco, commonly called the Great River; and now he began to consult with me what course he should take; for the ship was leaky, and very much disabled, and he was for going directly back to the coast of Brazil.

I was positively against that; and looking over the charts of the seacoast of America with him, we concluded there was no inhabited country for us to have recourse to till we came within the circle of the Carribbee Islands, and therefore resolved to stand away for Barbadoes; which, by keeping off at sea, to avoid the indraft of the bay or gulf of Mexico, we might easily perform, as we hoped, in about fifteen days' sail; whereas we could not possibly make our voyage to the coast of Africa without some assistance both to our ship and ourselves.

With this design we changed our course, and steered away N.W. by W., in order to reach some of our English islands, where I hoped for relief; but our voyage was other wise determined; for, being in the latitude of twelve degrees eighteen minutes, a second storm came upon us, which carried us away with the same impetuosity westward, and drove us so out of the way of all human commerce that, had all our lives been saved as to the sea, we were rather in danger of being devoured by savages than ever returning to our own country.

In this distress, the wind still blowing very hard, one of our men early one morning cried out, "Land!" and we had no sooner run out of the cabin to look out, in hopes of seeing whereabouts in the world we were than the ship struck upon the sand, and in a moment, her motion being so stopped, the sea broke over her in such a manner that we expected we should all have perished immediately; and we were even driven into our close quarters, to shelter us from the very foam and spray of the sea.

It is not easy for any one who has not been in the like condition to describe or conceive the consternation of men in such circumstances. We knew nothing where we were, or upon what land it was we were driven; whether an island or the main, whether inhabited or not inhabited. As the rage of the wind was still great, though rather less than at first, we could not so much as hope to have the ship hold many minutes without breaking in pieces, unless the winds, by a kind of miracle, should turn immediately about. In a word, we sat looking one upon another, and expecting death every moment, and every man acting accordingly, as preparing for another world; for there was little or nothing more for us to do in this; that which was our present comfort, and all the comfort we had, was that, contrary to our expectation, the ship did not break yet, and that the master said the wind began to abate.

Now, though we thought the wind did a little abate, yet the ship having thus struck upon the sand, and sticking too fast for us to expect her getting off, we were in a dreadful condition indeed, and had nothing to do but to think of saving our lives as well as we could. We had a boat at our stern just before the storm, but she was first staved by dashing against the ship's rudder, and in the next place she broke away, and either sunk, or was driven off to sea; so there was no hope from her. We had another boat on board, but how to get her off into the sea was a doubtful thing; however, there was no room to debate, for we fancied the ship would break in pieces every minute, and some told us she was actually broken already.

In this distress, the mate of our vessel lays hold of the boat, and with the help of the rest of the men, they got her flung over the ship's side; and getting all into her, we let go, and committed ourselves, being eleven in number to God's mercy and the wild sea: for though the storm was abated considerably, yet the sea went dreadfully high upon the shore, and might be well called *den wild zee*, as the Dutch call the sea in a storm.

And now our case was very dismal indeed; for we all saw plainly that the sea went so high that the boat could not escape, and that we should be inevitably drowned. As to making sail, we had none, nor, if we had, could we have done anything with it; so we worked at the oar towards the land, though with heavy hearts, like men going to execution; for we all knew that when the boat came near the shore, she would be dashed in a thousand pieces by the breach of the sea. However, we committed our souls to God in the most earnest manner; and the wind driving us towards the shore, we hastened our destruction with our own hands, pulling as well as we could towards land.

What the shore was, whether rock or sand, whether steep or shoal, we knew not; the only hope that could rationally give us the least shadow of expectation was if we might happen into some bay or gulf, or the mouth of some river, where by great chance we might have run our boat in, or got under the lea of the land, and perhaps made smooth water. But there was nothing of this appeared; but as we made nearer and nearer the shore, the land looked more frightful than the sea.

After we had rowed, or rather driven, about a league and a half, as we reckoned it, a raging wave, mountainlike, came rolling astern of us, and plainly bade us expect the *coup de grace*. In a word, it took us with such a fury that it overset the boat at once; and separating us as well from the boat as from one another, gave us not time hardly to say "O God!" for we were all swallowed up in a moment.

Nothing can describe the confusion of thought which I felt, when I sank into the water; for though I swam very well, yet I could not deliver myself from the waves so as to draw breath, till that wave having driven me, or rather carried me, a vast way on towards the shore, and having spent itself, went back, and left me upon the land almost dry, but half dead with the water I took in. I had so much presence of mind, as well as breath left, that seeing myself nearer the mainland than I expected, I got upon my feet, and endeavoured to make on towards the land as fast as I could, before another wave should return and take me up again; but I soon found it was impossible to avoid it; for I saw the sea come after me as high as a great hill, and as furious as an enemy, which I had no means or strength to contend with: my business was to hold my breath, and raise myself upon the water, if I could; and so by swimming to preserve my breathing, and pilot myself towards the shore if possible, my greatest concern now being that the wave, as it would carry me a great way towards the shore when it came on, might not carry me back again with it when it gave back towards the sea.

The wave that came upon me again buried me at once twenty or thirty feet deep in its own body, and I could feel myself carried with a mighty force and swiftness towards the shore a very great way; but I held my breath, and assisted myself to swim still forward with all my might. I was ready to burst with holding my breath, when as I felt myself rising up to my immediate relief, I found my head and hands shoot out above the surface of the water; and though it was not two seconds of time that I could keep myself so, yet it relieved me greatly, gave me breath and new courage. I was covered again with water a good while, but not so long but I held it out; and finding the water had spent itself, and began to return, I struck forward against the return of the waves, and felt ground again with my feet. I stood still a few moments to recover breath, and till the waters went from me, and then took to my heels, and ran with what strength I had, farther towards the shore. But neither would this deliver me from the fury of the sea, which came pouring in after me again; and twice more I was lifted up by the waves and carried forwards as before, the shore being very flat.

The last time of these two had well-nigh been fatal to me; for the sea having hurried me along, as before, landed me, or rather dashed me, against a piece of a rock, and that with such force, as it left me senseless, and indeed helpless, as to my own deliverance; for the blow taking my side and breast, beat the breath as it were quite out of my body; and had it returned again immediately, I must have been strangled in the water; but I recovered a little before the return of the waves, and seeing I should be covered again with water, I resolved to hold fast by a piece of the rock, and so to hold my breath, if possible, till the wave went back. Now, as the waves were not so high as at first, being nearer land, I held my hold till the wave abated, and then fetched another run, which brought me so near the shore, that the next wave, though it went over me, yet did not so swallow me up as to carry me away; and the next run I took, I got to the mainland; where, to my great comfort, I clambered up the cliffs of the shore, and sat me down upon the grass, free from danger, and quite out of the reach of the water.

I was now landed and safe on shore, and began to look up and thank God that my life was saved, in a case wherein there was some minutes before scarce any room to hope. I believe it is impossible to express, to the life, what the ecstasies and transports of the soul are, when it is so saved, as I may say, out of the very grave: and I do not wonder now at that custom, when a malefactor, who has the halter about his neck, is tied up, and just going to be turned off, and has a reprieve brought to him—I say, I do not wonder that they bring a surgeon with it, to let him blood that very moment they tell him of it, that the surprise may not drive the animal spirits from the heart, and overwhelm him,

For sudden joys, like griefs, confound at first.

I walked about on the shore, lifting up my hands, and my whole being, as I may say, wrapt up in a contemplation of my deliverance; making a thousand gestures and motions, which I cannot describe; reflecting upon all my comrades that were drowned, and that there should not be one soul saved but myself; for, as for them, I never saw them afterwards, or any sign of them, except three of their hats, one cap and two shoes that were not fellows.

I cast my eyes to the stranded vessel, when, the breach and froth of the sea being so big, I could hardly see it, it lay so far off; and considered, Lord! how was it possible I could get on shore?

After I had solaced my mind with the comfortable part of my condition, I began to look round me, to see what kind of place I was in, and what was next to be done: and I soon found my comforts abate, and that, in a word, I had a dreadful deliverance: for I was wet, had no clothes to shift me, nor anything to eat or drink, to comfort me;

47

neither did I see any prospect before me but that of perishing with hunger, or being devoured by wild beasts: and that which was particularly afflicting to me was that I had no weapon, either to hunt and kill any creature for my sustenance, or to defend myself against any other creature that might desire to kill me for theirs. In a word, I had nothing about me but a knife, a tobacco-pipe, and a little tobacco in a box. This was all my provision; and this threw me into terrible agonies of mind, that for awhile I ran about like a madman. Night coming upon me, I began, with a heavy heart, to consider what would be my lot if there were any ravenous beasts in that country, seeing at night they always come abroad for their prey.

All the remedy that offered to my thoughts, at that time, was to get up into a thick, bushy tree, like a fir, but thorny, which grew near me, and where I was resolved to sit all night, and consider the next day what death I should die, for as yet I saw no prospect of life. I walked about a furlong from the shore, to see if I could find any fresh water to drink, which I did, to my great joy; and having drunk, and put a little tobacco in my mouth to prevent hunger, I went to the tree, and getting up into it, endeavoured to place myself so that if I should sleep I might not fall. And having cut me a short stick, like a truncheon, for my defence, I took up my lodging; and being excessively fatigued I fell fast asleep, and slept as comfortably as, I believe, few could have done in my condition, and found myself more refreshed with it than I think I ever was on such an occasion.

CHAPTER IV

WHEN I waked it was broad day, the weather clear, and the storm abated, so that the sea did not rage and swell as before; but that which surprised me most was, that the ship was lifted off in the night from the sand where she lay, by the swelling of the tide, and was driven up almost as far as the rock which I at first mentioned, where I had been so bruised by the wave dashing me against it. This being within about a mile from the shore where I was, and the ship seeming to stand upright still, I wished myself on board, that at least I might save some necessary things for my use.

When I came down from my apartment in the tree, I looked about me again, and the first thing I found was the boat, which lay, as the wind and sea had tossed her up, upon the land, about two miles on my right hand. I walked as far as I could upon the shore to have got to her; but found a neck or inlet of water between me and the boat which was about half a mile broad; so I came back for the present, being more intent upon getting at the ship, where I hoped to find something for my present subsistence.

A little after noon I found the sea very calm, and the tide ebbed so far out, that I could come within a quarter of a mile of the ship. And here I found a fresh renewing of my grief; for I saw evidently that, if we had kept on board, we had been all safe; that is to say, we had all got safe on shore, and I had not been so miserable as to be left entirely destitute of all comfort and company as I now was. This forced tears to my eyes again; but as there was little relief in that, I resolved, if possible, to get to the ship, so I pulled off my clothes, for the weather was hot to extremity, and took the water. But when I came to the ship, my difficulty was still greater to know how to get on board; for, as she lay aground, and high out of the water, there was nothing within my reach to lay hold of. I swam round her twice, and the second time I espied a small piece of rope, which I wondered I did not see at first, hanging down by the fore-chains so low, that with great difficulty I got hold of it, and by the help of that rope got up into the forecastle of the ship. Here I found that the ship was bulged, and had a great deal of water in her hold; but that she lay so on the side of a bank of hard sand, or rather earth, that her stern lay lifted up upon the bank, and her head low, almost to the water. By this means all her quarter was free and all that was in that part was dry; for you may be sure my first work was to search, and to see what was spoiled and what was free. And, first, I found that all the ship's provisions were dry and untouched by the water, and being very well disposed to eat, I went to the bread-room, and filled my pockets with biscuit, and ate it as I went about other things, for I had no time to lose. I also found some rum in the great cabin, of which I took a large dram, and which I had, indeed, need enough of to spirit me for what was before me. Now I wanted nothing but a boat, to furnish myself with many things which I foresaw would be very necessary to me.

It was in vain to sit still and wish for what was not to be had; and this extremity roused my application. We had several spare yards, and two or three large spars of wood, and a spare topmast or two in the ship: I resolved to fall to work with them, and I flung as many of them overboard as I could manage for their weight, tying every one with a rope, that they might not drive away. When this was done, I went down the ship's side, and pulling them to me, I tied four of them together at both ends, as well as I could, in the form of a raft, and laying two or three short pieces of plank upon them, crossways, I found I could walk upon it very well, but that it was not able to bear any great weight, the pieces being too light. So I went to work, and with the carpenter's saw I cut a spare topmast into three lengths, and added them to my raft, with a great deal of labour and pains. But the hope of furnishing myself with necessaries encouraged me to go beyond what I should have been able to have done upon another occasion.

My raft was now strong enough to bear any reasonable weight. My next care was what to load it with, and how to preserve what I laid upon it from the surf of the sea: but I was not long in considering this. I first laid all the planks or boards upon it that I could get, and having considered well what I most wanted, I first got three of the seamen's chests, which I had broken open and emptied, and lowered them down upon my raft; the first of these I filled with provisions—viz., bread, rice, three Dutch cheeses, five pieces of dried goat's flesh (which we lived much upon), and a little remainder of European corn, which had been laid by for some fowls which we brought to sea with us, but the fowls were killed. There had been some barley and wheat together; but, to my great disappointment, I found afterwards that the rats had eaten or spoiled it all. As for liquors, I found several cases of bottles belonging to our skipper, in which were some cordial waters; and in all, about five or six gallons of arrack. These I stowed by themselves, there being no need to put them into the chest, nor any room for them. While I was doing this, I found the tide began to flow, though very calm; and I had the mortification to see my coat, shirt, and waistcoat, which I had left on shore upon the sand, swim away. As for my breeches, which were only linen, and open-kneed, I swam on board in them and my stockings. However, this put me upon rummaging for clothes, of which I found enough, but took no more than I wanted for present use, for I had other things which my eye was more upon; as, first, tools to work with on shore; and it was after long searching that I found out the carpenter's chest, which was indeed a very useful prize to me, and much more valuable than a ship-lading of gold would have been at that time. I got it down to my raft, whole as it was, without losing time to look into it, for I knew in general what it contained.

My next care was for some ammunition and arms. There were two very good fowling pieces in the great cabin, and two pistols. These I secured first, with some powder-horns, a small bag of shot, and two old rusty swords. I knew there were three barrels of powder in the ship, but knew not where our gunner had stowed them; but with much search I found them, two of them dry and good, the third had taken water. Those two I got to my raft, with the arms. And now I thought myself pretty well freighted, and began to think how I should get to shore with them, having neither sail, oar, nor rudder; and the least capful of wind would have overset all my navigation.

I had three encouragements: first, a smooth, calm sea; secondly, the tide rising, and setting into the shore; thirdly, what little wind there was blew me towards the land. And thus, having found two or three broken oars belonging to the boat, and besides the tools which were in the chest, two saws, an axe, and a hammer; with this cargo I put to sea. For a mile, or thereabouts, my raft went very well, only that I found it drive a little distant from the place where I had landed before; by which I perceived that there was some indraft of the water, and consequently, I hoped to find some creek or river there, which I might make use of as a port to get to land with my cargo.

As I imagined, so it was. There appeared before me a little opening of the land. I found a strong current of the tide set into it; so I guided my raft as well as I could, to keep in the middle of the stream.

But here I had like to have suffered a second shipwreck, which, if I had, I think verily would have broken my heart; for knowing nothing of the coast, my raft ran aground at one end of it upon a shoal, and not being aground at the other end, it wanted but a little that all of my cargo had slipped off towards the end that was afloat, and so fallen into the water. I did my utmost, by setting my back against the chests, to keep them in their places, but could not thrust off the raft with all my strength; neither durst I stir from the posture I was in; but holding up the chests with all my might, I stood in that manner near half an hour, in which time the rising of the water brought me a little more upon a level; and, a little after, the water still rising, my raft floated again, and I thrust her off with the oar I had into the channel, and then driving up higher, I at length found myself in the mouth of a little river, with land on both sides, and a strong current or tide running up. I looked on both sides for a proper place to get to shore, for I was not willing to be driven too high up the river; hoping in time to see some ship at sea, and therefore resolved to place myself as near the coast as I could.

At length I spied a little cove on the right shore of the creek, to which, with great pain and difficulty, I guided my raft, and at last got so near that, reaching ground with my oar, I could thrust her directly in. But here I had like to have dipped all my cargo into the sea again; for that shore lying pretty steep—that is to say, sloping—there was no place to land, but where one end of my float, if it ran on shore, would lie so high, and the other sink lower, as before, that it would endanger my cargo again. All that I could do was to wait till the tide was at the highest, keeping the raft with my oar like an anchor, to hold the side of it fast to the shore, near a flat piece of ground, which I expected the water would flow over; and so it did. As soon as I found water enough, for my raft drew about a foot of water, I thrust her upon that flat piece of ground, and there fastened or moored her, by sticking my two broken oars into the ground—one on one side, near one end, and one on the other side, near the other end; and thus I lay till the water ebbed away, and left my raft and all my cargo safe on shore.

My next work was to view the country, and seek a proper place for my habitation, and where to stow my goods, to secure them from whatever might happen. Where I was, I yet knew not; whether on the continent or an island; whether inhabited or not inhabited; whether in danger of wild beasts or not. There was a hill not above a mile from me, which rose up very steep and high, and which seemed to overtop some other hills, which lay as in a ridge from it, northward. I took out one of the fowling-pieces, and one of the pistols, and a horn of powder; and thus armed, I travelled for discovery up to the top of that hill, where, after I had with great labour and difficulty got to the top, I saw my fate, to my great affliction—viz., that I was in an island environed every way with the sea: no land to be seen except some rocks, which lay a great way off, and two small islands, less than this, which lay about three leagues to the west.

I found also that the island I was in was barren, and, as I saw good reason to believe, uninhabited, except by wild beasts, of which, however, I saw none. Yet I saw abundance of fowls, but knew not their kinds; neither, when I killed them, could I tell what was fit for food, and what was not. At my coming back, I shot at a great bird, which I saw sitting upon a tree, on the side of a great wood. I believe it was the first gun that had been fired there since the creation of the world. I had no sooner fired, but from all parts of the wood there arose an innumerable number of fowls of many sorts, making a confused screaming and crying, every one according to his usual note, but not one of them of any kind that I knew. As for the creature I killed, I took it to be a kind of a hawk, its colour and beak resembling it, but it had no talons or claws more than common. Its flesh was carrion, and fit for nothing.

Contented with this discovery, I came back to my raft, and fell to work to bring my cargo on shore, which took me up the rest of the day: what to do with myself at night I knew not, nor indeed where to rest, for I was afraid to

ROBINSON CRUSOE

lie down on the ground, not knowing but some wild beast might devour me; though, as I afterwards found, there was really no need for those fears.

However, as well as I could, I barricaded myself round with chests and boards that I had brought on shore, and made a kind of hut for that night's lodging. As for food, I yet saw not which way to supply myself, except that I had seen two or three creatures, like hares, run out of the wood where I shot the fowl.

I now began to consider that I might yet get a great many things out of the ship, which would be useful to me, and particularly some of the rigging and sails, and such other things as might come to land; and I resolved to make another voyage on board the vessel, if possible. And as I knew that the first storm that blew must necessarily break her all in pieces, I resolved to set all other things apart, till I got everything out of the ship that I could get. Then I called a council—that is to say, in my thoughts—whether I should take back the raft; but this appeared impracticable: so I resolved to go as before, when the tide was down; and I did so, only that I stripped before I went from my hut, having nothing on but a checkered shirt, a pair of linen drawers, and a pair of pumps on my feet.

I got on board the ship as before, and prepared a second raft; and, having had experience of the first, I neither made this so unwieldy, nor loaded it so hard, and yet I brought away several things very useful to me; as, first, in the carpenter's stores I found two or three bags full of nails and spikes, a great screw-jack, a dozen or two of hatchets, and, above all, that most useful thing called a grindstone. All these I secured, together with several things belonging to the gunner, particularly two or three iron crows, and two barrels of musket bullets, seven muskets, and another fowling piece, with some small quantity of powder more; a large bagful of small shot, and a great roll of sheet lead; but this last was so heavy I could not hoist it up to get it over the ship's sides.

Besides these things, I took all the men's clothes that I could find, and a spare fore-topsail, a hammock, and some bedding; and with this I loaded my second raft, and brought them all safe on shore, to my very great comfort.

I was under some apprehension during my absence from the land, that at least my provisions might be devoured on shore; but when I came back, I found no sign of any visitor; only there sat a creature like a wildcat, upon one of the chests, which when I came towards it, ran away a little distance, and then stood still. She sat very composed and unconcerned, and looked full in my face, as if she had a mind to be acquainted with me. I presented my gun to her, but, as she did not understand it, she was perfectly unconcerned at it, nor did she offer to stir away; upon which I tossed her a bit of biscuit, though, by the way, I was not very free of it, for my store was not great; however, I spared her a bit, I say, and she went to it, smelled at it, and ate it, and looked (as pleased) for more; but I thanked her, and could spare no more; so she marched off.

Having got my second cargo on shore—though I was obliged to open the barrels of powder, and bring them by parcels, for they were too heavy, being large casks—I went to work to make me a little tent, with the sail, and some poles which I cut for that purpose; and into this tent I brought everything that I knew would spoil either with rain or sun; and I piled all the empty chests and casks up in a circle round the tent, to fortify it from any sudden attempt, either from man or beast.

When I had done this, I blocked up the door of the tent with some boards within, and an empty chest set up on end without; and spreading one of the beds upon the ground, laying my two pistols just at my head, and my gun at length by me, I went to bed the first time, and slept very quietly all night. I was very weary and heavy; for the night before I had slept little, and had laboured very hard all day, as well to fetch those things from the ship as to get them on shore.

I had the biggest magazine of all kinds now that ever was laid up, I believe, for one man; but still I was not satisfied, for while the ship sat upright in that posture, I thought I ought to get everything out of her that I could; so every day, at low water, I went on board, and brought away something or other; but particularly the third time I went, I brought away as much of the rigging as I could, as also all the small ropes and rope twine I could get, with a piece of spare canvas, which was to mend the sails upon occasion, and the barrel of wet gunpowder. In a word I brought away all the sails, first and last; only that I was fain to cut them in pieces, and bring as much at a time as I could, for they were no more useful to me for sails, but as mere canvas only.

But that which comforted me more still was, that at last of all, after I had made five or six such voyages as these, and thought I had nothing more to expect from the ship that was worth my meddling with—I say, after all this, I found a great hogshead of bread, three large runlets of rum, or spirits, a box of fine sugar, and a barrel of fine flour: this was surprising to me, because I had given over expecting any more provisions except what was spoiled by the water. I soon emptied the hogshead of the bread, and wrapped it up, parcel by parcel, in pieces of the sails, which I cut out; and, in a word, I got all this safe on shore also, though at several times.

The next day I made another voyage, and now, having plundered the ship of what was portable and fit to hand out, I began with the cable; cutting the great cable into pieces such as I could move, I got two cables and a hawser on shore, with all the iron-work I could get; and having cut down the spritsail-yard and the mizzen-yard, and everything I could to make a large raft, I loaded it with all those heavy goods and came away; but my good luck began to leave me, for this raft was so unwieldy, and so overladen, that after I was entered the little cove, where I had landed the rest of my goods, not being able to guide it so handily as I did the other, it overset, and threw me and all my cargo into the water; as for myself, it was no great harm, for I was near the shore; but as to my cargo, it was great part lost, especially the iron, which I expected would have been of great use to me; however, when the tide was out, I got most of the pieces of cable ashore, and some of the iron, though with infinite labour; for I was fain to dip for it into the water, a work which fatigued me very much. After this, I went every day on board, and brought away what I could get.

I had now been thirteen days on shore, and had been eleven times on board the ship, in which time I had brought away all that one pair of hands could well be supposed capable of bringing; though I verily believe, had the calm weather held, I should have brought away the whole ship, piece by piece; but preparing the twelfth time to go on board, I found the wind began to rise; however, at low water I went on board, and though I thought I had rummaged the cabin so effectually that nothing more could be found, yet I discovered a locker with drawers in it, in one of which I found two or three razors, and one pair of large scissors, with some ten or a dozen of good knives and forks; in another I found about thirty-six pounds' value in money—some European coin, some Brazil, some pieces of eight, some gold, and some silver.

I smiled to myself at the sight of this money. "Oh, drug!" said I aloud, "what art thou good for? Thou art not worth to me—no, not the taking off the ground; one of those knives is worth all this heap; I have no manner of use for thee; e'en remain where thou art, and go to the bottom, as a creature whose life is not worth saving." However, upon second thoughts, I took it away; and wrapping all in a piece of canvas, I began to think of making another raft; but while I was preparing this, I found the sky overcast, and the wind began to rise, and in a quarter of an hour it blew a fresh gale from the shore. It presently occurred to me that it was in vain to pretend to make a raft with the wind offshore; and that it was my business to be gone before the tide of flood began, otherwise I might not be able to reach the shore at all. Accordingly, I let myself down into the water, and swam across the channel which lay between the ship and the sands, and even that with difficulty enough, partly with the weight of the things I had about me, and partly from the roughness of the water; for the wind rose very hastily, and before it was quite high water it blew a storm.

But I was gotten home to my little tent, where I lay, with all my wealth about me very secure, It blew very hard all that night, and in the morning, when I looked out, behold, no more ship was to be seen. I was a little surprised, but recovered myself with this satisfactory reflection, that I had lost no time, nor abated any diligence, to get everything out of her that could be useful to me; and that, indeed, there was little left in her that I was able to bring away, if I had had more time.

I now gave over any more thoughts of the ship, or of anything out of her, except what might drive on shore from her wreck; as, indeed, divers pieces of her afterwards did; but those things were of small use to me.

My thoughts were now wholly employed about securing myself against either savages, if any should appear, or wild beasts, if any were in the island; and I had many thoughts of the method how to do this, and what kind of dwelling to make—whether I should make me a cave in the earth, or a tent upon the earth; and in short, I resolved upon both; the manner and description of which it may not be improper to give an account of.

I soon found that the place I was in was not fit for my settlement, particularly because it was upon a low moorish ground near the sea, and I believed would not be wholesome, and more particularly because there was no fresh water near it; so I resolved to find a more healthy and more convenient spot of ground.

I consulted several things in my situation, which I found

would be proper for me: first, health and fresh water, I just now mentioned; secondly, shelter from the heat of the sun; thirdly, security from ravenous creatures, whether man or beast; fourthly, a view of the sea, that if God sent any ship in sight, I might not lose any advantage for my deliverance, of which I was not willing to banish my expectation yet.

In search of a place proper for this, I found a little plain on the side of a rising hill, whose front towards this little plain was steep as a house-side, so that nothing could come down upon me from the top. On the side of the rock there was a hollow place, worn a little way in, like the entrance or door of a cave; but there was not really any cave, or way into the rock, at all.

On the flat of the green, just below this hollow place, I resolved to pitch my tent. This plain was not above a hundred yards broad, and about twice as long, and lay like a green before my door; and, at the end of it, descended irregularly every way down into the low ground by the seaside. It was on the N.N.W. side of the hill; so that it was sheltered from the heat every day, till it came to the W. and by S. sun, or thereabouts, which, in those countries, is near the setting.

Before I set up my tent, I drew a half-circle before the hollow place, which took in about ten yards in its semi-diameter, from the rock, and twenty yards in its diameter from its beginning and ending.

In this half-circle I pitched two rows of strong stakes, driving them into the ground till they stood very firm like piles, the biggest end being out of the ground about five feet and a half, and sharpened on the top. The two rows did not stand above six inches from one another.

Then I took the pieces of cable which I had cut in the ship, and laid them in rows, upon one another, within the circle, between these two rows of stakes, up to the top, placing other stakes on the inside, leaning against them, about two feet and a half high, like a spur to a post;

and this fence was so strong that neither man nor beast could get into it or over it. This cost me a great deal of time and labour, especially to cut the piles in the woods, bring them to the place, set them up, drive them into the earth, and make them firm.

The entrance into this place I made to be, not by a door, but by a short ladder to go over the top; which ladder, when I was in, I lifted over after me; and so I was completely fenced in and fortified, as I thought, from all the world, and consequently slept secure in the night, which otherwise I could not have done; though, as it appeared afterwards, there was no need of all this caution from the enemies that I apprehended danger from.

Into this fence, or fortress, with infinite labour, I carried all my riches, all my provisions, ammunition, and stores, of which you have the account above; and I made me a large tent also, to preserve me from the rains, that in one part of the year are very violent there. I made it double—viz., one smaller tent within, and one larger tent above it; and covered the uppermost part of it with a large tarpaulin, which I had saved among the sails.

And now I lay no more for a while in the bed which I had brought on shore, but in a hammock which was indeed a very good one, and belonged to the mate of the ship.

Into this tent I brought all my provisions, and everything that would spoil by the wet; and having thus inclosed all my goods, I made up the entrance, which till now I had left open, and so passed and repassed as I said, by a short ladder.

When I had done this, I began to work my way into the rock, and bringing all the earth and stones that I dug down, out through my tent, I laid them up within my fence, in the nature of a terrace, so that it raised the ground within about a foot and a half; and thus I made me a cave, just behind my tent, which served me like a cellar to my house.

ROBINSON CRUSOE

It cost me much labour and many days before all these things were brought to perfection, and therefore I must go back to some other things which took up some of my thoughts. At the same time it occurred, after I had laid my scheme for the setting up the tent, and making the cave, that a storm of rain falling from a thick, dark cloud, a sudden flash of lightning happened, and after that, a great clap of thunder, as is naturally the effect of it. I was not so much surprised with the lightning, as I was with the thought which darted into my mind as swift as the lightning itself. "Oh, my powder!" My very heart sank within me, when I thought that, at one blast, all my powder might be destroyed; on which not my defence only, but the providing me food, as I thought, entirely depended. I was nothing near so anxious about my own danger; though, had the powder took fire, I had never known who had hurt me.

Such impression did this make upon me that, after the storm was over, I laid aside all my work, my building and fortifying, and applied myself to make bags and boxes to separate my powder, and to keep it a little and a little in a parcel, in hopes, that whatever might come, it might not all take fire at once; and to keep it so apart that it should not be possible to make one part fire another. I finished this work in about a fortnight; and I think my powder, which in all was about one hundred and forty pounds' weight, was divided into no less than a hundred parcels. As to the barrel that had been wet, I did not apprehend any danger from that; so I placed it in my new cave, which, in my fancy, I called my kitchen; and the rest I hid up and down in holes among the rocks, so that no wet might come to it, marking very carefully where I had laid it.

In the interval of time while this was doing I went out at least once every day with my gun, as well to divert myself, as to see if I could kill anything fit for food; and, as near as I could, to acquaint myself with what the island produced. The first time I went out, I presently discovered that there were goats in the island, which was a great satisfaction to me; but then it was attended with this misfortune to me, viz., that they were so shy, so subtle, and so swift of foot, that it was the most difficult thing in the world to come at them; but I was not discouraged at this, not doubting but I might now and then shoot one, as it soon happened; for after I had found their haunts a little, I laid wait in this manner for them: I observed if they saw me in the valleys, though they were upon the rocks, they would run away, as in a terrible fright; but if they were feeding in the valleys, and I was upon the rocks, they took no notice of me; from whence I concluded that, by the position of their optics, their sight was so directed downward that they did not readily see objects that were above them; so afterwards I took this method— I always climbed the rocks first, to get above them, and then had frequently a fair mark.

The first shot I made among these creatures I killed a she-goat, which had a little kid by her, which she gave suck to, which grieved me heartily; for, when the old one fell, the kid stood stock still by her, till I came and took her up; and not only so, but when I carried the old one with me upon my shoulders, the kid followed me quite to my inclosure, upon which I laid down the dam, and took the kid in my arms, and carried it over my pale, in hopes to have bred it up tame; but it would not eat; so I was forced to kill it and eat it myself. These two supplied me with flesh a great while, for I ate sparingly, and saved my provisions, my bread especially, as much as I possibly could.

Having now fixed my habitation, I found it absolutely necessary to provide a place to make a fire in, and fuel to burn; and what I did for that, as also how I enlarged my cave, and what conveniences I made, I shall give a full account of in its place; but I must now give some little account of myself, and of my thoughts about living, which, it may well be supposed, were not a few.

I had a dismal prospect of my condition, for as I was not cast away upon that island without being driven, as is said, by a violent storm quite out of the course of our intended voyage, and a great way, viz., some hundreds of leagues, out of the ordinary course of the trade of mankind, I had great reason to consider it as a determination of Heaven, that in this desolate place, and in this desolate manner, I should end my life. The tears would run plentifully down my face when I made these reflections: and sometimes I would expostulate with myself why Providence should thus completely ruin its creatures, and render them so absolutely miserable, so without help abandoned, and so entirely depressed, that it could hardly be rational to be thankful for such a life.

But something always returned swift upon me to check these thoughts, and to reprove me; and particularly one day walking with my gun in my hand by the seaside, I was very pensive upon the subject of my present condition, when Reason, as it were, put in expostulating with me the other way, thus: "Well, you are in a desolate condition, it is true; but, pray remember, where are the rest of you? Did not you come eleven of you into the boat? Where are the ten? Why were not they saved, and you lost? Why are you singled out? Is it better to be here or there?" And then I pointed to the sea. All evils are to be considered with the good that is in them, and with what worse attended them.

Then it occurred to me again, how well I was furnished for my subsistence, and what would have been my case if it had not happened (which was a hundred thousand to one) that the ship floated from the place where first she struck, and was driven so near to the shore, that I had time to get all these things out of her? What would have been my case, if I had been forced to have lived in the condition in which I at first came on shore, without necessaries of life, or any means to supply and procure them? "Particularly," said I aloud (though to myself), "what should I have done without a gun, without ammunition, without any tools to make anything, or to work with? without clothes, bedding, a tent, or any manner of coverings?" and that now I had all these to a sufficient quantity, and was in a fair way to provide myself in such a manner as to live without my gun, when my ammunition was spent: so that I had a tolerable view of subsisting without any want as long as I lived; for I considered from the beginning how I would provide for the accidents that might happen, and for the time that was to come, even not only after my ammunition should be spent, but even after my health and strength should decay.

I confess I had not then entertained any notion of my ammunition being destroyed at one blast—I mean, my powder being blown up by lightning; and this made the thought of it surprising to me, when it lightened and thundered, as I observed just now.

And now, being about to enter into melancholy relation of a scene of silent life, such, perhaps, as was never heard of in the world before, I shall take it from its beginning, and continue it in its order. It was, by my account, the 30th of September, when, in the manner as above said, I first set foot upon this horrid island; when the sun being to us in its autumnal equinox, was almost just over my head: for I reckoned myself, by observation, to be in the latitude of nine degrees twenty-two minutes north of the line.

After I had been there about ten or twelve days, it came into my thoughts that I should lose my reckoning of time for want of books, and pen, and ink, and should even forget the Sabbath-day from the working-days; but to prevent this, I cut it with my knife upon a large post, in capital letters; and making it into a great cross, I set it up on the shore where I first landed, viz., "I càme on shore here on the 30th of September, 1659."

Upon the sides of this square post I cut every day a notch with my knife, and every seventh notch was as

ROBINSON CRUSOE

long again as the rest, and every first day of the month
as long again as that long one; and thus I kept my calendar,
or weekly, monthly, and yearly reckoning of time.

In the next place, we are to observe that, among the
many things which I brought from the ship in the several
voyages which, as above mentioned, I made to it, I got
several things of less value, but not at all less useful to
me, which I omitted setting down before; as, in particular,
pens, ink, and paper; several parcels in the captain's,
mate's, gunner's, and carpenter's keeping; three or four
compasses, some mathematical instruments, dials, perspec-
tives, charts, and books of navigation; all of which I
huddled together, whether I might want them or no; also
I found three very good Bibles, which came to me in my
cargo from England, and which I had packed up among
my things; some Portuguese books also; and, among them,
two or three Popish prayer-books, and several other books;
all which I carefully secured. And I must not forget that
we had in the ship a dog and two cats, of whose eminent
history I must have occasion to say something in its place,
for I carried both the cats with me; and as for the dog, he
jumped out of the ship of himself, and swam on shore to
me the day after I went on shore with my first cargo, and
was a trusty servant to me many years; I wanted nothing
that he could fetch me, nor any company that he could
make up to me; I only wanted to have him talk to me,
but that he could not do. As I observed before, I found
pens, ink, and paper, and I husbanded them to the
utmost; and I shall show that while my ink lasted, I kept
things very exact; but after that was gone I could not, for
I could not make any ink by any means that I could devise.

And this put me in mind that I wanted many things,
notwithstanding all that I had amassed together; and of
these, ink was one; as also a spade, pick-axe, and shovel,
to dig or remove the earth; needles, pins, and thread;
as for linen, I soon learned to want that without much
difficulty.

This want of tools made every work I did go on heavily; and it was near a whole year before I had entirely finished my little pale, or surrounded habitation. The piles or stakes, which were as heavy as I could well lift, were a long time in cutting and preparing in the woods, and more, by far, in bringing home; so that I spent sometimes two days in cutting and bringing home one of those posts, and a third day in driving it into the ground; for which purpose I got a heavy piece of wood at first, but at last bethought myself of one of the iron crows; which, however, though I found it, yet made driving those posts or piles very laborious and tedious work. But what need I have been concerned at the tediousness of anything I had to do, seeing I had time enough to do it in? nor had I any other employment, if that had been, over at least that I could foresee, except the ranging the island to seek for food, which I did, more or less, every day.

I now began to consider seriously my condition, and the circumstances I was reduced to; and I drew up the state of my affairs in writing, not so much to leave them to any that were to come after me, for I was like to have but few heirs, as to deliver my thoughts from daily poring upon them, and afflicting my mind: and as my reason began now to master my despondency, I began to comfort myself as well as I could, and to set the good against the evil, that I might have something to distinguish my case from worse, and I stated it very impartially, like debtor and creditor, the comfort I enjoyed, against the miseries I suffered, thus:

EVIL.	GOOD.
I am cast upon a horrible, desolate island; void of all hope of recovery.	But I am alive; and not drowned, as all my ship's company was.
I am singled out and separated, as it were, from all the world, to be miserable.	But I am singled out, too, from all the ship's crew, to be spared from death; and He that miraculously saved me from death can deliver me from this condition.

ROBINSON CRUSOE

EVIL.	GOOD.
I am divided from mankind, a solitary; one banished from human society.	But I am not starved and perishing on a barren place, affording no sustenance.
I have no clothes to cover me.	But I am in a hot climate, where if I had clothes, I could hardly wear them.
I am without any defence, or means to resist any violence of man or beast.	But I am cast on an island where I see no wild beasts to hurt me, as I saw on the coast of Africa; and what if I had been shipwrecked there?
I have no soul to speak to or relieve me.	But God wonderfully sent the ship in near enough to the shore, that I have got out so many necessary things as will either supply my wants or enable me to supply myself, even as long as I live.

Upon the whole, here was an undoubted testimony that there was scarce any condition in the world so miserable, but there was something negative, or something positive, to be thankful for in it: and let this stand as a direction, from the experience of the most miserable of all conditions in this world—that we may always find in it something to comfort ourselves from, and to set, in the description of good and evil, on the credit side of the account.

Having now brought my mind a little to relish my condition, and giving over looking out to sea, to see if I could spy a ship; I say, giving over these things, I began to apply myself to accommodate my way of living, and to make things as easy to me as I could.

I have already described my habitation, which was a tent under the side of a rock, surrounded with a strong pale of posts and cables; but I might now rather call it a wall, for I raised a kind of wall up against it of turfs about two feet thick on the outside: and after some time (I think it was a year and a half) I raised rafters from it, leaning to the rock, and thatched or covered it with boughs of trees, and such things as I could get to keep out the rain, which I found at some times of the year very violent.

I have already observed how I brought all my goods into this pale, and into the cave which I had made behind me. But I must observe, too, that at first this was a confused heap of goods, which, as they lay in no order, so they took up all my place; I had no room to turn myself: so I set myself to enlarge my cave, and worked farther into the earth; for it was a loose, sandy rock, which yielded easily to the labour I bestowed on it: and so when I found I was pretty safe as to beasts of prey, I worked sideways to the right hand, into the rock; and then turning to the right again, worked quite out, and made me a door to come out on the outside of my pale or fortification.

This gave me not only egress and regress, as it was a back way to my tent and to my storehouse, but gave me room to stow my goods.

And now I began to apply myself to make such necessary things as I found I most wanted, particularly a chair and a table; for without these I was not able to enjoy the few comforts I had in the world; I could not write, or eat, or do several things with so much pleasure without a table.

So I went to work; and here I must needs observe that as reason is the substance and original of the mathematics, so by stating and squaring everything by reason, and by making the most rational judgment of things, every man may be, in time, master of every mechanic art. I had never handled a tool in my life; and yet in time, by labour, application, and contrivance, I found at last that I wanted nothing but I could have made it, especially if I had had tools. However, I made abundance of things, even without tools; and some with no more tools than an adze and a hatchet, which, perhaps, were never made that way before, and that with infinite labour. For example, if I wanted a board, I had no other way but to cut down a tree, set it on an edge before me, and hew it flat on either side with my axe till I had brought it to be as thin as a plank, and then dub it smooth with my adze. It is true, by this method I could make but one board out of a whole tree; but this I had no remedy for but patience, any more than I had for the prodigious deal of time and labour which it took me to make a plank or board; but my time and labour was little worth, and so it was as well employed one way as another.

However, I made me a table and a chair, as I observed above, in the first place; and this I did out of the short pieces of boards that I brought on my raft from the ship. But when I had wrought out some boards as above, I made large shelves, of the breadth of a foot and a half, one over another, all along one side of my cave, to lay all my tools, nails, and ironwork on; and, in a word, to separate everything at large into their places, that I might come easily at them; also I knocked pieces into the wall of the rock, to hang my guns and all things that would hang up: so that had my cave been to be seen, it looked like a general magazine of all necessary things; and I had everything so ready at my hand, that it was a great pleasure to me to see all my goods in such order, and especially to find my stock of all necessaries so great.

And now it was when I began to keep a journal of every day's employment; for, indeed, at first, I was in too much hurry, and not only in hurry as to labour, but in too much discomposure of mind; and my journal would have been full of many dull things; for example, I must have said thus:

"*September* 30.—After I had got to shore, and had escaped drowning, instead of being thankful to God for my deliverance, having first vomited, with the great quantity of salt water which was gotten into my stomach, and recovering myself a little, I ran about the shore wringing my hands and beating my head and face, exclaiming at my misery, and crying out I was undone, undone! till, tired and faint, I was forced to lie down on the ground for repose, but durst not sleep, for fear of being devoured.

"Some days after this, and after I had been on board the ship, and had got all I could out of her, I could not forbear getting up to the top of a little mountain, and looking out to sea, in hopes of seeing a ship: then fancy at a vast distance I spied a sail, please myself with the hopes of it, and then, after looking steadily, till I was almost blind, lose it quite, and sit down and weep like a child, and thus increase my misery by my folly."

But having gotten over these things in some measure, and having settled my household stuff and habitation, made me a table and chair, and all as handsome about me as I could, I began, I say, to keep my journal; of which I shall here give you the copy (though in it will be told all these particulars over again), as long as it lasted; for at last, having no more ink, I was forced to leave it off.

CHAPTER V

THE JOURNAL

SEPTEMBER 30, 1659.—I, poor miserable Robinson Crusoe, being shipwrecked during a dreadful storm in the offing, came on shore on this dismal, unfortunate island, which I called "The Island of Despair"; all the rest of the ship's company being drowned, and myself almost dead.

All the rest of the day I spent in afflicting myself at the dismal circumstances I was brought to; viz., I had neither food, house, clothes, weapon, nor place to fly to; and in despair of any relief, saw nothing but death before me; either that I should be devoured by wild beasts, murdered by savages, or starved to death for want of food. At the approach of night I slept in a tree, for fear of wild creatures; but slept soundly, though it rained all night.

October 1.—In the morning I saw, to my great surprise, the ship had floated with the high tide, and was driven on shore again, much nearer the island; which, as it was some comfort, on one hand (for seeing her sit upright, and not broken to pieces, I hoped, if the wind abated, I might get on board, and get some food and necessaries out of her for my relief), so, on the other hand, it renewed my grief at the loss of my comrades, who, I imagined, if we had all stayed on board, might have saved the ship, or at least, that they would not have been all drowned, as they were; and that, had the men been saved, we might perhaps have built us a boat out of the ruins of the ship, to have carried us to some other part of the world. I spent great part of this day in perplexing myself on these things;

but, at length, seeing the ship almost dry, I went upon the sand as near as I could, and then swam on board. This day also it continued raining, though with no wind at all.

From the 1st of October to the 24th.—All these days entirely spent in many several voyages to get all I could out of the ship, which I brought on shore, every tide of flood, upon rafts. Much rain also, in those days, though with some intervals of fair weather; but it seems this was the rainy season.

October 24.—I overset my raft, and all the goods I had got upon it; but being in shoal water, and the things being chiefly heavy, I recovered many of them when the tide was out.

October 25.—It rained all night and all day, with some gusts of wind; during which time the ship broke in pieces, the wind blowing a little harder than before, and was no more to be seen, except the wreck of her, and that only at low water. I spent this day in covering and securing the goods which I saved, that the rain might not spoil them.

October 26.—I walked about the shore almost all day, to find out a place to fix my habitation, greatly concerned to secure myself from any attack in the night, either from wild beasts or men. Towards night I fixed upon a proper place, under a rock, and marked out a semicircle for my encampment, which I resolved to strengthen with a work, wall, or fortification, made of double piles, lined within with cables, and without with turf.

From the 26th to the 30th, I worked very hard in carrying all my goods to my new habitation, though some part of the time it rained exceeding hard.

The 31st, in the morning, I went out into the island with my gun, to seek for some food, and discover the country; when I killed a she-goat, and her kid followed me home, which I afterwards killed also, because it would not feed.

November 1.—I set up my tent under a rock, and lay there for the first night; making it as large as I could, with stakes driven in to swing my hammock upon.

November 2.—I set up all my chests and boards, and the pieces of timber which made my rafts, and with them formed a fence round me, a little within the place I had marked out for my fortification.

November 3.—I went out with my gun, and killed two fowls like ducks, which were very good food. In the afternoon went to work to make me a table.

November 4.—This morning I began to order my times of work, of going out with my gun, time of sleep, and time of diversion; viz., every morning I walked out with my gun for two or three hours, if it did not rain; then employed myself to work till about eleven o'clock; then ate what I had to live on; and from twelve to two I lay down to sleep, the weather being excessive hot: and then, in the evening, to work again. The working part of this day and the next were wholly employed in making this table, for I was yet but a very sorry workman, though time and necessity made me a complete natural mechanic soon after, as I believe they would do any one else.

November 5.—This day I went abroad with my gun and my dog, and killed a wildcat; her skin pretty soft, but her flesh good for nothing; every creature I killed, I took off the skins and preserved them. Coming back by the seashore, I saw many sorts of sea-fowls, which I did not understand; but was surprised, and almost frighted, with two or three seals, which, while I was gazing at, not well knowing what they were, got into the sea and escaped me for that time.

November 6.—After my morning walk, I went to work with my table again, and finished it, though not to my liking; nor was it long before I learned to mend it.

November 7.—Now it began to be settled fair weather. The 7th, 8th, 9th, 10th, and part of the 12th (for the 11th was Sunday according to my reckoning), I took wholly up to make me a chair, and with much ado brought it to a tolerable shape, but never to please me; and even in the making I pulled it to pieces several times.

Note.—I soon neglected keeping Sundays; for, omitting my mark for them on my post, I forgot which was which.

November 13.—This day it rained, which refreshed me exceedingly, and cooled the earth: but it was accompanied with terrible thunder and lightning, which frighted me dreadfully, for fear of my powder. As soon as it was over, I resolved to separate my stock of powder into as many little parcels as possible, that it might not be in danger.

November 14, 15, 16.—These three days I spent in making little square chests, or boxes, which might hold about a pound, or two pounds at most, of powder; and so, putting the powder in, I stowed it in places as secure and remote from one another as possible. On one of these three days I killed a large bird that was good to eat, but I knew not what to call it.

November 17.—This day I began to dig behind my tent into the rock, to make room for my further conveniency.

Note.—Three things I wanted exceedingly for this work; viz., a pickaxe, a shovel, and a wheelbarrow, or basket; so I desisted from my work, and began to consider how to supply that want, and make me some tools. As for the pickaxe, I made use of the iron crows, which were proper enough, though heavy; but the next thing was a shovel, or spade; this was so absolutely necessary, that, indeed, I could do nothing effectually without it; but what kind of one to make I knew not.

November 18.—The next day, in searching the woods, I found a tree of that wood, or like it, which, in the Brazils, they call the iron tree, for its exceeding hardness; of this, with great labour, and almost spoiling my axe, I cut a piece, and brought it home, with difficulty enough, for it was exceeding heavy. The excessive hardness of the wood, and having no other way, made me a long while upon this machine, for I worked it effectually by little and little into the form of a shovel or spade; the handle shaped exactly like ours in England, only that the board part having no iron shod upon it at bottom, it would not last me so long; however, it served well enough for the uses which I had occasion to put it to; but never was a shovel, I believe, made after that fashion, or so long making.

I was still deficient, for I wanted a basket, or a wheel-barrow. A basket I could not make by any means, having no such things as twigs that would bend to make wicker-ware—at least, none yet found out; and as to the wheel-barrow, I fancied I could make all but the wheel; but that I had no notion of; neither did I know how to go about it; besides, I had no possible way to make iron gudgeons for the spindle or axis of the wheel to run in; so I gave it over, and so, for carrying away the earth which I dug out of the cave, I made me a thing like a hod, which the labourers carry mortar in, when they serve the bricklayers. This was not so difficult to me as the making of the shovel; and yet this and the shovel, and the attempt which I made in vain to make a wheel-barrow, took me up no less than four days, I mean always excepting my morning's walk with my gun, which I seldom failed, and very seldom failed also of bringing home something fit to eat.

November 23.—My other work having stood still, because of my making these tools, when they were finished I went on, and working every day, as my strength and time allowed, I spent eighteen days entirely in widening and deepening my cave, that it might hold my goods commodiously.

Note.—During all this time I worked to make this room, or cave, spacious enough to accommodate me as a warehouse, or magazine, a kitchen, a dining-room, and a cellar. As for a lodging, I kept to the tent; except that sometimes, in the wet season of the year, it rained so hard that I could not keep myself dry, which caused me afterwards to cover all my place within my pale with long poles, in the form of rafters, leaning against the rock, and load them with flags and large leaves of trees, like a thatch.

December 10.—I began now to think my cave or vault finished, when on a sudden (it seems I had made it too large) a great quantity of earth fell down from the top and one side; so much that, in short, it frighted me, and not without reason, too; for if I had been under it, I had never wanted a grave-digger. Upon this disaster I had a great deal of work to do over again, for I had the loose earth to carry out; and, which was of more importance, I had the ceiling to prop up, so that I might be sure no more would come down.

December 11.—This day I went to work with it accordingly, and got two shores or posts pitched upright to the top, with two pieces of board across over each post; this I finished the next day, and setting more posts up with boards, in about a week more I had the roof secured; and the posts, standing in rows, served me for partitions to part off my house.

December 17.—From this day to the 20th I placed shelves and knocked up nails on the posts, to hang everything up that could be hung up; and now I began to be in some order within doors.

December 20.—Now I carried everything into the cave, and began to furnish my house, and set up some pieces of board like a dresser, to order my victuals upon; but boards began to be very scarce with me; also I made me another table.

December 24.—Much rain all night and all day; no stirring out.

December 25.—Rain all day.

December 26.—No rain, and the earth much cooler than before, and pleasanter.

December 27.—Killed a young goat, and lamed another so that I catched it, and led it home on a string; when I had it at home, I bound and splintered up its leg, which was broke.

N.B.—I took such care of it that it lived, and the leg grew well and as strong as ever; but by nursing it so long it grew tame and fed upon the little green at my door, and would not go away. This was the first time that I entertained a thought of breeding up some tame creatures, that I might have food when my powder and shot were all spent.

December 28, 29, 30, 31.—Great heats and no breeze, so that there was no stirring abroad, except in the evening, for food; this time I spent in putting all my things in order within doors.

January 1.—Very hot still: but I went abroad early and late with my gun, and lay still in the middle of the day. This evening, going farther into the valleys which lay towards the centre of the island, I found there was plenty of goats, though exceedingly shy, and hard to come at; however, I resolved to try if I could not bring my dog to hunt them down.

January 2.—Accordingly, the next day, I went out with my dog, and set him upon the goats; but I was mistaken, for they all faced about upon the dog, and he knew his danger too well, for he would not come near them.

January 3.—I began my fence, or wall; which, being still jealous of my being attacked by somebody, I resolved to make very thick and strong.

N.B.—This wall being described before, I purposely omit what was said in the Journal; it is sufficient to observe that I was no less time than from the 3rd of January to the 14th of April working, finishing, and perfecting this wall, though it was no more than about twenty-four yards in length, being a half-circle, from one place in the rock to another place, about eight yards from it, the door of the cave being in the centre behind it.

All this time I worked very hard, the rains hindering me many days, nay, sometimes weeks together; but I thought I should never be perfectly secure till this wall was finished; and it is scarce credible what inexpressible labour everything was done with, especially the bringing piles out of the woods, and driving them into the ground; for I made them much bigger than I needed to have done.

When this wall was finished, and the outside double-fenced with a turf wall raised up close to it, I persuaded myself that, if any people were to come on shore there, they would not perceive anything like a habitation; and it was very well I did so, as may be observed hereafter, upon a very remarkable occasion.

During this time I made rounds in the woods for game every day, when the rain permitted me, and made frequent discoveries in these walks of something or other to my advantage; particularly I found a kind of wild pigeons, which build, not as woodpigeons in a tree, but rather as house pigeons, in the holes of rocks; and taking some young ones, I endeavoured to breed them up tame, and did so; but when they grew older they flew all away, which perhaps was at first for want of feeding them, for I had nothing to give them; however, I frequently found their nests, and got their young ones, which were very good meat.

And now, in the managing my household affairs, I found myself wanting in many things, which I thought at first it was impossible for me to make; as, indeed, as to some of them it was: for instance, I could never make a cask to be hooped. I had a small runlet or two, as I observed before; but I could never arrive to the capacity of making one of them, though I spent many weeks about it; I could neither put in the heads, nor join the staves so true to one another as to make them hold water; so I gave that also over.

In the next place, I was at a great loss for candles; so that, as soon as it was dark, which was generally by seven o'clock, I was obliged to go to bed. I remembered the lump of beeswax with which I made candles in my African adventure; but I had none of that now; the only remedy I had was, that when I had killed a goat I saved the tallow, and with a little dish made of clay, which I baked in the sun, to which I added a wick of some oakum, I made me a lamp; and this gave me light, though not a clear, steady light like a candle. In the middle of all my labours it happened that, rummaging my things, I found a little bag, which, as I hinted before, had been filled with corn for the feeding of poultry—not for this voyage, but before, as I suppose, when the ship came from Lisbon. What little remainder of corn had been in the bag was all devoured by the rats, and I saw nothing in the bag but husks and dust; and being willing to have the bag for some other use (I think it was to put powder in, when I divided it for fear of the lightning, or some such use), I shook the husks of corn out of it on one side of my fortification, under the rock.

It was a little before the great rains just now mentioned that I threw this stuff away, taking no notice of anything, and not so much as remembering that I had thrown anything there, when, about a month after, or thereabouts, I saw some few stalks of something green shooting up on the ground, which I fancied might be some plant I had not seen; which I was surprised, and perfectly astonished when, after a little longer time, I saw about ten or twelve ears come out, which were perfect green barley, of the same kind as our European —nay, as our English barley.

It is impossible to express the astonishment and confusion of my thoughts on this occasion; I had hitherto acted upon no religious foundation at all; indeed, I had very few notions of religion in my head, nor had entertained any sense of anything that had befallen me, otherwise than a chance, or, as we lightly say, what pleases God, without so much as inquiring into the end of Providence in these things, or his order in governing events in the world. But after I saw barley grow there in a climate which

I knew was not proper for corn, and especially that I knew not how it came there, it startled me strangely, and I began to suggest that God had miraculously caused this grain to grow without any help of seed sown, and that it was so directed purely for my sustenance in that wild, miserable place.

This touched my heart a little, and brought tears out of my eyes, and I began to bless myself that such a prodigy of Nature should happen upon my account; and this was the more strange to me, because I saw near it still, all along by the side of the rock, some other straggling stalks, which proved to be stalks of rice, and which I knew because I had seen it grow in Africa, when I was ashore there.

I not only thought these the pure productions of Providence for my support, but not doubting but that there was more in the place, I went all over that part of the island where I had been before, peering in every corner and under every rock, to see for more of it, but I could not find any. At last it occurred to my thoughts that I had shaken the bag of chickens' meat out in that place; and the wonder began to cease; and I must confess, my religious thankfulness to God's providence began to abate too, upon the discovering that all this was nothing but what was common; though I ought to have been as thankful for so strange and unforeseen providence, as if it had been miraculous; for it was really the work of Providence as to me, that should order or appoint that ten or twelve grains of corn should remain unspoiled, when the rats had destroyed all the rest, as if it had been dropped from heaven; as also that I should throw it out in that particular place, where, it being in the shade of a high rock, it sprang up immediately; whereas, if I had thrown it anywhere else at that time it had been burnt up and destroyed.

I carefully saved the ears of this corn, you may be sure, in their season, which was about the end of June; and laying up every corn, I resolved to sow them all again, hoping in time, to have some quantity, sufficient to supply me with bread. But it was not till the fourth year that I would allow myself the least grain of this corn to eat, and even then but sparingly, as I shall say afterwards, in its order; for I lost all that I sowed the first season, by not observing the proper time; for I sowed it just before the dry season, so that it never came up at all, at least not as it would have done; of which in its place.

Besides this barley, there were, as above, twenty or thirty stalks of rice, which I preserved with the same care, and whose use was of the same kind, or to the same purpose, viz., to make me bread, or other food; for I found ways to cook it up without baking, though I did that also after some time.

But to return to my Journal:

I worked excessive hard these three or four months, to get my wall done; and the 14th of April, I closed it up, contriving to go into it, not by a door, but over a wall, by a ladder, that there might be no sign on the outside of my habitation.

April 16.—I finished the ladder; so I went up the ladder to the top, and then pulled it up after me, and let it down on the inside: this was a complete inclosure to me; for within I had room enough, and nothing could come at me from without, unless it could first mount my wall.

The very next day after this wall was finished, I had almost had all my labours overthrown at once, and myself killed. The case was thus: As I was busy in the inside of it, behind my tent, just in the entrance into my cave, I was terribly frightened with a most dreadful surprising thing indeed; for all on a sudden, I found the earth came tumbling down from the roof of my cave, and from the edge of the hill over my head, and two of the posts I had set up in the cave cracked in a frightful manner. I was heartily scared; but thought nothing of what really was the cause, only thinking that the top of my cave was fallen in, as some of it had done before; and for fear I should be buried in it, I ran forwards to my ladder, and not thinking myself safe there neither, I got over my wall for fear of the pieces of the hill, which I expected might roll down upon me. I was no sooner stepped down upon the firm ground, than I plainly saw it was a terrible earthquake; for the ground I stood on shook three times at about eight minutes' distance, with three such shocks as would have overturned the strongest building that could be supposed to have stood upon the earth; and a great piece of the top of the rock, which stood about half a mile from me, next the sea, fell down with such a terrible noise as I never heard in all my life. I perceived also the very sea was put into a violent motion by it; and I believe the shocks were stronger under the water than on the island.

I was so amazed with the thing itself, having never felt the like, or discoursed with any one that had, that I was like one dead or stupefied; and the motion of the earth made my stomach sick like one that was tossed at sea; but the noise of the falling of the rock awaked me, as it were, and rousing me from the stupefied condition I was in, filled me with horror, and I thought of nothing then but the hill falling upon my tent and all my household goods, and burying all at once; and this sunk my very soul within me a second time.

After the third shock was over, and I felt no more for some time, I began to take courage; and yet I had not heart enough to get over my wall again, for fear of being buried alive, but still sat upon the ground, greatly cast down and disconsolate, not knowing what to do. All this while I had not the least serious religious thought; nothing but the common "Lord, have mercy upon me!" and when it was over, that went away too.

While I sat thus, I found the air overcast, and it grew cloudy, as if it would rain; soon after that, the wind arose by little and little, so that in less than half an hour it blew a most dreadful hurricane of wind; the sea was, all on a sudden, covered with foam and froth; the shore was covered with the breach of the water; the trees were torn up by the roots; and a terrible storm it was. This held about three hours and then began to abate; and then in two hours more it was calm, and began to rain very hard. All this while I sat upon the ground very much terrified and dejected; when on a sudden it came into my thoughts, that these winds and rain being the consequences of the earthquake, the earthquake itself was spent and over, and I might venture into my cave again. With this thought, my spirits began to revive; and the rain also helping to persuade me, I went in and sat down in my tent; but the rain was so violent that my tent was ready to be beaten down with it; and I was forced to go into my cave, though very much afraid and uneasy, for fear it should fall on my head. This violent rain forced me to a new work, viz., to cut a hole through my new fortifications, like a sink, to let the water go out, which would else have drowned my cave. After I had been in my cave some time, and found still no more shocks of the earthquake follow, I began to be more composed. And now to support my spirits, which indeed wanted it very much, I went to my little store, and took a small sup of rum; which, however, I did then and always very sparingly, knowing I could have no more when that was gone. It continued raining all that night, and great part of the next day, so that I could not stir abroad; but my mind being more composed, I began to think of what I had best to do; concluding, that if the island was subject to these earthquakes, there would be no living for me in a cave, but I must consider of building me some little hut in an open place which I might surround with a wall, as I had done here, and so make myself secure from wild beasts or men; for I concluded if I stayed where I was, I should certainly, one time or other, be buried alive.

With these thoughts, I resolved to move my tent from the place where it now stood, which was just under the hanging precipice of the hill; and which, if it should be shaken again, would certainly fall upon my tent; and I spent the two next days, being the 19th and 20th of April, in contriving where and how to remove my habitation. The fear of being swallowed up alive made me that I never slept in quiet; and yet the apprehensions of lying abroad without any fence were almost equal to it: but still, when I looked about, and saw how everything was put in order, how pleasantly concealed I was, and how safe from danger, it made me loath to remove. In the meantime, it occurred to me that it would require a vast deal of time for me to do this, and that I must be contented to run the venture where I was, till I had formed a camp for myself, and had secured it so as to remove to it. So with this resolution I composed myself for a time, and resolved that I would go to work with all speed to build me a wall with piles and cables, etc., in a circle, as before, and set my tent up in it, when it was finished; but that I would venture to stay where I was till it was finished, and fit to remove to. This was the 21st.

April 22.—The next morning I began to consider of means to put this resolve in execution; but I was at a great loss about my tools. I had three large axes, and abundance of hatchets (for we carried the hatchets for traffic with the Indians), but with much chopping and cutting knotty hard wood, they were all full of notches, and dull; and though I had a grindstone, I could not turn it and grind my tools too. This caused me as much thought as a statesman would have bestowed upon a grand point of politics, or judge upon the life and death of a man. At length, I contrived a wheel with a string, to turn it with my foot, that I might have both my hands at liberty.

Note.—I had not seen any such thing in England, or at least not to take notice how it was done, though I have observed it was very common there; besides that, my grindstone was very large and heavy. This machine cost me a full week's work to bring it to perfection.

April 28, 29.—These two whole days I took up in grind-
ing my tools, my machine for turning my grindstone
performing very well.

April 30.—Having perceived my bread had been low
a great while, I now took a survey of it, and reduced myself
to one biscuit-cake a day, which made my heart very
heavy.

CHAPTER VI

*M*AY 1.—In the morning, looking towards the sea-side, the tide being low, I saw something lie on the shore bigger than ordinary, and it looked like a cask; when I came to it, I found a small barrel, and two or three pieces of the wreck of the ship, which were driven on shore by the late hurricane; and looking towards the wreck itself, I thought it seemed to lie higher out of the water than it used to do. I examined the barrel which was driven on shore, and soon found it was a barrel of gunpowder; but it had taken water, and the powder was caked as hard as a stone: however, I rolled it farther on shore for the present, and went on upon the sand, as near as I could to the wreck of the ship, to look for more.

When I came down to the ship, I found it strangely removed. The forecastle, which lay before buried in sand, was heaved up at least six feet, and the stern, which was broken to pieces and parted from the rest by the force of the sea soon after I had left rummaging of her, was tossed, as it were, up, and cast on one side; and the sand was thrown so high on that side next the stern, that whereas there was a great place of water before, so that I could not come within a quarter of a mile of the wreck without swimming, I could now walk quite up to her when the tide was out. I was surprised with this at first, but soon concluded it must be done by the earthquake; and as by this violence the ship was more broken open than formerly, so many things came daily on shore, which the sea had loosened, and which the winds and water rolled by degrees to the land.

This wholly diverted my thoughts from the design of removing my habitation and I busied myself mightily, that day especially, in searching whether I could make any way into the ship; but I found nothing was to be expected of that kind, for that all the inside of the ship was choked up with sand. However, as I had learned not to despair of anything, I resolved to pull everything to pieces that I could of the ship, concluding that everything I could get from her would be of some use or other to me.

May 3.—I began with my saw, and cut a piece of beam through, which held some of the upper part or quarterdeck together, and when I had cut it through, I cleared away the sand as well as I could from the side which lay highest and was quite out of the water; but the tide coming in, I was obliged to give over for that time.

May 4.—I went a-fishing, but caught not one fish that I durst eat of, till I was weary of my sport; when, just going to leave off, I caught a young dolphin. I had made me a long line of some rope-yarn, but I had no hooks; yet I frequently caught fish enough, as much as I cared to eat; all which I dried in the sun, and ate them dry.

May 5.—Worked on the wreck; cut another beam asunder, and brought three great fire planks off from the decks, which I tied together, and made swim on shore when the tide of flood came on.

May 6.—Worked on the wreck; got several iron bolts out of her, and other pieces of ironwork; worked very hard, and came home very much tired and had thoughts of giving it over.

May 7.—Went to the wreck again, with an intent not to work, but found the weight of the wreck had broken itself down, the beams being cut; that several pieces of the ship seemed to lie loose, and the inside of the hold lay so open that I could see into it; but it was almost full of water and sand.

May 8.—Went to the wreck, and carried an iron crow to wrench up the deck, which lay now quite clear of the water or sand. I wrenched open two planks, and brought them on shore also with the tide. I left the iron crow in the wreck for next day.

May 9.—Went to the wreck, and with the crow made way into the body of the wreck, and felt several casks, and loosened them with the crow, but could not break them up. I felt also a roll of English lead, and could stir it, but it was too heavy to move.

May 10, 11, 12, 13, 14.—Went every day to the wreck; and got a great deal of pieces of timber, and boards, or planks, and two or three hundred weight of iron.

May 15.—I carried two hatchets, to try if I could not cut a piece off the roll of lead, by placing the edge of one hatchet, and driving it with the other; but as it lay about a foot and a half in the water, I could not make any blow to drive the hatchet.

May 16.—It had blown hard in the night, and the wreck appeared more broken by the force of the water; but I stayed so long in the woods, to get pigeons for food, that the tide prevented me going to the wreck that day.

May 17.—I saw some pieces of the wreck blown on shore, at a great distance, near two miles off me, but resolved to see what they were, and found they were pieces of the head, but too heavy for me to bring away.

May 24.—Every day, to this day, I worked on the wreck; and with hard labour I loosened some things so much with the crow that the first flowing tide several casks floated out, and two of the seamen's chests; but the wind blowing from the shore nothing came to land that day but pieces of timber, and a hogshead which had some Brazil pork in it; but the salt water and the sand had spoiled it. I continued this work every day to the 15th of June, except the time necessary to get food, which I always appointed, during this part of my employment, to be when the tide was up, that I might be ready when it was ebbed out; and by this time I had gotten timber and plank, and iron-work enough to have built a good boat, if I had known how; and also I got, at several times, and in several pieces, near one hundredweight of the sheet lead.

June 16.—Going down to the seaside, I found a large tortoise, or turtle. This was the first I had seen, which, it seems, was only my misfortune, not any defect of the place or the scarcity; for had I happened to be on the other side of the island, I might have had hundreds of them every day, as I found afterwards; but perhaps had paid dear enough for them.

June 17.—I spent in cooking the turtle. I found in her threescore eggs; and her flesh was to me, at that time, the most savoury and pleasant that ever I tasted in my life, having had no flesh, but of goats and fowls, since I landed in this horrible place.

June 18.—Rained all the day, and I stayed within. I thought, at this time, the rain felt cold, and I was somewhat chilly, which I knew was not usual in that latitude.

June 19.—Very ill, and shivering, as if the weather had been cold.

June 20.—No rest all night; violent pains in my head, and feverish.

June 21.—Very ill; frighted almost to death with the apprehensions of my sad condition—to be sick, and no help: prayed to God, for the first time since the storm off of Hull, but scarce knew what I said or why; my thoughts being all confused.

June 22.—A little better; but under dreadful apprehensions of sickness.

June 23.—Very bad again; cold and shivering, and then a violent headache.

June 24.—Much better.

June 25.—An ague very violent: the fit held me seven hours; cold fit, and hot with faint sweats after it.

June 26.—Better; and having no victuals to eat, took my gun, but found myself very weak; however, I killed a she-goat, and with much difficulty got it home, and broiled some of it, and ate. I would fain have stewed it, and made some broth, but had no pot.

June 27.—The ague again so violent that I lay a-bed all day, and neither ate nor drank. I was ready to perish for thirst; but so weak I had no strength to stand up, or to get myself any water to drink. Prayed to God again, but was light-headed; and when I was not, I was so ignorant that I knew not what to say; only I lay and cried, "Lord, look upon me! Lord, pity me! Lord, have mercy upon me!" I suppose I did nothing else for two or three hours; till the fit wearing off, I fell asleep, and did not awake till far in the night. When I awoke, I found myself much refreshed, but weak, and exceeding thirsty; however, as I had no water in my whole habitation, I was forced to lie till morning, and went to sleep again. In this second sleep I had this terrible dream: I thought that I was sitting on the ground, on the outside of my wall, where I sat when the storm blew after the earthquake, and that I saw a man descend from a great black cloud, in a bright flame of fire, and light upon the ground: he was all over as bright as a flame, so that I could but just bear to look towards him: his countenance was most inexpressibly dreadful, impossible for words to describe; when he stepped upon the ground with his feet, I thought the earth trembled, just as it had done before in the earthquake, and all the air looked, to my apprehension, as if it had been filled with flashes of fire. He was no sooner landed upon the earth, but he moved forwards towards me with a long spear or weapon in his hand to kill me; and when he came to a rising ground, at some distance, he spoke to me— or I heard a voice so terrible that it is impossible to express the terror of it. All that I can say I understood was this:— "Seeing all these things have not brought thee to repentance now thou shalt die";—at which words, I thought he lifted up the spear that was in his hand to kill me.

No one that shall ever read this account will expect that I should be able to describe the horrors of my soul at this terrible vision. I mean, that even while it was a dream, I even dreamed of those horrors. Nor is it any more possible to describe the impression that remained upon my mind when I awaked, and found it was but a dream.

I had, alas! no divine knowledge. What I had received by the good instruction of my father was then worn out by an uninterrupted series, for eight years of seafaring, wickedness, and a constant conversation with none but such as were, like myself, wicked and profane to the last degree. I do not remember that I had, in all that time, one thought that so much as tended either to looking upwards towards God, or inwards towards a reflection upon my own ways: but a certain stupidity of soul without desire of good, or conscience of evil, had entirely overwhelmed me; and I was all that the most hardened, unthinking, wicked creature among our common sailors can be supposed to be—not having the least sense, either of the fear of God in dangers, or of thankfulness to God in deliverances.

In the relating what is already past of my story, this will be the more easily believed when I shall add, that through all the variety of miseries that had to this day befallen me, I never had so much as once thought of its being the hand of God, or that it was a just punishment for my sins—my rebellious behaviour against my father—or my present sins, which were great—or so much as a punishment for the general course of my wicked life. When I was on the desperate expedition on the desert shores of Africa, I never had so much as one thought of what would become of me, or one wish to God to direct me whither I should go, or to keep me from the danger which apparently surrounded me, as well from voracious creatures as cruel savages; but I was merely thoughtless of God or a Providence—I acted like a mere brute, from the principles of nature, and by the dictates of common sense only, and indeed hardly that. When I was delivered and taken up at sea by the Portugal captain, well used, and dealt justly and honourably with, as well as charitably, I had not the least thankfulness in my thoughts. When, again, I was shipwrecked, ruined, and in danger of drowning on this island, I was as far from remorse, or looking on it as a judgment. I only said to myself often, that I was an unfortunate dog, and born to be always miserable.

It is true, when I got on shore first here, and found all my ship's crew drowned, and myself spared, I was surprised, with a kind of ecstasy, and some transports of soul, which, had the grace of God assisted, might have come up to true thankfulness; but it ended where it began, in a mere common flight of joy, or, as I may say, being glad I was alive, without the least reflection upon the distinguishing goodness of the Hand which had preserved me, and had singled me out to be preserved when all the rest were destroyed, or an inquiry why Providence had been thus merciful to me. Even just the same common sort of joy which seamen generally have, after they have got safe ashore from a shipwreck, all which they drown in the next bowl of punch and forget almost as soon as it is over: and all the rest of my life was like it. Even when I was afterwards, on due consideration, made sensible of my condition, how I was cast on this dreadful place, out of the reach of human kind, out of all hope of relief, or prospect of redemption, as soon as I saw a probability of living, and that I should not starve and perish for hunger, all the sense of my affliction wore off; and I began to be very easy, applied myself to the works proper for my preservation and supply, and was far enough from being afflicted at my condition, as a judgment from Heaven, or as the hand of God against me: these were thoughts which very seldom entered into my head.

The growing up of the corn, as is hinted in my journal, had at first some little influence upon me, and began to affect me with seriousness, as long as I thought it had something miraculous in it; but as soon as ever that part of the thought was removed, all the impression which was raised from it wore off also, as I have noted already. Even the earthquake, though nothing could be more terrible in its nature, or more immediately directing to the invisible Power which alone directs such things, yet no sooner was the first fright over, but the impression it had made went off also. I had no more sense of God or his judgment—much less of the present affliction of my circumstances being from his hand—than if I had been in the most prosperous condition of life. But now, when I began to be sick, and a leisurely view of the miseries of death came to place itself before me; when my spirits began to sink under the burden of a strong distemper, and nature was exhausted with the violence of the fever, conscience, that had slept so long, began to awake, and I began to reproach myself with my past life, in which I had so evidently, by uncommon wickedness, provoked the justice of God to lay me under uncommon strokes, and to deal with me in so vindictive a manner. These reflections oppressed me from the second or third day of my distemper; and in the violence as well of the fever as of the dreadful reproaches of my conscience, extorted some words from me like praying to God, though I cannot say they were either a prayer attended with desires or with hopes: it was rather the voice of mere fright and distress. My thoughts were confused, the convictions great upon my mind, and the horror of dying in such a miserable condition raised vapors into my head with the mere apprehensions; and in these hurries of my soul, I knew not what my tongue might express. But it was rather exclamation, such as, "Lord, what a miserable creature am I! If I should be sick, I shall certainly die for want of help, and what will become of me?" Then the tears burst out of my eyes, and I could say no more for a good while. In this interval, the good advice of my father came to my mind, and presently his prediction, which I mentioned at the beginning of this story, viz., that if I did take this foolish step, God would not bless me, and I would have leisure hereafter to reflect upon having neglected his counsel, when there might be none to assist me in my recovery. "Now," I said aloud, "my dear father's words are come to pass; God's justice has overtaken me, and I have none to help or hear me. I rejected the voice of Providence, which had mercifully put me in a posture or station of life wherein I might have been happy and easy; and I would neither see it myself, nor learn to know the blessing of it from my parents. I left them to mourn over my folly; and now I am left to mourn under the consequences of it. I refused their help and assistance, who would have lifted me into the world, and would have made everything easy to me; and now I have difficulties to struggle with too great for even nature itself to support, and no assistance, no help, no comfort, no advice." Then I cried out, "Lord, be my help, for I am in great distress." This was the first prayer, if I might call it so, that I had made for many years. But I return to my journal.

June 28.—Having been somewhat refreshed with the sleep I had had, and the fit being entirely off, I got up; and though the fright and terror of my dream was very great, yet I considered that the fit of the ague would return again the next day, and now was my time to get something to refresh and support myself when I should be ill; and the first thing I did, I filled a large square case-bottle with water, and set it upon my table, in reach of my bed; and to take off the chill or aguish disposition of the water, I put about a quarter of a pint of rum into it, and mixed them together. Then I got me a piece of the goat's flesh, and broiled it on the coals, but could eat very little; I walked about, but was very weak, and withal very sad and heavy-hearted in the sense of my miserable condition, dreading the return of my distemper the next day. At night, I made my supper of three of the turtle's eggs, which I roasted in the ashes, and ate, as we call it, in the shell, and this was the first bit of meat I had ever asked

God's blessing to, even as I could remember, in my whole life.

After I had eaten, I tried to walk, but found myself so weak that I could hardly carry the gun, for I never went out without that; so I went out but a little way, and sat down upon the ground, looking out upon the sea, which was just before me, and very calm and smooth. As I sat here, some thoughts such as these occurred to me: What is the earth and sea, of which I have seen so much? Whence is it produced? And what am I, and all the other creatures, wild and tame, human and brutal? Whence are we? Sure we are all made by some secret Power, who formed the earth and sea, the air and sky. And who is that? Then it followed most naturally, It is God that has made it all. Well, but then, it came on strongly, if God has made all these things, he guides and governs them all, and all things that concern them; for the Being that could make all things must certainly have power to guide and direct them. If so, nothing could happen in this great circuit of his works, either without his knowledge or appointment.

And if nothing happens without his knowledge, he knows that I am here, and am in this dreadful condition; and if nothing happens without his appointment, he has appointed all this to befall me. Nothing occurred to my thoughts to contradict any of these conclusions, and therefore it rested upon me with the greater force, that it must needs be that God had appointed all this to befall me; that I was brought to this miserable circumstance by his direction, he having the sole power, not of me only, but of everything that happened in the world. Immediately it followed, Why has God done this to me? What have I done to be thus used? My conscience presently checked me in that inquiry, as if I had blasphemed, and methought it spoke to me like a voice, "Wretch! dost *thou* ask what thou hast done? Look back upon a dreadful mis-spent life, and ask thyself, what hast thou *not* done? Ask, why is it that

thou wert not long ago destroyed? Why wert thou not
drowned in Yarmouth Roads? killed in the fight, when
the ship was taken by the Sallee man-of-war? devoured
by the wild beasts off the coast of Africa? or drowned
here, when all the crew perished but thyself? Dost *thou*
ask, What have I done?" I was struck dumb with these
reflections, as one astonished, and had not a word to say,
—no, not to answer to myself,—but rose up pensive and
sad, walked back to my retreat, and went up over my
wall, as if I had been going to bed; but my thoughts were
sadly disturbed, and I had no inclination to sleep: so I
sat down in my chair, and lighted my lamp, for it began
to be dark. Now, as the apprehensions of the return of
my distemper terrified me very much, it occurred to my
thought, that the Brazilians take no physic but their
tobacco for almost all their distempers, and I had a piece
of a roll of tobacco in one of the chests, which was quite
cured, and some also that was green, and not quite cured.

I went, directed by Heaven, no doubt; for in this chest
I found a cure both for soul and body. I opened the
chest, and found what I looked for, viz., the tobacco; and
as the few books I had saved lay there too, I took out
one of the Bibles which I mentioned before, and which
to this time I had not found leisure, or so much as inclination to look into. I say I took it out, and brought both
that and the tobacco with me to the table. What use to
make of the tobacco I knew not, as to my distemper, or
whether it was good for it or no; but I tried several experiments with it, as if I was resolved it should heal one way
or the other. I first took a piece of leaf, and chewed it
in my mouth, which indeed, at first, almost stupefied my
brain, the tobacco being green and strong, and that I had
not been much used to it. Then I took some and steeped
it an hour or two in some rum, and resolved to take a dose
of it when I lay down; and, lastly, I burnt some upon a
pan of coals, and held my nose close over the smoke of
it as long as I could bear it, as well for the heat as the

virtue of it, and I held it almost to suffocation. In the interval of this operation, I took up the Bible and began to read, but my head was too much disturbed with the tobacco to bear reading, at least at that time; only, having opened the book casually, the words first that occurred to me were these, "Call upon me in the day of trouble, and I will deliver thee, and thou shalt glorify me." These words were very apt to my case, and made some impression upon my thoughts at the time of reading them, though not so much as they did afterwards; for, as for being *delivered*, the word had no sound, as I may say, to me, the thing was so remote, so impossible in my apprehension of things, that I began to say, as the children of Israel did when they were promised flesh to eat, "Can God spread a table in the wilderness?" so I began to say, "Can God himself deliver me from this place?" And as it was not for many years that any hopes appeared, this prevailed very often upon my thoughts; but, however, the words made a great impression upon me, and I mused upon them very often. It grew now late, and the tobacco had, as I said, dozed my head so much that I inclined to sleep: so I left my lamp burning in the cave, lest I should want anything in the night, and went to bed. But before I lay down, I did what I never had done in all my life; I kneeled down, and prayed to God to fulfill the promise to me, that if I called upon him in the day of trouble, he would deliver me. After my broken and imperfect prayer was over, I drank the rum in which I had steeped the tobacco, which was so strong and rank of the tobacco, that indeed I could scarcely get it down; immediately upon this I went to bed; and I found presently it flew up into my head violently; but I fell into a sound sleep, and waked no more till, by the sun, it must necessarily be near three o'clock in the afternoon the next day: nay, to this hour I am partly of opinion that I slept all the next day and night, and till almost three the day after; for otherwise, I know not how I should lose a day out of my reckoning in the days of the week, as it appeared some years after I had done; for if I had lost it by crossing and recrossing the line, I should have lost more than one day; but in my account it was lost, and I never knew which way. Be that, however, one way or other, when I awaked I found myself exceedingly refreshed, and my spirits lively and cheerful; when I got up I was stronger than I was the day before, and my stomach better, for I was hungry; and, in short, I had no fit the next day, but continued much altered for the better. This was the 29th.

The 30th was my well day, of course, and I went abroad with my gun, but did not care to travel too far. I killed a sea-fowl or two, something like a brant goose, and brought them home; but was not very forward to eat them; so I ate some more of the turtle's eggs, which were very good. This evening I renewed the medicine, which I had supposed did me good the day before, viz., the tobacco steeped in rum; only I did not take so much as before, nor did I chew any of the leaf, or hold my head over the smoke; however, I was not so well the next day, which was the first of July, as I hoped I should have been; for I had a little spice of the cold fit, but it was not much.

July 2.—I renewed the medicine all three ways; and dosed myself with it as at first, and doubled the quantity which I drank.

July 3.—I missed the fit for good and all, though I did not recover my full strength for some weeks after. While I was thus gathering strength, my thoughts ran exceedingly upon this Scripture, "I will deliver thee"; and the impossibility of my deliverance lay much upon my mind, in bar of my ever expecting it; but as I was discouraging myself with such thoughts, it occurred to my mind that I pored so much upon my deliverance from the main affliction that I disregarded the deliverance I had received, and I was, as it were, made to ask myself such questions as these, viz., Have I not been delivered, and wonderfully too, from sickness? from the most distressed condition that could be, and that was so frightful to me? and what notice had I taken of it? Had I done my part? God had delivered me, but I had not glorified him; that is to say, I had not owned and been thankful for that as a deliverance; and how could I expect greater deliverance? This touched my heart very much; and immediately I kneeled down, and gave God thanks aloud for my recovery from my sickness.

July 4.—In the morning I took the Bible; and beginning at the New Testament, I began seriously to read it, and imposed upon myself to read a while every morning and every night; not tying myself to the number of chapters, but as long as my thoughts should engage me. It was not long after I set seriously to this work, till I found my heart more deeply and sincerely affected with the wickedness of my past life. The impression of my dream revived; and the words, "All these things have not brought thee to repentance," ran seriously in my thoughts. I was earnestly begging of God to give me repentance, when it happened providentially, the very day, that, reading the Scripture, I came to these words: "He is exalted a Prince and a Saviour, to give repentance and to give remission." I threw down the book; and with my heart as well as my hands lifted up to heaven, in a kind of ecstasy of joy, I cried out aloud, "Jesus, thou Son of David! Jesus, thou exalted Prince and Saviour! give me repentance!" This was the first time I could say, in the true sense of the words, that I prayed in all my life; for now I prayed with a sense of my condition, and with a true Scripture view of hope, founded on the encouragement of the Word of God; and from this time, I may say, I began to have hope that God would hear me.

Now I began to construe the words mentioned above, "Call on me, and I will deliver thee," in a different sense from what I had ever done before, for then I had no notion of anything being called *deliverance*, but my being delivered from the captivity I was in: for though I was indeed at large in the place, yet the island was certainly a prison to me, and that in the worst sense in the world. But now I learned to take it in another sense: now I looked back upon my past life with such horror, and my sins appeared so dreadful, that my soul sought nothing of God but deliverance from the load of guilt that bore down all my comfort. As for my solitary life, it was nothing; I did not so much as pray to be delivered from it, or think of it; it was all of no consideration, in comparison of this. And I added this part here, to hint to whoever shall read it, that whenever they come to a true sense of things, they will find deliverance from sin a much greater blessing than deliverance from trouble and affliction.

But, leaving this part, I return to my journal:

My condition began now to be, though not less miserable as to my way of living, yet much easier to my mind: and my thoughts being directed, by a constant reading the Scripture and praying to God, to things of a higher nature, I had a great deal of comfort within, which, till now, I knew nothing of; also, my health and strength returned, I bestirred myself to furnish myself with everything that I wanted, and make my way of living as regular as I could.

From the 4th of July to the 14th, I was chiefly employed in walking about with my gun in my hand, a little and a little at a time, as a man that was gathering up his strength after a fit of sickness; for it is hardly to be imagined how low I was, and to what weakness I was reduced. The application which I made use of was perfectly new, and perhaps what had never cured an ague before, neither can I recommend it to any one to practice, by this experiment; and though it did carry off the fit, yet it rather contributed to weaken me; for I had frequent convulsions in my nerves and limbs for some time; I learned from it also this, in particular, that being abroad in the rainy season was the most pernicious thing to my health that could be, especially in those rains which came attended with storms and hurricanes of wind; for as the rain which came in a dry season was always most accompanied with such storms, so I found this rain was much more dangerous than the rain which fell in September and October.

I had now been in this unhappy island above ten months; all possibility of deliverance from this condition seemed to be entirely taken from me; and I firmly believed that no human shape had ever set foot upon that place. Having now secured my habitation, as I thought, fully to my mind, I had a great desire to make a more perfect discovery of the island, and to see what other productions I might find, which yet I knew nothing of.

It was the 15th of July that I began to take a more particular survey of the island itself. I went up the creek first, where, as I hinted, I brought my rafts on shore. I found, after I came about two miles up, that the tide did not flow any higher; and that it was no more than a little brook of running water, and very fresh and good; but this being the dry season, there was hardly any water in some parts of it; at least, not enough to run in any stream, so as it could be perceived. On the banks of this brook, I found many pleasant savannas of meadows, plain, smooth, and covered with grass; and on the rising parts of them, next to the higher grounds, where the water, as it might be supposed, never overflowed, I found a great deal of tobacco, green, and growing to a great and very strong stalk; there were divers other plants, which I had no notion of or understanding about, and might, perhaps, have virtues of their own, which I could not find out. I searched for the cassava root, which the Indians in all that climate make their bread of, but I could find none. I saw large plants of aloes, but did not then understand them. I saw several sugar-canes, but wild, and for want of cultivation imperfect. I contented myself with these discoveries for this time, and came back, musing with myself what course I might take to know the virtue and goodness of any of the fruits of plants which I should discover; but could bring it to no conclusion; for, in short, I had made so little observation while I was in the Brazils, that I knew little of the plants of the field; at least, very little that might serve me to any purpose now in my distress.

The next day, the 16th, I went up the same way again; and after going something further than I had gone the day before, I found the brook and savannas cease, and the country became more woody than before. In this part I found different fruits, and particularly I found melons upon the ground, in great abundance; and grapes upon the trees; the vines had spread indeed over the trees, and the clusters of grapes were just now in their prime, very ripe and rich. This was a surprising discovery, and I was exceedingly glad of them; but I was warned by my experience to eat sparingly of them; but, remembering that, when I was ashore in Barbary, the eating of grapes killed several of our Englishmen, who were slaves there, by throwing them into fluxes and fevers. But I found an excellent use for these grapes; and that was to cure or dry them in the sun, and keep them as dried grapes or raisins are kept, which I thought would be, as indeed they were, as wholesome and as agreeable to eat, when no grapes might be had.

I spent all that evening there, and went not back to my habitation, which, by the way, was the first night, as I might say, I had lain from home. In the night, I took my first contrivance, and got up into a tree, where I slept well; and the next morning proceeded upon my discovery, travelling nearly four miles, as I might judge by the length of the valley, keeping still due north, with a ridge of hills on the south and north side of me. At the end of this march I came to an opening, where the country seemed to descend to the west: and a little spring of fresh water, which issued out of the side of the hill by me, ran the other way, that is, due east; and the country appeared so fresh, so green, so flourishing, everything being in a constant verdure, or flourish of spring, that it looked like a planted garden. I descended a little on the side of that delicious valley, surveying it with a secret kind of pleasure, though mixed with other afflicting thoughts, to think that this was all my own; that I was king and lord of all this country indefeasibly, and had a right of possession; and, if I could convey it, I might have it in inheritance as completely as any lord of a manor in England. I saw here abundance of cocoa trees, orange and lemon and citron trees; but all wild, and few bearing any fruit, at least not then. However, the green limes that I gathered were not only pleasant to eat, but very wholesome; and I mixed their juice afterwards with water, which made it very wholesome; and very cool and refreshing. I found now I had business enough to gather and carry home, and I resolved to lay up a store as well of grapes as limes and lemons, to furnish myself for the wet season, which I knew was approaching. In order to do this, I gathered a great heap of grapes in one place, a lesser heap in another place, and a great parcel of limes and lemons in another place; and taking a few of each with me I travelled homeward, and resolved to come again, and bring a bag or sack, or what I could make to carry the rest home. Accordingly, having spent three days in this journey, I came home (so I must now call my tent and my cave); but before I got thither, the grapes were spoiled; the richness of the fruit, and the weight of the juice, having broken them and bruised them, they were good for little or nothing; as to the limes, they were good, but I could bring but a few.

The next day, being the 19th, I went back, having made me two small bags to bring home my harvest; but I was surprised when, coming to my heap of grapes, which were so rich and fine when I gathered them, I found them all spread abroad, trodden to pieces, and dragged about, some here, some there, and abundance eaten and devoured. By this I concluded there were some wild creatures thereabouts, which had done this; but what they were I knew not. However, as I found there was no laying them up on heaps, and no carrying them away in a sack, but that one way they would be destroyed, and the other way they would be crushed with their own weight, I took another course;

for I gathered a large quantity of the grapes, and hung them upon the out branches of the trees, that they might cure and dry in the sun; and as for the limes and lemons, I carried as many back as I could stand under.

When I came home from this journey, I contemplated with great pleasure the fruitfulness of that valley and the pleasantness of the situation; the security from storm on that side of the water, and the wood; and concluded that I had pitched upon a place to fix my abode, which was by far the worst part of the country. Upon the whole, I began to consider of removing my habitation, and to look out for a place equally safe as where now I was situate, if possible, in that pleasant, fruitful part of the island.

This thought ran long in my head, and I was exceeding fond of it for some time, the pleasantness of the place tempting me; but when I came to a nearer view of it, I considered that I was now by the seaside, where it was at least possible that something might happen to my advantage; and that the same ill fate that brought me hither might bring some other unhappy wretches to the same place; and though it was scarce probable that any such thing should ever happen, yet to inclose myself among the hills and woods in the centre of the island, was to anticipate my bondage, and to render such an affair not only improbable, but impossible; and that therefore I ought not by any means to remove. However I was so enamoured with this place that I spent much of my time there for the whole remaining part of the month of July; and though, upon second thoughts, I resolved as above not to remove, yet I built me a little kind of a bower, and surrounded it at a distance with a strong fence, being a double hedge, as high as I could reach, well staked, and filled between with brushwood; and here I lay very secure, sometimes two or three nights together, always going over it with a ladder as before; so that I fancied now I had my country house and my seacoast house; and this work took me up to the beginning of August.

ROBINSON CRUSOE

I had but newly finished my fence, and began to enjoy my labour, when the rains came on, and made me stick close to my first habitation; for though I had made me a tent like the other, with a piece of a sail, and spread it very well, yet I had not the shelter of a hill to keep me from storms, nor a cave behind me to retreat into when the rains were extraordinary.

CHAPTER VII

ABOUT the beginning of August, as I said, I had finished my bower, and began to enjoy myself. The 3rd of August, I found the grapes I had hung up were perfectly dried, and indeed were excellent good raisins of the sun; so I began to take them down from the trees, and it was very happy that I did so, for the rains which followed would have spoiled them, and I had lost the best part of my winter food; for I had above two hundred large bunches of them. No sooner had I taken them all down, and carried most of them home to my cave, but it began to rain; and from hence, which was the 14th of August, it rained, more or less, every day till the middle of October, and sometimes so violently, that I could not stir out of my cave for several days.

In this season I was much surprised with the increase of my family; I had been concerned for the loss of one of my cats, who ran away from me, or, as I thought, had been dead, and I heard no more tidings of her till to my astonishment, she came home about the end of August, with three kittens. This was the more strange to me, because, though I had killed a wildcat, as I called it, with my gun, yet I thought it was a quite different kind from our European cats; but the young cats were the same kind of house-breed as the old one; and both my cats being females, I thought it very strange. But from these three cats I afterwards came to be so pestered with cats that I was forced to kill them like vermin or wild beasts, and to drive them from my house as much as possible.

From the 14th of August to the 26th, incessant rain, so that I could not stir, and was now very careful not to be much wet. In this confinement, I began to be straitened for food; but venturing out twice, I one day killed a goat; and the last day, which was the 26th, found a very large tortoise, which was a treat to me, and my food was regulated thus: I ate a bunch of raisins for my breakfast; a piece of the goat's flesh, or of the turtle, for my dinner, broiled (for, to my great misfortune, I had no vessel to boil or stew anything), and two or three of the turtle's eggs for supper.

During this confinement in my cover by the rain, I worked daily two or three hours at enlarging my cave, and by degrees worked it on towards one side, till I came to the outside of the hill, and made a door or way out, which came beyond my fence or wall; and so I came in and out this way. But I was not perfectly easy at lying so open; for, as I had managed myself before, I was in a perfect inclosure; whereas now, I thought, I lay exposed, and yet I could not perceive that there was any living thing to fear; the biggest creature that I had yet seen upon the island being a goat.

September 30.—I was now come to the unhappy anniversary of my landing. I cast up the notches on my post, and found I had been on shore three hundred and sixty-five days. I kept this day as a solemn fast, setting it apart for religious exercise, prostrating myself on the ground with the most serious humiliation, confessing my sins to God, acknowledging his righteous judgment upon me, and praying to him to have mercy on me through Jesus Christ; and having not tasted the least refreshment for twelve hours, even till the going down of the sun, I then ate a biscuit-cake and a bunch of grapes, and went to bed, finishing the day as I began it. I had all this time observed no Sabbath-day; for as at first I had no sense of religion upon my mind, I had, after some time, omitted to distinguish the weeks, by making a longer notch than ordinary for the Sabbath-day, and so did not really know what any of the days were; but now, having cast up the days as above, I found I had been there a year: so I divided it into weeks, and set apart every seventh day for a Sabbath;

though I found at the end of my account I had lost a day in my reckoning. A little after this my ink began to fail me, and so I contented myself to use it more sparingly, and to write down only the most remarkable events of my life; without continuing a daily memorandum of other things.

The rainy season and the dry season began now to appear regular to me, and I learned to divide them so as to provide for them accordingly; but I bought all my experience before I had it, and this I am going to relate was one of the most discouraging experiments that I made at all.

I have mentioned that I had saved the few ears of barley and rice which I had so surprisingly found spring up, as I thought, of themselves; and I believe there were about thirty stalks of rice and about twenty of barley; and now I thought it a proper time to sow it, after the rains, the sun being in his southern position, going from me. Accordingly, I dug up a piece of ground as well as I could with my wooden spade, and dividing it into two parts, I sowed my grain; but as I was sowing, it casually occurred to my thoughts that I would not sow it all at first, because I did not know when was the proper time for it, so I sowed about two-thirds of the seed, leaving about a handful of each. It was a great comfort to me afterwards that I did so, for not one grain of that I sowed this time came to anything; for the dry months following, the earth having had no rain after the seed was sown, it had no moisture to assist its growth, and never came up at all till the wet season had come again, and then it grew as if it had been newly sown. Finding my first seed did not grow, which I easily imagined was by the drought, I sought for a moister piece of ground to make another trial in, and I dug up a piece of ground near my new bower, and sowed the rest of my seed in February, a little before the vernal equinox; and this having the rainy months of March and April to water it, sprang up very pleasantly, and yielded a very good crop; but having part of the seed left only, and not daring to sow all that I had got, I had but a small quantity at last, my whole crop not amounting to above half a peck of each kind. But by this experiment I was made master of my business, and knew exactly when the proper season was to sow, and that I might expect two seed-times and two harvests every year. While this corn was growing I made a little discovery, which was of use to me afterwards. As soon as the rains were over, and the weather began to settle, which was about the month of November, I made a visit up the country to my bower, where, though I had not been some months I found all things just as I left them. The circle or double hedge that I had made was not only firm and entire, but the stakes which I had cut off of some trees that grew thereabouts were all shot out and grown with long branches, as much as a willow-tree usually shoots the first year after lopping its head. I could not tell what tree to call it that these stakes were cut from. I was surprised, and yet very well pleased, to see the young trees grow; and I pruned them, and led them up to grow as much alike as I could; and it is scarcely credible how beautiful a figure they grew into in three years; so that though the hedge made a circle of about twenty-five yards in diameter, yet the trees, for such I might now call them, soon covered it, and it was a complete shade, sufficient to lodge under all the dry season. This made me resolve to cut some more stakes and make me a hedge like this, in a semicircle round my wall (I mean that of my first dwelling), which I did; and placing the trees or stakes in a double row, at about eight yards distance from my first fence, they grew presently, and were at first a fine cover to my habitation, and afterwards served for a defence also, as I shall observe in its order.

I found now that the seasons of the year might generally be divided, not into summer and winter, as in Europe, but into the rainy seasons and the dry seasons, which were generally thus:

The half of August, the whole of September, and the half of April—rainy, the sun being then on or near the equinox.

The half of April, the whole of May, June, and July, and the half of August—dry, the sun being then to the north of the line.

The half of August, the whole of September, and the half of October—rainy, the sun being then come back.

The half of October, the whole of November, December, and January, and the half of February—dry, the sun being then to the south of the line.

The rainy seasons sometimes held longer or shorter as the winds happened to blow, but this was the general observation I made. After I had found, by experience, the ill consequence of being abroad in the rain, I took care to furnish myself with provisions beforehand, that I might not be obliged to go out, and I sat within doors as much as possible during the wet months. In this time I found much employment, and very suitable also to the time, for I found great occasion of many things which I had no way to furnish myself with but by hard labour and constant application; particularly, I tried many ways to make myself a basket, but all the twigs I could get for the purpose proved so brittle that they would do nothing. It proved of excellent advantage to me now that, when I was a boy, I used to take great delight in standing at a basket-maker's, in the town where my father lived, to see them make their wicker-ware; and being, as boys usually are, very officious to help, and a great observer of the manner how they worked those things, and sometimes lent a hand, I had by this means so full knowledge of the methods of it, that I wanted nothing but the materials; when it came into my mind that the twigs of that tree from whence I cut my stakes that grew might possibly be as tough as the sallows, willow and osiers in England, and I resolved to try. Accordingly, the next day I went to my country house, as I called it, and cutting some of the smaller twigs, I found them to my purpose as much as I could desire; whereupon I came the next time prepared with a hatchet to cut down a quantity, which I soon found, for there was a great plenty of them.

These I set up to dry, within my circle or hedges, and when they were fit for use, I carried them to my cave; and here, during the next season, I employed myself in making, as well as I could, a great many baskets, both to carry earth or to carry or lay up anything, as I had occasion; and though I did not finish them very handsomely, yet I made them sufficiently serviceable for my purpose; and thus, afterwards, I took care never to be without them; and as my wickerware decayed, I made more, especially strong, deep baskets to place my corn in, instead of sacks, when I should come to have any quantity of it.

Having mastered this difficulty, and employed a world of time about it, I bestirred myself to see, if possible, how to supply two wants. I had no vessel to hold anything that was liquid, except two runlets, which were almost full of rum, and some glass bottles—some of the common size, and others which were case-bottles, square, for the holding of water, spirits, etc. I had not so much as a pot to boil anything in, except a great kettle, which I saved out of the ship, and which was too big for such uses as I desired it for—viz., to make broth, and stew a bit of meat by itself. The second thing I fain would have had was a tobacco-pipe, but it was impossible for me to make one; however, I found a contrivance for that, too, at last. I employed myself in planting my second row of stakes or piles, and in this wickerwork, all the summer or dry season, when another business took me up more time than it could be imagined I could spare.

I mentioned before that I had a great mind to see the whole island, and that I had travelled up the brook, and so on to where I built my bower, and where I had an opening quite to the sea, on the other side of the island. I now resolved to travel quite across to the seashore on that side; so, taking my gun, a hatchet, and my dog, and a larger quantity of powder and shot than usual, with two biscuit-cakes and a great bunch of raisins in my pouch for my store, I began my journey. When I had passed the vale where my bower stood, as above, I came within view of the sea to the west, and it being a very clear day, fairly descried land—whether an island or a continent I could not tell; but it lay very high, extending from the W. to the W.S.W., at a very great distance; by my guess, it could not be less than fifteen or twenty leagues off.

I could not tell what part of the world this might be, otherwise than that I knew it must be part of America, and, as I concluded, by all my observations, must be near the Spanish dominions, and perhaps was all inhabited by savages, where, if I should have landed, I had been in a worse condition than I was now; and therefore I acquiesced in the dispositions of Providence, which I began now to own and to believe ordered everything for the best; I say I quieted my mind with this, and left afflicting myself with fruitless wishes of being there.

Besides, after some pause upon this affair, I considered that if this land was the Spanish coast, I should certainly, one time or other, see some vessel pass or repass one way or other; but if not, then it was the savage coast between the Spanish country and the Brazils, which were indeed the worst of savages; for they are cannibals, and fail not to murder and devour all the human bodies that fall into their hands.

With these considerations, I walked very leisurely forward. I found that side of the island where I now was much pleasanter than mine—the open savanna fields sweet, adorned with flowers and grass, and full of very fine woods. I saw abundance of parrots, and fain would I have caught one, if possible, to have kept it to be tame, and taught it to speak to me. I did, after some painstaking, catch a young parrot, for I knocked it down with a stick, and having recovered it, I brought it home; but it was some years before I could make him speak; however, at last, I taught him to call me by my name very familiarly. But the accident that followed, though it be a trifle, will be very diverting in its place.

I was exceedingly diverted with this journey. I found in the low ground hares (as I thought them to be) and foxes; but they differed greatly from all the other kinds I had met with, nor could I satisfy myself to eat them, though I killed several. But I had no need to be venturous, for I had no want of food, and of that which was very good, too, especially these three sorts, viz., goats, pigeons, and turtle, or tortoise, which, added to my grapes, Leadenhall Market could not have furnished a table better than I, in proportion to the company; and though my case was deplorable enough, yet I had great cause for thankfulness that I was not driven to any extremities for food, but had rather plenty, even to dainties.

I never travelled in this journey above two miles outright in a day, or thereabouts; but I took so many turns and returns to see what discoveries I could make, that I came weary enough to the place where I resolved to sit down for all night; and then I either reposed myself in a tree, or surrounded myself with a row of stakes set upright in the ground, either from one tree to another, or so as no wild creature could come at me without waking me. As soon as I came to the seashore I was surprised to see that I had taken up my lot on the worst side of the island, for here, indeed, the shore was covered with innumerable turtles, whereas on the other side I had found but three in a year and a half. Here was also an infinite number of fowls of many kinds, some of which I had not seen before, and many of them very good meat, but such as I knew not the names of, except those called penguins.

I could have shot as many as I pleased, but was very sparing of my powder and shot, and therefore had more mind to kill a she-goat, if I could, which I could better feed on; and though there were many goats here, more than on the other side of the island, yet it was with much more difficulty that I could come near them, the country being flat and even, and they saw me much sooner than when I was on the hills.

I confess this side of the country was much pleasanter than mine; but yet I had not the least inclination to remove, for as I was fixed in my habitation it became natural to me, and I seemed all the while I was here to be as it were upon a journey, and from home. However, I travelled along the shore of the sea toward the east, I suppose about twelve miles, and then setting up a great pole upon the shore for a mark, I concluded I would go home again, and that the next journey I took should be on the other side of the island east from my dwelling, and so round till I came to my post again, of which in its place.

I took another way to come back than that I went, thinking I could easily keep all the island so much in my view that I could not miss finding my first dwelling by viewing the country; but I found myself mistaken, for, being come about two or three miles, I found myself descended into a very large valley, but so surrounded with hills, and those hills covered with wood, that I could not see which was my way by any direction but that of the sun, nor even then, unless I knew very well the position of the sun at that time of the day. It happened, to my further misfortune, that the weather proved hazy for three or four days while I was in this valley, and not being able to see the sun, I wandered about very uncomfortable, and at last was obliged to find out the seaside, look for my post, and come back the same way I went: and then, by easy journeys, I turned homeward, the weather being exceeding hot, and my gun, ammunition, hatchet, and other things, very heavy.

In this journey my dog surprised a young kid, and seized upon it, and I running in to take hold of it, caught it, and saved it alive from the dog. I had a great mind to bring it home if I could, for I had often been musing whether it might not be possible to get a kid or two, and so raise a breed of tame goats, which might supply me when my powder and shot should be spent. I made a collar to this little creature, and with a string, which I made of some rope-yarn which I always carried about me, I led him along, though with some difficulty, till I came to my bower, and there I inclosed him and left him, for I was very impatient to be at home, from whence I had been absent above a month.

I cannot express what a satisfaction it was to me to come into my old hutch, and lie down in my hammock-bed. This little wandering journey, without settled place of abode, had been so unpleasant to me that my own house, as I called it to myself, was a perfect settlement to me, compared to that; and it rendered everything about me so comfortable, that I resolved I would never go a great way from it again, while it should be my lot to stay on the island.

I reposed myself here a week, to rest and regale myself after my long journey; during which, most of the time was taken up in the weighty affair of making a cage for my Poll, who began now to be a mere domestic, and to be mighty well acquainted with me. Then I began to think of the poor kid which I had pent in within my little circle, and resolved to go and fetch it home, or give it some food; accordingly I went, and found it where I left it, for indeed it could not get out, but was almost starved for want of food. I went and cut boughs of trees, and branches of such shrubs as I could find, and threw them over, and having fed it, I tied it as I did before, to lead it away; but it was so tame with being hungry, that I had no need to have tied it, for it followed me like a dog; and as I continually fed it, the creature became so loving, so gentle, and so fond, that it became from that time one of my domestics also, and would never leave me afterwards.

The rainy season of the autumnal equinox was now come, and I kept the 30th of September in the same solemn manner as before, being the anniversary of my landing on the island, having now been there two years, and no more prospect of being delivered than the first day I came there. I spent the whole day in humble and thankful acknowledgments of the many wonderful mercies which my solitary condition was attended with, and without which it might have been infinitely more miserable. I gave humble and hearty thanks that God had been pleased to discover to me that it was possible I might be more happy in this solitary condition than I should have been in a liberty of society, and in all the pleasures of the world; that he could fully make up to me the deficiencies of my solitary state, and the want of human society, by his presence, and the communication of his grace to my soul; supporting, comforting, and encouraging me to depend upon his providence here, and hope for his eternal presence hereafter.

It was now that I began sensibly to feel how much more happy the life I now led was, with all its miserable circumstances, than the wicked, cursed, abominable life I led all the past part of my days; and now having changed both my sorrows and my joys, my very desires altered, my affections changed their gusts, and my delights were perfectly new from what they were at first coming, or, indeed, for the two years past.

Before, as I walked about, either on my hunting, or for viewing the country, the anguish of my soul at my condition would break out upon me on a sudden, and my very heart would die within me, to think of the woods, the mountains, the deserts I was in, and how I was a prisoner, locked up with the eternal bars and bolts of the ocean, in an uninhabited wilderness, without redemption. In the midst of the greatest composures of my mind, this would break out upon me like a storm and make me wring my hands, and weep like a child; sometimes it would take me in the middle of my work, and I would immediately sit down and sigh, and look upon the ground for an hour or two together; and this was still worse to me, for if I could burst out into tears, or vent myself by words, it would go off, and the grief having exhausted itself would abate.

But now I began to exercise myself with new thoughts. I daily read the Word of God, and applied all the comforts of it to my present state. One morning, being very sad, I opened the Bible upon these words, "I will never leave thee, nor forsake thee." Immediately I thought that these words were to me; why else should they be directed in such a manner, just at the moment when I was mourning over my condition, as one forsaken of God and man? "Well, then," said I, "if God does not forsake me, of what ill consequence can it be, or what matters it, though the world should all forsake me, seeing on the other hand, if I had all the world, and should lose the favour and blessing of God, there would be no comparison in the loss?"

From this moment I began to conclude in my mind that it was possible for me to be more happy in this forsaken, solitary condition, than it was probable I should ever have been in any other particular state in the world; and with this thought I was going to give thanks to God for bringing me to this place. I know not what it was, but something shocked my mind at that thought, and I durst not speak the words. "How canst thou become such a hypocrite," said I, even audibly, "to pretend to be thankful for a condition, which, however thou mayest endeavour to be contented with, thou wouldst rather pray heartily to be delivered from?" So I stopped there; but though I could not say I thanked God for being there, yet I sincerely gave thanks to God for opening my eyes, by whatever afflicting providences, to see the former condition of my life, and to mourn for my wickedness, and repent. I never opened the Bible, or shut it, but my very soul within me blessed God for directing my friend in England, without any order of mine, to pack it up among my goods, and for assisting me afterwards to save it out of the wreck of the ship.

Thus, and in this disposition of mind, I began my third year; and though I have not given the reader the trouble of so particular an account of my works this year as the first; yet in general it may be observed that I was very seldom idle, but having regularly divided my time according to several daily employments that were before me, such as, first, my duty to God, and the reading the Scriptures, which I constantly set apart some time for, thrice every day; secondly, the going abroad with my gun for food, which generally took up three hours in every morning, when it did not rain; thirdly, the ordering, curing, preserving, and cooking what I had killed or caught for my supply: these took up great part of the day; also, it is to be considered, that in the middle of the day, when the sun was in the zenith, the violence of the heat was too great to stir out; so that about four hours in the evening was all the time I could be supposed to work in, with this exception, that sometimes I changed my hours of hunting and working, and went to work in the morning, and abroad with my gun in the afternoon.

To this short time allowed for labour, I desire may be added the exceeding laboriousness of my work; the many hours which for want of tools, want of help, and want of skill, everything I did took up out of my time: for example, I was full two-and-forty days in making a board for a long shelf, which I wanted in my cave; whereas two sawyers, with their tools and a saw-pit, would have cut six of them out of the same tree in half a day.

My case was this: it was to be a large tree which was to be cut down, because my board was to be a broad one. This tree I was three days a-cutting down, and two more cutting off the boughs, and reducing it to a log, or piece of timber. With inexpressible hacking and hewing, I reduced both the sides of it into chips till it began to be light enough to move; then I turned it, and made one side of it smooth and flat as a board from end to end; then, turning that side downward, cut the other side till I brought the plank to be about three inches thick, and smooth on both sides. Any one may judge the labour of my hands in such a piece of work; but labour and patience carried me through that, and many other things; I only observe this in particular, to show the reason why so much of my time went away with so little work, viz., that what might be a little to be done with help and tools, was a vast labour and required a prodigious time to do alone, and by hand. But notwithstanding this, with patience and labour I went through many things, and indeed everything that my circumstances made necessary to me to do, as will appear by what follows.

I was now, in the months of November and December, expecting my crop of barley and rice. The ground I had manured or dug up for them was not great; for, as I observed, my seed of each was not above the quantity of half a peck, for I had lost one whole crop by sowing in the dry season: but now my crop promised very well, when on a sudden I found I was in danger of losing it all again by enemies of several sorts, which it was scarcely possible to keep from it; as, first, the goats, and wild creatures which I called hares, which, tasting the sweetness of the blade, lay in it night and day, as soon as it came up, and ate it so close that it could get no time to shoot up into stalk.

This I saw no remedy for, but by making an inclosure about it with a hedge, which I did with a great deal of toil, and the more, because it required a great deal of speed; the creatures daily spoiling my corn. However, as my arable land was but small, suited to my crop, I got it totally well fenced in about three weeks' time; and shooting some of the creatures in the daytime, I set my dog to guard it in the night, tying him up to a stake at the gate, where he would stand and bark all night long; so in a little time the enemies forsook the place, and the corn grew very strong and well, and began to ripen apace.

But as the beasts ruined me before, while my corn was in the blade, so the birds were as likely to ruin me now, when it was in the ear; for going along by the place to see how it throve, I saw my little crop surrounded with fowls, of I know not how many sorts, who stood, as it were, watching till I should be gone. I immediately let fly among them, for I always had my gun with me. I had no sooner shot, but there rose up a little cloud of fowls, which I had not seen at all, from among the corn itself.

This touched me sensibly, for I foresaw that in a few days they would devour all my hopes; that I should be starved, and never be able to raise a crop at all; and what to do I could not tell; however, I resolved not to lose my corn, if possible, though I should watch it night and day. In the first place, I went among it to see what damage was already done, and found they had spoiled a good deal of it; but that as it was yet too green for them, the loss was not so great, but the remainder was likely to be a good crop, if it could be saved.

I stayed by it to load my gun, and then coming away, I could easily see the thieves sitting upon all the trees about me, as if they only waited till I was gone away, and the event proved it to be so; for as I walked off, as if I was gone, I was no sooner out of their sight, but they dropped down one by one into the corn again. I was so provoked that I could not have patience to stay till more came on, knowing that every grain that they ate now was, as it might be said, a peck-loaf to me, in the consequence; but coming up to the hedge, I fired again, and killed three of them. This was what I wished for; so I took them up, and served them as we serve notorious thieves in England, viz., hanged them in chains, for a terror to others. It is impossible to imagine almost that this should have had such an effect as it had, for the fowls would not only not come at the corn, but, in short, they forsook all that part of the island, and I could never see a bird near the place as long as my scarecrows hung there. This I was very glad of, you may be sure, and about the latter end of December, which was our second harvest of the year, I reaped my corn.

I was sadly put to it for a scythe or sickle to cut it down, and all I could do was to make one, as well as I could, out of one of my broadswords, or cutlasses, which I saved among the arms out of the ship. However, as my crop was but small, I had no great difficulty to cut it down; in short, I reaped it in my way, for I cut nothing off but the ears, and carried it away in a great basket which I had made, and so rubbed it out with my hands; and at the end of all my harvesting, I found that out of my half-peck of seed I had near two bushels of rice, and above two bushels and a half of barley; that is to say, by my guess, for I had no measure at that time.

However, this was a great encouragement to me, and I foresaw that in time it would please God to supply me with bread; and yet here I was perplexed again, for I neither knew how to grind or make meal of my corn, or indeed how to clean it and part it; nor, if made into meal how to make bread of it; and if how to make it, yet I knew not how to bake it; these things being added to my desire of having a good quantity for store, and to secure a constant supply, I resolved not to taste any of this crop, but to preserve it all for seed against the next season; and in the meantime, to employ all my study and hours of working to accomplish this great work of providing myself with corn and bread.

It might be truly said that now I worked for my bread. It is a little wonderful, and what I believe few people have thought much upon, viz., the strange multitude of little things necessary in providing, producing, curing, dressing, making, and finishing this one article of bread.

I, that was reduced to a mere state of nature, found this to my daily discouragement and was made more and more sensible of it every hour, even after I had got the first handful of seed-corn which, as I have said, came unexpectedly, and indeed to a surprise.

First, I had no plough to turn the earth; no spade or shovel to dig it. Well, this I conquered by making me a wooden spade, as I observed before; but this did my work only in a wooden manner; and though it cost me a great many days to make it, yet, for want of iron, it not only wore out the sooner, but made my work the harder, and made it be performed much worse. However, this I bore with too, and was content to work it out with patience, and bear with the badness of the performance. When the corn was sown, I had no harrow, but was forced to go over it myself, and drag a great heavy bough of a tree over it to scratch it, as it may be called, rather than rake or harrow it. When it was growing, or grown, I have observed already how many things I wanted to fence it, secure it, mow or reap it, cure and carry it home, thrash, part it from the chaff, and save it. Then I wanted a mill to grind it, sieves to dress it, yeast and salt to make it into bread, and an oven to bake it in; and all these things I did without, as shall be observed; and yet the corn was an inestimable comfort and advantage to me too. But this, as I said, made everything laborious and tedious to me; but that there was no help for; neither was my time so much loss to me, because, as I divided it, a certain part of it was every day appointed to these works; and as I had resolved to use none of the corn for bread till I had a greater quantity by me, I had the next six months to apply myself wholly, by labour and invention, to furnish myself with utensils proper for the performing all the operations necessary for making the corn, when I had it fit for my use.

But first I was to prepare more land, for I had now seed enough to sow above an acre of ground. Before I did this, I had a week's work at least to make me a spade, which, when it was done, was but a sorry one indeed, and very heavy, and required double labour to work with it. However, I went through that, and sowed my seed in two large flat pieces of ground, as near my house as I could find them to my mind, and fenced them in with a good hedge, the stakes of which were all cut of that wood which I had set before, which I knew would grow; so that, in one year's time, I knew I should have a quick or living hedge, that would want but little repair. This work was not so little as to take me up less than three months, because great part of that time was of the wet season, when I could not go abroad. Within-door, that is when it rained, and I could not go out, I found employment in the following occupations—always observing that all the while I was at work I diverted myself with talking to my parrot, and teaching him to speak; and I quickly learnt him to know his own name, and at last to speak it out pretty loud, "Poll," which was the first word I ever heard spoken in that island by any mouth but my own. This, therefore, was not my work, but an assistant to my work; for now, as I said, I had a great employment upon my hands, as follows: viz., I had long studied, by some means or other, to make myself some earthen vessels, which, indeed, I wanted sorely, but knew not where to come at them. However, considering the heat of the climate, I did not doubt but if I could find out any clay, I might botch up some such pot as might, being dried by the sun, be hard enough and strong enough to bear handling, and to hold anything that was dry, and required to be kept so; and as this was necessary in preparing corn, meal, etc., which was the thing I was upon, I resolved to make some as large as I could, and fit only to stand like jars, to hold what should be put into them.

It would make the reader pity me, or rather laugh at me, to tell how many awkward ways I took to raise this paste; what odd, misshapen, ugly things I made; how many of them fell in, and how many fell out—the clay not being stiff enough to bear its own weight; how many cracked by the over-violent heat of the sun, being set out too hastily; and how many fell to pieces with only removing, as well before as after they were dried; and, in a word, how, after having laboured hard to find the clay—to dig it, to temper it, to bring it home, and work it—I could not make above two large earthen ugly things (I cannot call them jars) in about two months' labour.

However, as the sun baked these two very dry and hard, I lifted them very gently up, and set them down again in two great wicker baskets, which I had made on purpose for them, that they might not break; and as between the pot and the basket there was a little room to spare, I stuffed it full of the rice and barley straw; and these two pots being to stand always dry, I thought would hold my dry corn, and perhaps the meal, when the corn was bruised.

Though I miscarried so much in my design for large pots, yet I made several smaller things with better success; such as little round pots, flat dishes, pitchers, and pipkins, and anything my hand turned to; and the heat of the sun baked them strangely hard.

But all this would not answer my end, which was to get an earthen pot to hold what was liquid, and bear the fire; which none of these could do. It happened after some time, making a pretty large fire for cooking my meat, when I went to put it out after I had done with it I found a broken piece of one of my earthenware vessels in the fire, burnt as hard as a stone, and red as a tile. I was agreeably surprised to see it, and said to myself that certainly they might be made to burn whole, if they could burn broken.

This set me to study how to order my fire so as to make it burn me some pots. I had no notion of a kiln, such as the potters burn in, or of glazing them with lead, though I had some lead to do it with; but I placed three large pipkins, and two or three pots, in a pile, one upon another, and placed my firewood all round it, with a great heap of embers under them. I plied the fire with fresh fuel round the outside, and upon the top, till I saw the pots in the inside red-hot quite through, and observed that they did not crack at all; when I saw them clear red, I let them stand in that heat about five or six hours, till I found one of them, though it did not crack, did melt or run; for the sand which was mixed with the clay melted by the violence of the heat, and would have run into glass if I had gone on; so I slacked my fire gradually till the pots began to abate of the red colour, and watching them all night, that I might not let the fire abate too fast, in the morning I had three very good (I will not say handsome) pipkins, and two other earthen pots, as hard burnt as could be desired, and one of them perfectly glazed with the running of the sand.

After this experiment, I need not say that I wanted no sort of earthenware for my use; but I must needs say as to the shapes of them they were very indifferent, as any one may suppose, when I had no way of making them but as the children make dirt pies, or as a woman would make pies that never learned to raise paste.

No joy at a thing of so mean a nature was ever equal to mine, when I found I had made an earthen pot that would bear the fire; and I had hardly patience to stay till they were cold before I set one on the fire again, with some water in it, to boil me some meat, which it did admirably well; and with a piece of a kid I made some very good broth, though I wanted oatmeal and several other ingredients requisite to make it as good as I would have liked.

CHAPTER VIII

MY next concern was to get me a stone mortar to stamp or beat some corn in; for as to the mill, there was no thought of arriving to that perfection of art with one pair of hands. To supply this want I was at a great loss; for, of all the trades in the world, I was as perfectly unqualified for a stone-cutter as for any whatever; neither had I any tools to go about it with. I spent many a day to find out a great stone big enough to cut hollow, and make fit for a mortar, and could find none at all, except what was in the solid rock, and which I had no way to dig or cut out; nor indeed were the rocks in the island of hardness sufficient, but were all of a sandy, crumbling stone, which would neither bear the weight of a heavy pestle, nor would break the corn without filling it with sand. So, after a great deal of time lost in searching for a stone, I gave it over, and resolved to look out a great block of hard wood, which I found indeed much easier; and getting one as big as I had strength to stir, I rounded it and formed it on the outside with my axe and hatchet, and then, with the help of fire and infinite labour, made a hollow place in it, as the Indians in Brazil make their canoes. After this, I made a great heavy pestle, or beater, of the wood called the iron-wood; and this I prepared and laid by against I had my next crop of corn, which I proposed to myself to grind, or rather pound my corn or meal, to make my bread.

My next difficulty was to make a sieve, or search, to dress my meal, and to part it from the bran and the husk; without which I did not see it possible I could have any bread. This was a most difficult thing, so much as but to think on, for to be sure I had nothing like the necessary things to make it with; I mean fine thin canvas, or stuff to search the meal through. And here I was at a full stop for many months; nor did I really know what to do. Linen I had none left but what was mere rags; I had goats' hair, but neither knew I how to weave or spin it; and had I known how, here were no tools to work with. All the remedy that I found for this was, that at last I did remember I had, among the seamen's clothes which were saved out of the ship, some neckcloths of calico or muslin; and with some pieces of these I made three small sieves, but proper enough for the work; and thus I made shift for a good many years; how I did afterwards, I shall show in its place.

The baking part was the next thing to be considered, and how I should make bread when I came to have corn; for, first, I had no yeast; as to that part, as there was no supplying the want, so I did not concern myself much about it. But for an oven, I was indeed in great pain. At length I found out an experiment for that also, which was this: I made some earth vessels very broad, but not deep, that is to say about two feet diameter, and not above nine inches deep; these I burned in the fire, as I had done the other, and laid them by; and when I wanted to bake, I made a great fire upon the hearth, which I had paved with some square tiles, of my own making and burning also; but I should not call them square.

When the firewood was burned pretty much into embers, or live coals, I drew them forward upon the hearth, so as to cover it all over, and there I let them lie till the hearth was very hot; then sweeping away all the embers, I set down my loaf or loaves, and whelming down the earthen pot upon them, drew the embers all round the outside of the pot, to keep in and add to the heat; and thus, as well as in the best oven in the world, I baked my barley loaves, and became, in little time, a good pastry-cook into the bargain; for I made myself several cakes and puddings of the rice; indeed I made no pies, neither had I anything to put into them, supposing I had, except the flesh either of fowls or goats.

It need not be wondered at if all these things took me up most part of the third year of my abode here; for, it is to be observed that, in the intervals of these things, I had my new harvest and husbandry to manage; for I reaped my corn in its season, and carried it home as well as I could, and laid it up in the ear, in my large baskets, till I had time to rub it out, for I had no floor to thrash it on, or instrument to thrash it with.

And now, indeed, my stock of corn increasing, I really wanted to build my barns bigger; I wanted a place to lay it up in, for the increase of the corn now yielded me so much that I had of the barley about twenty bushels, and of the rice as much, or more; insomuch that I now resolved to begin to use it freely; for my bread had been quite gone a great while; also I resolved to see what quantity would be sufficient for me a whole year, and to sow but once a year.

Upon the whole, I found that the forty bushels of barley and rice were much more than I could consume in a year; so I resolved to sow just the same quantity every year that I sowed the last, in hopes that such a quantity would fully provide me with bread.

All the while these things were doing, you may be sure my thoughts ran many times upon the prospect of land which I had seen from the other side of the island; and I was not without secret wishes that I was on shore there, fancying that, seeing the mainland, and an inhabited country, I might find some way or other to convey myself farther, and perhaps at last find some means of escape.

But all this while I made no allowance for the dangers of such a condition, and how I might fall into the hands of savages, and perhaps such as I might have reason to think far worse than the lions and tigers of Africa: that if I once came into their power I should run a hazard more than a thousand to one of being killed, and perhaps of being eaten; for I had heard that the people of the Caribbean coasts were cannibals, or men-eaters and I knew by the latitude that I could not be far off from that shore! That suppose they were not cannibals, yet they might kill me, as many Europeans who had fallen into their hands had been served, even when they had been ten or twenty together—much more I, that was but one, and could make little or no defence; all these things, I say, which I ought to have considered well of, and I did cast up in my thoughts afterwards, yet took up none of my apprehensions at first, and my head ran mightily upon the thought of getting over to that shore.

Now, I wished for my boy Xury, and the longboat with the shoulder-of-mutton sail, with which I sailed above a thousand miles on the coast of Africa: but this was in vain; then I thought I would go and look at our ship's boat, which, as I have said, was blown up upon the shore a great way, in the storm, when we were first cast away. She lay almost where she did at first, but not quite, and was turned, by the force of the waves and the winds, almost bottom upward, against the high ridge of beachy, rough sands, but no water about her as before. If I had had hands to have refitted her, and to have launched her into the water, the boat would have done well enough, and I might have gone back into the Brazils with her easily enough; but I might have easily forseen that I could no more turn her and set her upright upon her bottom than I could remove the island; however, I went to the wood, and cut levers and rollers, and brought them to the boat, resolved to try what I could do; suggesting to myself, that if I could but turn her down, I might easily repair the damage she had received, and she would be a very good boat, and I might go to sea in her very easily.

I spared no pains, indeed, in this piece of fruitless toil, and spent, I think, three or four weeks about it; at last, finding it impossible to heave it up with my little strength, I fell to digging away the sand, to undermine it, and so to make it fall down, setting pieces of wood to thrust and guide it right in the fall.

But when I had done this, I was unable to stir it up again, or to get under it, much less to move it forward towards the water; so I was forced to give it over; and yet, though I gave over the hopes of the boat, my desire to venture over for the main increased rather than decreased, as the means for it seemed impossible.

This at length set me upon thinking whether it was not possible to make myself a canoe, or periagua, such as the natives of those climates make, even without tools, or, as I might say, without hands—viz., of the trunk of a great tree. This I not only thought possible, but easy, and pleased myself extremely with my thoughts of making it, and with my having much more convenience for it than any of the Negroes or Indians; but not at all considering the particular inconveniences which I lay under more than the Indians did, viz., want of hands to move it into the water when it was made—a difficulty much harder for me to surmount than all the consequences of want of tools could be to them. For what was it to me, that when I had chosen a vast tree in the wood, I might with great trouble cut it down, if after I might be able with my tools to hew and dub the outside into the proper shape of a boat, and burn or cut out the inside to make it hollow, so as to make a boat of it—if, after all this, I must leave it just there where I found it, and was not able to launch it into the water?

One would have thought I could not have had the least reflection upon my mind of my circumstances while I was making this boat, but I should have immediately thought how I should get it into the sea: but my thoughts were so intent upon my voyage over the sea in it, that I never once considered how I should get it off the land; and it was really, in its own nature, more easy for me to guide it over forty-five miles of sea, than about forty-five fathoms of land, where it lay, to set it afloat in the water.

I went to work upon this boat the most like a fool that ever man did, who had any of his senses awake. I pleased myself with the design without determining whether I was ever able to undertake it; not but that the difficulty of launching my boat came often into my head; but I put a stop to my inquiries into it, by this foolish answer which I gave myself: "Let me first make it; I warrant I shall find some way or other to get it along when it is done."

This was a most preposterous method; but the eagerness of my fancy prevailed, and to work I went, and felled a cedar tree. I question much whether Solomon ever had such a one for the building the Temple at Jerusalem; it was five feet ten inches diameter at the lower part next the stump, and four feet eleven inches diameter at the end of twenty-two feet; after which it lessened for a while, and then parted into branches. It was not without infinite labour that I felled this tree. I was twenty days hacking and hewing at it at the bottom; I was fourteen more getting the branches and limbs and the vast spreading head of it cut off, which I hacked and hewed through with axe and hatchet and inexpressible labour: after this, it cost me a month to shape it and dub it to a proportion, and to something like the bottom of a boat, that it might swim upright as it ought to do. It cost me near three months more to clear the inside and work it out so as to make an exact boat of it; this I did, indeed, without fire, by mere mallet and chisel, and by the dint of hard labour, till I had brought it to be a very handsome periagua, and big enough to have carried six-and-twenty men, and consequently big enough to have carried me and all my cargo.

When I had gone through this work, I was extremely delighted with it. The boat was really much bigger than ever I saw a canoe or a periagua, that was made of one tree, in my life. Many a weary stroke it had cost, you may be sure—for there remained nothing but to get it into the water; and had I gotten it into the water, I made no question but I should have begun the maddest voyage, and the most unlikely to be performed, that ever was undertaken.

But all my devices to get it into the water failed me; though they cost infinite labour too. It lay about one hundred yards from the water, and not more; but the first inconvenience was, it was uphill towards the creek. Well, to take away this discouragement, I resolved to dig into the surface of the earth, and so make a declivity. This I began, and it cost me a prodigious deal of pains (but who grudge pains that have their deliverance in view?); but when this was worked through, and this difficulty managed it was still much at one, for I could no more stir the canoe than I could the other boat. Then I measured the distance of the ground, and resolved to cut a dock or canal, to bring the water up to the canoe, seeing I could not bring the canoe down to the water. Well, I began this work; and when I began to enter into it, and calculate how deep it was to be dug, how broad, how the stuff was to be thrown out, I found that, by the number of hands I had, being none but my own, it must have been ten or twelve years before I could have gone through with it; for the shore lay so high that at the upper end it must have been at least twenty feet deep; so at length though with great reluctancy, I gave this attempt over also.

This grieved me heartily; and now I saw, though too late, the folly of beginning a work before we count the cost, and before we judge rightly of our own strength to go through with it.

In the middle of this work, I finished my fourth year in this place, and kept my anniversary with the same devotion, and with as much comfort as ever before; for, by a constant study and serious application of the Word of God, and by the assistance of his grace, I gained a different knowledge from what I had before. I entertained different notions of things. I looked now upon the world as a thing remote, which I had nothing to do with, no expectation from, and, indeed, no desires about: in a word I had nothing indeed to do with it, nor was ever likely to have. So I thought it looked, as we may perhaps look upon it hereafter, viz., as a place I had lived in, but was come out of it; and well might I say, as Father Abraham to Dives, "Between me and thee is a great gulf fixed."

In the first place I was removed from all the wickedness of the world here; I had neither the lust of the flesh, the lust of the eye, nor the pride of life. I had nothing to covet, for I had all I was now capable of enjoying; I was lord of the whole manor; or, if I pleased, I might call myself king or emperor over the whole country which I had possession of. There were no rivals; I had no competitor, none to dispute sovereignity or command with me. I might have raised ship-ladings of corn, but I had no use for it; so I let as little grow as I thought enough for my occasion. I had tortoises or turtles enough, but now and then one was as much as I could put to any use. I had timber enough to have built a fleet of ships; and I had grapes enough to have made wine, or to have cured into raisins, to have loaded that fleet when it had been built.

But all I could make use of was all that was valuable: I had enough to eat and to supply my wants, and what was all the rest to me? If I killed more flesh than I could eat, the dog must eat it, or the vermin; if I sowed more corn than I could eat, it must be spoiled; the trees that I cut down were lying to rot on the ground; I could make no more use of them than for fuel, and that I had no occasion for but to dress my food.

In a word, the nature and experience of things dictated to me, upon just reflection, that all the good things of this world are no further good to us than they are for our use; and that, whatever we may heap up indeed to give others we may enjoy as much as we can use and no more. The most covetous, griping miser in the world would have been cured of the vice of covetousness, if he had been in my case; for I possessed infinitely more than I knew what to do with. I had no room for desire, except it was of things which I had not, and they were but trifles, though, indeed, of great use to me. I had, as I hinted before, a parcel of money, as well gold as silver, about thirty-six pounds sterling. Alas! there the nasty, sorry, useless stuff lay! I had no manner of business for it; and I often thought with myself that I would have given a handful of it for a gross of tobacco-pipes; or for a handmill to grind my corn; nay, I would have given it all for sixpenny-worth of turnip and carrot seed out of England, or for a handful of peas and beans and a bottle of ink. As it was, I had not the least advantage by it, or benefit from it; but there it lay in a drawer, and grew mouldy with the damp of the cave in the wet seasons; and if I had had the drawer full of diamonds, it had been the same case, they had been of no manner of value to me, because of no use.

I had now brought my state of life to be much easier in itself than it was at first and much easier to my mind, as well as to my body. I frequently sat down to meat with thankfulness, and admired the hand of God's providence, which had thus spread my table in the wilderness. I learned to look more upon the bright side of my condition, and less upon the dark side, and to consider what I enjoyed rather than what I wanted; and this gave me sometimes such secret comforts that I cannot express them; and which I take notice of here, to put those discontented people in mind of it, who cannot enjoy comfortably what God has given them, because they see and covet something that he has not given them. All our discontents about what we want appeared to me to spring from the want of thankfulness for what we have.

Another reflection was of great use to me, and doubtless would be so to any one that should fall into such distress as mine was; and this was, to compare my present con-dition with what I at first expected it would be; nay, with what it would certainly have been, if the good providence of God had not wonderfully ordered the ship to be cast up nearer to the shore, where I not only could come at her, but could bring what I got out of her to the shore, for my relief and comfort; without which, I had wanted for tools to work, weapons for defence, and gunpowder and shot for getting my food.

I spent whole hours, I may say whole days, in representing to myself, in the most lively colours, how I must have acted if I had got nothing out of the ship. How I could not have so much as got any food, except fish and turtles; and that, as it was long before I found any of them, I must have perished first; that I should have lived, if I had not perished, like a mere savage; that if I had killed a goat or a fowl, by any contrivance, I had no way to flay or open it, or part the flesh from the skin and the bowels, or to cut it up; but must gnaw it with my teeth, and pull it with my claws, like a beast.

These reflections made me very sensible of the goodness of Providence to me, and very thankful for my present condition, with all its hardships and misfortunes; and this part also I cannot but recommend to the reflection of these who are apt, in their misery, to say, "Is any affliction like mine?" Let them consider how much worse the cases of some people are, and their case might have been, if Providence had thought fit.

I had another reflection, which assisted me also to comfort my mind with hopes; and this was comparing my present situation with what I had deserved, and had therefore reason to expect from the hand of Providence. I had lived a dreadful life, perfectly destitute of the knowledge and fear of God. I had been well instructed by father and mother; neither had they been wanting to me, in their early endeavours to infuse a religious awe of God into my mind, a sense of my duty, and what the nature and end of my being required of me. But alas! falling early into the seafaring life, which, of all lives, is the most destitute of the fear of God, though his terrors are always before them; I say, falling early into the seafaring life, and into seafaring company, all that little sense of religion which I entertained was laughed out of me by my messmates; by a hardened despising of dangers, and the views of death, which grew habitual to me; by my long absence from all manner of opportunities to converse with anything but what was like myself, or to hear anything of what was good, or tended towards it.

So void was I of everything that was good, or of the least sense of what I was, or was to be, that, in the greatest deliverances I enjoyed—such as my escape from Sallee; my being taken up by the Portuguese master of the ship; my being planted so well in the Brazils; my receiving the cargo from England, and the like—I never once had the words, "Thank God!" so much as on my mind, or in my mouth; nor in the greatest distress had I so much thought as to pray to him, or so much as to say, "Lord, have mercy upon me!" no, not to mention the name of God, unless it was to swear by, and blaspheme it.

I had terrible reflections upon my mind for many months as I have already observed, on the account of my wicked and hardened life past; and when I looked about me, and considered what particular providences had attended me since my coming into this place, and how God had dealt bountifully with me—had not only punished me less than my iniquity had deserved but had so plentifully provided for me—this gave me great hopes that my repentance was accepted, and that God had yet mercies in store for me.

With these reflections, I worked my mind up, not only to resignation to the will of God in the present disposition of my circumstances, but even to a sincere thankfulness for my condition; and that I, who was yet a living man, ought not to complain, seeing I had not the due punishment of my sins. That I enjoyed so many mercies which I had no reason to have expected in that place. That I ought never more to repine at my condition, but to rejoice, and to give daily thanks for that daily bread, which nothing but a crowd of wonders could have brought. That I ought to consider I had been fed even by a miracle, even as great as that of feeding Elijah by ravens; nay, by a long series of miracles. And that I could hardly have named a place in the uninhabited part of the world where I could have been cast more to my advantage; a place where, as I had no society, which was my affliction on one hand, so I found no ravenous beasts, no furious wolves or tigers, to threaten my life; no venomous creatures or poisonous, which I might have fed on to my hurt; no savages to murder and devour me. In a word, as my life was a life of sorrow one way, so it was a life of mercy another, and I wanted nothing to make it a life of comfort but to be able to make my sense of God's goodness to me, and care over me in this condition, be my daily consolation; and after I made a just improvement of these things, I went away and was no more sad. I had now been here so long, that many things which I brought on shore for my help were either quite gone, or very much wasted and near spent.

My ink, as I observed, had been gone some time, all but a very little, which I eked out with water, a little and a little, till it was so pale, it scarce left any appearance of black upon the paper. As long as it lasted I made use of it to minute down the days of the month on which any remarkable thing happened to me; and first, by casting up times past, I remembered that there was a strange concurrence of days in the various providences which befell me, and which, if I had been superstitiously inclined to observe days as fatal or fortunate, I might have had reason to have looked upon with a great deal of curiosity.

First, I observed, that the same day that I broke away from my father and my friends, and ran away to Hull, in order to go to sea, the same day afterwards I was taken by the Sallee man-of-war, and made a slave; the same day of the year that I escaped out of the wreck of that ship in Yarmouth Roads, that same day of the year afterwards I made my escape from Sallee in a boat; the same day of the year I was born on, viz., the 30th of September, the same day I had my life so miraculously saved twenty-six years after, when I was cast on shore in this island; so that my wicked life and solitary life began both on a day.

The next thing to my ink being wasted was that of my bread. I mean the biscuit which I brought out of the ship; this I had husbanded to the last degree, allowing myself but one cake of bread a day for above a year; and yet I was quite without bread for a year before I got any corn of my own; and great reason I had to be thankful that I had any at all, the getting it being, as has been already observed, next to miraculous.

My clothes too, began to decay mightily; as to linen, I had had none a good while, except some checkered shirts which I found in the chests of the other seamen, and which I carefully preserved; because many times I could bear no other clothes on but a shirt; and it was a very great help to me that I had, among all the men's clothes of the ship, almost three dozen of shirts. There were also several thick watch-coats of the seamen's which were left behind, but they were too hot to wear: and though it is true that the weather was so violently hot that there was no need of clothes, yet I could not go quite naked—no, though I had been inclined to it, which I was not; nor could I abide the thoughts of it, though I was all alone. One reason why I could not go naked was, I could not bear the heat of the sun so well when quite naked as with some clothes on; nay, the very heat frequently blistered my skin; whereas, with a shirt on, the air itself made some motion, and whistling under the shirt, was twofold cooler than without it. No more could I ever bring myself to go out in the heat of the sun without a cap or a hat; the heat of the sun, beating with such violence as it does in that place, would give me the headache presently, by darting so directly on my head, without a cap or hat on, so that I could not bear it; whereas, if I put on my hat, it would presently go away.

Upon these views, I began to consider about putting the few rags I had, which I called clothes, into some order; I had worn out all the waistcoats I had, and my business was now to try if I could not make jackets out of the great watch-coats which I had by me, and with such other materials as I had; so I set to work, tailoring, or rather, indeed, botching, for I made most piteous work of it. However, I made shift to make two or three waistcoats, which I hoped would serve me a great while; as for breeches or drawers, I made but a very sorry shift indeed till afterwards.

I have mentioned that I saved the skins of all the creatures that I killed, I mean four-footed ones, and I had them hung up stretched out with sticks in the sun, by which means some of them were so dry and hard that they were fit for little, but others, it seems, were very useful. The first thing I made of these was a great cap for my head, with the hair on the outside, to shoot off the rain; and this I performed so well, that after, I made me a suit of clothes wholly of those skins—that is to say, a waistcoat, and breeches open at the knees, and both loose, for they were rather wanting to keep me cool than to keep me warm. I must not omit to acknowledge that they were wretchedly made; for if I was a bad carpenter, I was a worse tailor. However, they were such as I made a very good shift with, and when I was abroad, if it happened to rain, the hair of the waistcoat and cap being outermost, I was kept very dry.

After this, I spent a great deal of time and pains to make an umbrella. I was indeed in great want of one, and had a great mind to make one. I had seen them made in the Brazils, where they are very useful in the great heats which are there, and I felt the heats every jot as great here, and greater too, being nearer the equinox; besides, as I was obliged to be much abroad, it was a most useful thing to me, as well for the rains as the heats. I took a world of pains at it, and was a great while before I could make anything likely to hold; nay, after I thought I had hit the way, I spoiled two or three before I made one to my mind. But at last I made one that answered indifferently well; the main difficulty I found was to make it to let down. I could make it spread, but if it did not let down too, and draw in, it would not be portable for me any way but just over my head, which would not do. However, at last, as I said, I made one to answer. I covered it with skins, the hair upwards, so that it cast off the rain like a pent-house and kept off the sun so effectually that I could walk out in the hottest of the weather with greater advantage than I could before in the coolest, and when I had no need of it, I could close it, and carry it under my arm.

Thus I lived mighty comfortably, my mind being entirely composed by resigning to the will of God, and throwing myself wholly upon the disposal of His providence. This made my life better than sociable, for when I began to regret the want of conversation, I would ask myself, whether thus conversing mutually with my own thoughts, and (as I hope I may say with even my Maker), by ejaculations and petitions, was not better than the utmost enjoyment of human society in the world?

I cannot say that, after this for five years, any extraordinary thing happened to me, but I lived on in the same course, in the same posture and place, just as before. The chief thing I was employed in, besides my yearly labour of planting my barley and rice, and curing my raisins— of both which I always kept up just enough to have sufficient stock of the year's provision beforehand—I say, besides this yearly labour, and my daily labour of going out with my gun, I had one labour to make me a canoe, which at last I finished; so that, by digging a canal to it of six feet wide and four feet deep, I brought it into the creek, almost half a mile. As for the first, which was so vastly big, as I made it without considering beforehand, as I ought to do, how I should be able to launch it, so never being able to bring it into the water, or bring the water to it, I was obliged to let it lie where it was, as a memorandum to teach me to be wiser the next time. Indeed, the next time, though I could not get a tree proper for it, and was in a place where I could not get the water to it at any less distance than, as I have said, of near half a mile, yet, as I saw it was practicable at last, I never gave it over; and though I was near two years about it, yet I never grudged my labour, in hopes of having a boat to go off to sea at last.

However, though my little periagua was finished, yet the size of it was not at all answerable to the design which I had in view when I made the first; I mean of venturing over to the *terra firma*, where it was above forty miles broad; accordingly, the smallness of my boat assisted to put an end to that design, and now I thought no more of it. As I had a boat, my next design was to make a tour round the island; for as I had been on the other side in one place, crossing, as I have already described it, over the land, so the discoveries I made in that journey made me very eager to see other parts of the coast; and now I had a boat, I thought of nothing but sailing round the island.

For this purpose, and that I might do everything with discretion and consideration, I fitted up a little mast in my boat, and made a sail to it out of some of the pieces of the ship's sails which lay in store, and of which I had a great store by me. Having fitted my mast and sail, and tried the boat, I found she would sail very well; then I made little lockers, or boxes, at each end of my boat, to put provisions, necessaries, ammunition, etc., into, to be kept dry, either from rain or the spray of the sea; and a little, long, hollow place I cut in the inside of the boat, where I could lay my gun, making a flap hang down over it, to keep it dry.

I fixed my umbrella also in a step at the stern, like a mast, to stand over my head, and keep the heat of the sun off of me, like an awning. And thus I every now and then took a little voyage upon the sea; but never went far out, nor far from the creek. At last, being eager to view the circumference of my little kingdom, I resolved upon my tour; and accordingly I victualed my ship for the voyage, putting in two dozen of loaves (cakes I should rather call them) of barley-bread, an earthen pot full of parched rice (a food I ate a great deal of), a little bottle of rum, half a goat, and powder with shot for killing more, and two large watch-coats, of those which, as I mentioned before, I had saved out of the seamen's chests; these I took, one to lie upon and the other to cover me in the night.

It was the 6th of November, in the sixth year of my reign, or my captivity, which you please, that I set out on this voyage, and I found it much longer than I expected; for though the island itself was not very large, yet when I came to the east side of it, I found a great ledge of rocks lie out about two leagues into sea, some above water, some under it; and beyond that a shoal of sand, lying dry half a league more so that I was obliged to go a great way out to sea to double that point.

When I first discovered them, I was going to give over my enterprise, and come back again, not knowing how far it might oblige me to go out to sea; and, above all, doubting how I should get back again; so I came to an anchor; for I had made a kind of an anchor with a piece of a broken grappling which I got out of the ship.

Having secured my boat, I took my gun and went on shore, climbing up a hill, which seemed to overlook that point where I saw the full extent of it, and resolved to venture.

In my viewing the sea from that hill where I stood, I perceived a strong and, indeed, a most furious current, which ran to the east, and even came close to the point; and I took the more notice of it, because I saw there might be some danger, that when I came into it, I might be carried out to sea by the strength of it, and not be able to make the island again. And, indeed, had I not got first upon this hill, I believe it would have been so; for there was the same current on the other side of the island, only that it set off at a farther distance, and I saw there was a strong eddy under the shore; so I had nothing to do but to get out of the first current, and I should presently be in an eddy.

I lay here, however, two days, because the wind blowing pretty fresh at E.S.E., and that being just contrary to the current, made a great breach of the sea upon the point; so that it was not safe for me to keep too close to the shore for the breach, nor to go too far off, because of the stream.

The third day, in the morning, the wind having abated overnight, the sea was calm, and I ventured. But I am a warning-piece to all rash and ignorant pilots; for no sooner was I come to the point, when I was not even my boat's length from the shore, but I found myself in a great depth of water, and a current like the sluice of a mill. It carried my boat along with it with such violence that all I could do could not keep her so much as on the edge of it; but I found it hurried me farther and farther out from the eddy, which was on my left hand. There was no wind stirring to help me, and all that I could do with my paddles signified nothing. And now I began to give myself over for lost; for, as the current was on both sides of the island, I knew in a few leagues' distance they must join again, and then I was irrecoverably gone; nor did I see any possibility of avoiding it; so that I had no prospect before me but of perishing, not by the sea, for that was calm enough, but of starving from hunger. I had, indeed, found a tortoise on the shore, as big almost as I could lift, and had tossed it into the boat; and I had a great jar of fresh water, that is to say, one of my earthen pots; but what was all this to being driven into the vast ocean, where, to be sure, there was no shore, no mainland or island, for a thousand leagues at least?

And now I saw how easy it was for the providence of God to make the most miserable condition that mankind could be in worse. Now I looked back upon my desolate, solitary island as the most pleasant place in the world, and all the happiness my heart could wish for was to be there again. I stretched out my hands to it, with eager wishes. "O happy desert!" said I, "I shall never see thee more. O miserable creature! whither am I going?" Then I reproached myself with my unthankful temper, and how I had repined at my solitary condition; and now what would I give to be on shore there again! Thus, we never see the true state of our condition till it is illustrated to us by its contraries, nor know how to value what we enjoy, but by the want of it. It is scarcely possible to imagine the consternation I was now in, being driven from my beloved island (for so it appeared to me now to be) into the wide ocean, almost two leagues, and in the utmost despair of ever recovering it again. However, I worked hard till, indeed, my strength was almost exhausted, and kept my boat as much to the northward —that is, towards the side of the current which the eddy lay on—as I possibly could; when about noon, as the sun passed the meridian, I thought I felt a little breeze of wind in my face, springing up from the S.S.E. This cheered my heart a little, and especially when, in about half an hour more, it blew a pretty small, gentle gale. By this time, I had got at a frightful distance from the island; and had the least cloudy or hazy weather intervened, I had been undone another way, too; for I had no compass on board, and should never have known how to have steered towards the island, if I had but once lost sight of it. But the weather continuing clear, I applied myself to get up my mast again, and spread my sail, standing away to the north as much as possible, to get out of the current.

Just as I had set my mast and sail, and the boat began to stretch away, I saw even by the clearness of the water some alteration of the current was near; for where the current was so strong the water was foul; but perceiving the water clear, I found the current abate; and presently I found to the east, at about half a mile, a breach of the sea upon some rocks. These rocks I found caused the current to part again, and as the main stress of it ran away more southerly, leaving the rocks to the northeast, so the other returned by the repulse of the rock, and made a strong eddy, which ran back again to the northwest, with a very sharp stream.

They who know what it is to have a reprieve brought to them upon the ladder, or to be rescued from thieves just going to murder them, or who have been in such extremities, may guess what my present surprise of joy was, and how gladly I put my boat into the stream of this eddy; and the wind also freshening, how gladly I spread my sail to it, running cheerfully before the wind, and with a strong tide or eddy underfoot.

This eddy carried me about a league in my way back again, directly towards the island, but about two leagues more towards the northward than the current lay which carried me away at first; so that when I came near the island, I found myself open to the northern shore of it, that is to say, the other end of the island, opposite to that which I went out from.

When I had made something more than a league of way by help of this current or eddy, I found it was spent, and saved me no farther. However, I found that being between two great currents, viz., that on the south side, which had hurried me away, and that on the north, which lay about two leagues on the other side; I say, between these two, in the wake of the island, I found the water at least still, and running no way; and having still a breeze of wind fair for me, I kept on steering directly for the island, though not making such fresh way as I did before.

About four o'clock in the evening, being then within about a league of the island, I found the point of the rocks which occasioned this disaster stretching out, as is described before, to the southward, and casting off the current more southerly, had, of course, made another eddy to the north; and this I found very strong, but directly setting the way my course lay, which was due west, but almost full north. However, having a fresh gale, I stretched across this eddy, slanting northwest; and in about an hour came within a mile of the shore, where, it being smooth water, I soon got to land.

When I was on shore, I fell on my knees, and gave God thanks for my deliverance, resolving to lay aside all thoughts of my deliverance by my boat; and refreshing myself with such things as I had, I brought my boat close to the shore, in a little cove that I had spied under some trees, and laid me down to sleep, being quite spent with the labour and fatigue of the voyage.

I was now at a great loss which way to get home with my boat! I had run so much hazard, and knew too much of the case, to think of attempting it by the way I went out; and what might be at the other side (I mean the west side) I knew not, nor had I any mind to run any more ventures. So I resolved on the next morning to make my way westward along the shore, and to see if there was no creek where I might lay up my frigate in safety so as to have her again, if I wanted her. In about three miles, or thereabouts, coasting the shore, I came to a very good inlet or bay, about a mile over, which narrowed till it came to a very little rivulet or brook, where I found a very convenient harbour for my boat, and where she lay as if she had been in a little dock made on purpose for her. Here I put in, and having stowed my boat very safe, I went on shore to look about me, and see where I was.

I soon found I had but a little passed by the place where I had been before, when I travelled on foot to that shore; so, taking nothing out of my boat but my gun and umbrella, for it was exceedingly hot, I began my march. The way was comfortable enough after such a voyage as I had been upon, and I reached my old bower in the evening, where I found everything standing as I left it; for I always kept it in good order, being, as I said before, my country-house.

I got over the fence, and laid me down in the shade to rest my limbs, for I was very weary, and fell asleep. But judge you, if you can, that read my story, what a surprise I must have been in when I was awakened out of my sleep by a voice, calling me by my name several times. "Robin, Robin, Robin Crusoe! poor Robin Crusoe! Where are you, Robin Crusoe? Where are you? Where have you been?"

I was so dead asleep at first, being fatigued with rowing or paddling, as it is called, the first part of the day, and walking the latter part, that I did not awake thoroughly; and dozing between sleeping and waking, thought I dreamed that somebody spoke to me; but as the voice continued to repeat, "Robin Crusoe! Robin Crusoe!" at last I began to awake more perfectly, and was at first dreadfully frightened, and started up in the utmost consternation. But no sooner were my eyes open, but I saw my Poll sitting on the top of the hedge, and immediately knew that it was he that spoke to me; for just in such a bemoaning language I had used to talk to him, and teach him; and he had learned it so perfectly that he would sit upon my finger, and lay his bill close to my face, and cry "Poor Robin Crusoe! Where are you? Where have you been? How came you here?" and such things as I had taught him.

However, even though I knew it was the parrot, and that indeed it could be nobody else, it was a good while before I could compose myself. First, I was amazed how the creature got thither; and then, how he should just keep about the place, and nowhere else; but as I was well satisfied it could be nobody but honest Poll, I got over it; and holding out my hand, and calling him by his name, "Poll," the sociable creature came to me, and sat upon my thumb, as he used to do, and continued talking to me, "Poor Robin Crusoe! How did you come here? Where have you been?" just as if he had been overjoyed to see me again; and so I carried him home along with me.

I had now had enough of rambling to sea for some time, and had enough to do for many days, to sit still, and reflect upon the danger I had been in. I would have been very glad to have had my boat again on my side of the island; but I knew not how it was practicable to get it about. As to the east side of the island, which I had gone round, I knew well enough there was no venturing that way; my very heart would shrink, and my very blood run chill, but to think of it; and as to the other side of the island, I did not know how it might be there. But supposing the current ran with the same force against the shore at the east as it passed by it on the other, I might run the same risk of being driven down the stream, and carried by the island, as I had been before of being carried away from it. So with these thoughts I contented myself to be without any boat, though it had been the product of so many months' labour to make it, and of so many more to get it into the sea.

In this government of my temper, I remained near a year; lived a very sedate, retired life, as you may well suppose; and my thoughts being very much composed as to my condition, and fully comforted in resigning myself to the dispositions of Providence, I thought I lived really very happily in all things, except that of society.

I improved myself in this time in all the mechanic exercises which my necessities put me upon applying myself to; and I believe I should, upon occasion, have made a very good carpenter, especially considering how few tools I had.

Besides this, I arrived at an unexpected perfection in my earthenware, and contrived well enough to make them with a wheel, which I found infinitely easier and better; because I made things round and shaped, which before were filthy things indeed to look on. But I think I was never more vain of my own performance, or more joyful for anything I found out, than for my being able to make a tobacco-pipe; and though it was a very ugly, clumsy thing when it was done, and only burnt red, like other earthenware, yet as it was hard and firm, and would draw the smoke, I was exceedingly comforted with it, for I had been always used to smoke; and there were pipes in the ship, but I forgot them at first, not thinking that there was tobacco in the island; and afterwards, when I searched the ship again, I could not come at any pipes.

In my wickerware also I improved much, and made abundance of necessary baskets, as well as my invention showed me; though not very handsome, yet they were such as were very handy and convenient for laying things up in, or fetching things home. For example, if I killed a goat abroad, I could hang it up in a tree, flay it, and dress it, and cut it in pieces, and bring it home in a basket: and the like by a turtle; I could cut it up, take out the eggs, and a piece or two of the flesh, which was enough for me, and bring them home in a basket, and leave the rest behind me. Also, large deep baskets were my receivers for my corn, which I always rubbed out as soon as it was dry, and cured; and kept it in great baskets, instead of a granary.

I began now to perceive my powder abated considerably; and this was a want which it was impossible for me to supply, and I began seriously to consider what I must do when I should have no more powder; that is to say, how I should do to kill any goats. I had, as I observed in the third year of my being here, kept a young kid, and bred her up tame; I was in hopes of getting a he-kid; but I could not by any means bring it to pass, till my kid grew to be an old goat; and as I could never find in my heart to kill her, she died at last of mere age.

CHAPTER IX

BEING now in the eleventh year of my residence, and as I have said, my ammunition growing low, I set myself to study some art to trap and snare the goats, to see whether I could not catch some of them alive; and particularly, I wanted a she-goat great with young. To this purpose, I made snares to hamper them; and I believe they were more than once taken in them; but my tackle was not good, for I had no wire, and always found them broken, and my bait devoured. At length, I resolved to try a pitfall: so I dug several large pits in the earth, in places where I had observed the goats used to feed, and over these pits I placed hurdles, of my own making too, with a great weight upon them; and several times I put ears of barley and dry rice, without setting the trap; and I could easily perceive that the goats had gone in and eaten up the corn, for I could see the marks of their feet. At length, I set three traps in one night, and going the next morning, I found them all standing, and yet the bait eaten and gone: this was very discouraging. However, I altered my traps; and, not to trouble you with particulars, going one morning to see my traps, I found in one of them a large old he-goat; and in one of the others three kids, a male and two females.

As to the old one, I knew not what to do with him; he was so fierce, I durst not go into the pit to him; that is to say, to go about to bring him away alive, which was what I wanted. I could have killed him, but that was not my business, nor would it answer my end; so I even let him out, and he ran away as if he had been frighted out of his wits; but I had forgot then what I learned afterwards, that hunger will tame a lion. If I had let him stay there three or four days without food, and then have carried him some water to drink, and then a little corn, he would have been as tame as one of the kids; for they are mighty sagacious, tractable creatures, where they are well used.

However, for the present I let him go, knowing no better at that time: then I went to the three kids, and taking them one by one, I tied them with strings together, and with some difficulty brought them all home.

It was a good while before they would feed; but throwing them some sweet corn, it tempted them, and they began to be tame. And now I found that if I expected to supply myself with goats' flesh, when I had no powder or shot left, breeding some up tame was my only way; when, perhaps, I might have them about my house like a flock of sheep. But, then, it occurred to me that I must keep the tame from the wild, or else they would always run wild when they grew up; and the only way for this was to have some inclosed piece of ground, well fenced either with hedge or pale, to keep them up so effectually, that those within might not break out, or those without break in.

This was a great undertaking for one pair of hands; yet as I saw there was an absolute necessity for doing it, my first piece of work was to find out a proper piece of ground; viz., where there was likely to be herbage for them to eat, water for them to drink, and cover to keep them from the sun.

Those who understand such inclosures will think I had very little contrivance, when I pitched upon a place proper for all these, being a plain, open piece of meadow land, or savanna (as our people call it in the western colonies), which had two or three little drills of fresh water in it, and at one end was very woody; I say, they will smile at my forecast, when I shall tell them I began by inclosing of this piece of ground in such a manner, that my hedge or pale must have been at least two miles about. Nor was the madness of it so great as to the compass, for if it was ten miles about, I was like to have time enough to do it in; but I did not consider that my goats would be as wild in so much compass as if they had had the whole island, and I should have so much room to chase them in that I should never catch them.

My hedge was begun and carried on, I believe, about fifty yards, when this thought occurred to me; so I presently stopped short, and, for the first beginning, I resolved to inclose a piece of about one hundred and fifty yards in length, and one hundred yards in breadth, which, as it would maintain as many as I should have in any reasonable time, so, as my flock increased, I could add more ground to my inclosure.

This was acting with some prudence, and I went to work with courage. I was about three months hedging in the first piece; and, till I had done it, I tethered the three kids in the best part of it, and used them to feed as near me as possible, to make them familiar; and very often I would go and carry them some ears of barley, or a handful of rice, and feed them out of my hand; so that, after my inclosure was finished, and I let them loose, they would follow me up and down, bleating after me for a handful of corn.

This answered my end, and in about a year and a half I had a flock of about twelve goats, kids and all; and in two years more I had three-and-forty, besides several that I took and killed for my food; and after that, I inclosed five several pieces of ground to feed them in, with little pens to drive them into, to take them as I wanted them, and gates out of one piece of ground into another.

But this was not all; for now I not only had goats' flesh to feed on when I pleased, but milk too—a thing which indeed in my beginning I did not so much as think of, and which, when it came into my thoughts, was really an agreeable surprise; for now I set up my dairy, and had sometimes a gallon or two of milk in a day. And as Nature, who gives supplies of food to every creature, dictates even naturally how to make use of it, so I, that never milked a cow, much less a goat, or saw butter or cheese made, very readily and handily, though after a great many essays and miscarriages, made me both butter and cheese at last, and never wanted it afterwards. How mercifully can our Creator treat his creatures, even in those conditions in which they seemed to be overwhelmed in destruction! How can he sweeten the bitterest providences, and give us cause to praise him for dungeons and prisons! What a table was here spread for me in a wilderness, where I saw nothing at first but to perish for hunger.

It would have made a Stoic smile to have seen me and my little family sit down to dinner. There was my majesty, the prince and lord of the whole island; I had the lives of all my subjects at absolute command; I could hang, draw, give life and liberty and take it away, and no rebels among all my subjects. Then to see how like a king I dined too, all alone, attended by my servants! Poll, as if he had been my favourite, was the only person permitted to talk to me; my dog, who was now grown very old and crazy, and had found no species to multiply his kind upon, sat always at my right hand; and two cats, one on one side the table, and one on the other, expecting now and then a bit from my hand, as a mark of special favour.

But these were not the two cats which I brought on shore at first, for they were both of them dead, and had been interred near my habitation by my own hand; but one of them having multiplied by I know not what kind of creature, these were two which I preserved tame; whereas the rest ran wild in the woods, and became indeed troublesome to me at last; for they would often come into my house, and plunder me too, till at last I was obliged to shoot them, and did kill a great many; at length they left me. With this attendance and in this plentiful manner I lived; neither could I be said to want anything but

society; and of that, in some time after this, I was likely
to have too much.

I was something impatient, as I have observed, to have
the use of my boat, though very loath to run any more
hazard; and therefore sometimes I sat contriving ways
to get her about the island, and at other times I sat myself
down contented enough without her. But I had a strange
uneasiness in my mind to go down to the point of the
island where, as I have said, in my last ramble, I went up
the hills to see how the shore lay, and how the current
set, that I might see what I had to do; this inclination
increased upon me every day, and at length I resolved
to travel thither by land; and following the edge of the
shore, I did so; but had any one in England met such a
man as I was, it must either have frightened them, or
raised a great deal of laughter: and as I frequently stood
still to look at myself, I could not but smile at the notion
of my travelling through Yorkshire with such an equipage,
and in such a dress. Be pleased to take a sketch of my figure,
as follows:

I had a great high shapeless cap, made of goat's skin,
with a flap hanging down behind, as well to keep the sun
from me as to shoot the rain off from running into my
neck; nothing being so hurtful in these climates as the
rain upon the flesh under the clothes.

I had a short jacket of goat's skin, the skirts coming
down to about the middle of the thighs, and a pair of
open-kneed breeches of the same; the breeches were made
of the skin of an old he-goat, whose hair hung down such
a length on either side, that, like pantaloons, it reached
to the middle of my legs. Stockings and shoes I had none,
but had made me a pair of somethings, I scarce knew
what to call them, like buskins, to flap over my legs, and
lace on either side like splatterdashes, but of a most barbarous shape, as indeed were all the rest of my clothes.

I had on a broad belt of goat's skin dried, which I drew
together with two thongs of the same, instead of buckles;

and in a kind of frog on either side of this, instead of a sword and dagger, hung a little saw and a hatchet, one on one side, one on the other. I had another belt not so broad, and fastened in the same manner, which hung over my shoulder; and at the end of it, under my left arm, hung two pouches, both made of goat's skin too, in one of which hung my powder, in the other my shot. At my back I carried my basket, on my shoulder my gun, and over my head a great clumsy, ugly, goat-skin umbrella, but which, after all, was the most necessary thing I had about me next to my gun. As for my face, the colour of it was really not so mulatto-like as one might expect from a man not at all careful of it, and living within nine or ten degrees of the equinox. My beard I had once suffered to grow till it was about a quarter of a yard long; but as I had both scissors and razors sufficient, I had cut it pretty short, except what grew on my upper lip, which I had trimmed into a large pair of Mahometan whiskers, such as I had seen worn by some Turks at Sallee, for the Moors did not wear such, though the Turks did; of these moustachios, or whiskers, I will not say they were long enough to hang my hat upon them, but they were of a length and shape monstrous enough, and such as in England would have passed for frightful.

But all this is by the bye; for, as to my figure, I had so few to observe me that it was of no manner of consequence, so I say no more to that part. In this kind of dress I went my new journey, and was out five or six days. I travelled first along the seashore, directly to the place where I first brought my boat to an anchor to get upon the rocks; and having no boat now to take care of, I went over the land a nearer way to the same height that I was upon before, when, looking forward to the point of the rock which lay out, and which I was obliged to double with my boat, as I said above, I was surprised to see the sea all smooth and quiet—no rippling, no motion, no current, any more there than in other places. I was at a strange loss to understand this, and resolved to spend some time in the observing it, to see if nothing from the sets of the tide had occasioned it; but I was presently convinced how it was, viz., that the tide of ebb setting from the west, and joining with the current of waters from some great river on the shore, must be the occasion of this current; and that according as the wind blew more forcibly from the west or from the north, this current came near, or went farther from the shore; for, waiting thereabouts till evening, I went up to the rock again, and then the tide of ebb being made, I plainly saw the current again as before, only that it ran farther off, being near half a league from the shore, whereas in my case it set close upon the shore, and hurried me in my canoe along with it, which at another time it would not have done.

This observation convinced me that I had nothing to do but to observe the ebbing and the flowing of the tide, and I might very easily bring my boat about the island again; but when I began to think about putting it in practice, I had such terror upon my spirits at the remembrance of the danger I had been in, that I could not think of it again with any patience; but, on the contrary, I took up another resolution, which was more safe, though more laborious—and this was, that I would build, or rather make me another periagua or canoe; and so have one for one side of the island, and one for the other.

You are to understand, that now I had, as I may call it, two plantations in the island; one my little fortification or tent, with the wall about it, under the rock, with the cave behind me, which by this time I had enlarged into several apartments, or caves, one within another. One of these, which was the driest and largest, and had a door out beyond my wall or fortification, that is to say, beyond where my wall joined to the rock, was all filled up with large earthen pots, of which I have given an account, and with fourteen or fifteen great baskets, which would hold five or six bushels each, where I laid up my stores of provision, especially my corn, some in the ear, cut off short from the straw, and the other rubbed out with my hand.

As for my wall, made, as before, with long stakes or piles, those piles grew all like trees, and were by this time grown so big, and spread so very much, that there was not the least appearance, to any one's view, of any habitation behind them.

Near this dwelling of mine, but a little farther within the land, and upon lower ground, lay my two pieces of corn land, which I kept duly cultivated and sowed, and which duly yielded me their harvest in its season; and whenever I had occasion for more corn, I had more land adjoining, as fit as that.

Besides this, I had my country-seat, and I had now a tolerable plantation there also; for first, I had my little bower, as I called it, which I kept in repair—that is to say, I kept the hedge, which circled it in, constantly fitted up to its usual height, the ladder standing always in the inside; I kept the trees, which at first were no more than my stakes, but were now grown very firm and tall, always so cut, that they might spread and grow thick and wild, and make the more agreeable shade, which they did effectually to my mind. In the middle of this I had my tent always standing, being a piece of a sail spread over poles set up for that purpose, and which never wanted any repair or renewing; and under this I had made me a squab or couch, with the skins of the creatures I had killed, and with other soft things, and a blanket laid on them, such as belonged to our sea-bedding, which I had saved; and a great watch-coat to cover me; and here, whenever I had occasion to be absent from my chief seat, I took up my country habitation.

Adjoining to this, I had my inclosures for my cattle, that is to say, my goats; and as I had taken an inconceivable deal of pains to fence and inclose this ground, I was so anxious to see it kept entire, lest the goats should break

through, that I never left off till, with infinite labour, I
had stuck the outside of the hedge so full of small stakes,
and so near to one another, that it was rather a pale than
a hedge, and there was scarce room to put a hand through
between them; which afterwards, when those stakes grew,
as they all did in the next rainy season, made the inclosure
strong like a wall—indeed stronger than any wall.

This will testify for me that I was not idle, and that I
spared no pains to bring to pass whatever appeared necessary for my comfortable support; for I considered the
keeping up a breed of the tame creatures thus at my hand
would be a living magazine of flesh, milk, butter, and
cheese for me as long as I lived in this place, if it were
to be forty years; and that keeping them in my reach
depended entirely upon my perfecting my inclosures to
such a degree that I might be sure of keeping them together;
which, by this method, indeed, I so effectually secured,
that when these little stakes began to grow, I had planted
them so very thick I was forced to pull some of them up
again.

In this place also I had my grapes growing, which I
principally depended on for my winter store of raisins, and
which I never failed to preserve very carefully, as the
best and most agreeable dainty of my whole diet; and,
indeed, they were not agreeable only, but physical, wholesome, nourishing, and refreshing to the last degree.

As this was also half-way between my other habitation
and the place where I had laid up my boat, I generally
stayed and lay here in my way thither, for I used frequently
to visit my boat; and I kept all things about, or belonging
to her, in very good order. Sometimes I went out in her to
divert myself, but no more hazardous voyages would I
go, scarcely ever above a stone's cast or two from the
shore, I was so apprehensive of being hurried out of my
knowledge again by the currents or winds, or any other
accident. But now I come to a new scene of my
life.

It happened one day, about noon, going towards my boat, I was exceedingly surprised with the print of a man's naked foot on the shore, which was very plain to be seen on the sand. I stood like one thunderstruck, or as if I had seen an apparition. I listened, I looked round me, but I could hear nothing, nor see anything; I went up to a rising ground to look farther; I went up the shore, and down the shore, but it was all one: I could see no other impression but that one. I went to it again to see if there were any more, and to observe if it might not be my fancy; but there was no room for that, for there was exactly the print of a foot—toes, heel, and every part of a foot. How it came thither, I knew not, nor could in the least imagine. But after innumerable fluttering thoughts like a man perfectly confused and out of himself, I came home to my fortification, not feeling, as we say, the ground I went on, but terrified to the last degree, looking behind me at every two or three steps, mistaking every bush and tree, and fancying every stump at a distance to be a man. Nor is it possible to describe how many various shapes my affrighted imagination represented things to me in; how many wild ideas were formed every moment in my fancy, and what strange unaccountable whimseys came into my thoughts by the way.

When I came to my castle (for so I think I called it ever after this), I fled into it like one pursued. Whether I went over by the ladder, as first contrived, or went in at the hole in the rock, which I called a door, I cannot remember; for never frighted hare fled to cover, or fox to earth, with more terror of mind than I to this retreat.

I had no sleep that night; the farther I was from the occasion of my fright, the greater my apprehensions were, which is something contrary to the nature of such things, and especially to the usual practice of all creatures in fear; but I was so embarrassed with my own frightful ideas of the thing, that I formed nothing but dismal imaginations to myself, even though I was now a great way off it.

Sometimes I fancied it must be the devil; and reason joined in with me upon this supposition: for how should any other thing in human shape come into the place? Where was the vessel that brought them? What marks were there of any other footsteps? And how was it possible a man should come there? But then to think that Satan should take human shape upon him in such a place, where there could be no manner of occasion for it, but to leave the print of his foot behind him, and that even for no purpose too, for he could not be sure I should see it—this was an amazement the other way. I considered that the devil might have found out abundance of other ways to have terrified me than this of the simple print of a foot; that as I lived quite on the other side of the island, he would never have been so simple as to leave a mark in a place where it was ten thousand to one whether I should ever see it or not, and in the sand too, which the first surge of the sea, upon a high wind, would have defaced entirely. All this seemed inconsistent with the thing itself, and with all the notions we usually entertain of the subtlety of the devil.

Abundance of such things as these assisted to argue me out of all apprehensions of its being the devil; and I presently concluded then, that it must be some more dangerous creature; viz., that it must be some of the savages of the mainland over against me, who had wandered out to sea in their canoes, and either driven by the currents or by contrary winds, had made the island, and had been on shore, but were gone away again to sea; being as loath, perhaps, to have stayed in this desolate island as I would have been to have had them.

While these reflections were rolling upon my mind, I was very thankful in my thought, that I was so happy as not to be thereabouts at that time, or that they did not see my boat, by which they would have concluded that some inhabitants had been in the place, and perhaps have searched farther for me. Then terrible thoughts racked my imagination about their having found my boat, and that there were people here; and that, if so, I should certainly have them come again in greater numbers, and devour me; that if it should happen that they should not find me, yet they would find my inclosure, destroy all my corn, and carry away all my flock of tame goats, and I should perish at last for mere want.

Thus my fear banished all my religious hope; all that former confidence in God, which was founded upon such wonderful experience as I had had of his goodness, now vanished; as if he that had fed me by miracle hitherto, could not preserve by his power the provision which he had made for me by his goodness. I reproached myself with my laziness, that would not sow any more corn one year than would just serve me till the next season, as if no accident could intervene to prevent my enjoying the crop that was upon the ground; and this I thought so just a reproof, that I resolved for the future to have two or three years' corn beforehand, so that, whatever might come, I might not perish for want of bread.

How strange a checkerwork of Providence is the life of man! and by what secret differing springs are the affections hurried about, as differing circumstances present! To-day we love what to-morrow we hate; to-day we seek what to-morrow we shun; to-day we desire what to-morrow we fear, nay, even tremble at the apprehensions of. This was exemplified in me at this time in the most lively manner imaginable; for I, whose only affliction was, that I seemed banished from human society, that I was alone, circumscribed by the boundless ocean, cut off from mankind, and condemned to what I call silent life; that I was as one whom Heaven thought not worthy to be numbered among the living, or to appear amongst the rest of his creatures; that to have seen one of my own species would have seemed to me a raising me from death to life, and the greatest blessing that Heaven itself, next to the supreme blessing of salvation, could bestow; I say, that I should now tremble at the very apprehensions of seeing a man, and was ready to sink into the ground at but the shadow or silent appearance of a man having set his foot on the island.

Such is the uneven state of human life; and it afforded me a great many curious speculations afterwards, when I had a little recovered my first surprise. I considered that this was the station of life the infinitely wise and good Providence of God had determined for me; that as I could not foresee what the end of Divine wisdom might be in all this, so I was not to dispute his sovereignty, who, as I was his creature, had an undoubted right by creation to govern and dispose of me absolutely as he thought fit; and who, as I was a creature who had offended him, had likewise a judicial right to condemn me to what punishment he thought fit; and that it was my part to submit to bear his indignation, because I had sinned against him. I then reflected that God, who was not only righteous, but omnipotent, as he had thought fit thus to punish and afflict me, so he was able to deliver me; that if he did not think fit to do it, it was my unquestioned duty to resign myself absolutely and entirely to his will; and, on the other hand, it was my duty also to hope in him, pray to him, and quietly to attend the dictates and directions of his daily providence.

These thoughts took me up many hours, days, nay, I may say weeks and months; and one particular effect of my cogitations on this occasion I cannot omit; viz., one morning early, lying in my bed, and filled with thoughts about my danger from the appearance of savages, I found it discomposed me very much; upon which those words of the Scripture came into my thoughts: "Call upon me in the day of trouble: I will deliver thee, and thou shalt glorify me." Upon this, rising cheerfully out of bed, my heart was not only comforted, but I was guided and encouraged to pray earnestly to God for deliverance: when I had done praying, I took up my Bible, and opening it to read, the first words that presented to me were, "Wait on the

Lord; be of good courage, and he shall strengthen thy heart: wait, I say, on the Lord." It is impossible to express the comfort this gave me, and in return I thankfully laid down the book, and was no more sad; at least, not on that occasion.

In the middle of these cogitations, apprehensions, and reflections, it came into my thoughts one day, that all this might be a mere chimera of my own, and that this foot might be the print of my own foot, when I came on shore from my boat; this cheered me up a little, too, and I began to persuade myself it was all a delusion; that it was nothing else but my own foot; and why might I not come that way from the boat, as well as I was going that way to the boat? Again I considered also, that I could by no means tell for certain where I had trod, and where I had not; and that if, at last, this was only the print of my own foot, I had played the part of those fools who try to make stories of spectres and apparitions, and then are themselves frighted at them more than anybody else.

Now I began to take courage, and to peep abroad again, for I had not stirred out of my castle for three days and nights, so that I began to starve for provision; for I had little or nothing within doors but some barley-cakes and water. Then I knew that my goats wanted to be milked too, which usually was my evening diversion; and the poor creatures were in great pain and inconvenience for want of it; and, indeed, it almost spoiled some of them, and almost dried up their milk.

Heartening myself, therefore, with the belief that this was nothing but the print of one of my own feet, and so I might be truly said to start at my own shadow, I began to go abroad again, and went to my countryhouse to milk my flock; but to see with what fear I went forward, how often I looked behind me, how I was ready, every now and then, to lay down my basket, and run for my life, it would have made any one have thought I was haunted with an evil conscience, or that I had been lately most terribly frightened; and so, indeed, I had. However, as I went down thus two or three days, and having seen nothing, I began to be a little bolder, and to think there was really nothing in it but my own imagination; but I could not persuade myself fully of this till I should go down to the shore again, and see this print of a foot, and measure it by my own, and see if there was any similitude or fitness, that I might be assured it was my own foot. But when I came to the place—first, it appeared evidently to me, that when I laid up my boat, I could not possibly be on shore anywhere thereabouts; secondly, when I came to measure the mark with my own foot, I found my foot not so large by a great deal. Both these things filled my head with new imaginations, and gave me the vapors again to the highest degree, so that I shook with cold like one in an ague; and I went home again, filled with the belief that some man or men had been on shore there; or, in short, that the island was inhabited, and I might be surprised before I was aware; and what course to take for my security I knew not.

Oh, what ridiculous resolutions men take when possessed with fear! It deprives them of the use of those means which reason offers for their relief. The first thing I proposed to myself was, to throw down my inclosures and turn all my tame cattle wild into the woods, that the enemy might not find them and then frequent the island in prospect of the same or the like booty; then the simple thing of digging up my two cornfields, that they might not find such a grain there, and still be prompted to frequent the island; then to demolish my bower and tent, that they might not see any vestiges of habitation, and be prompted to look farther, in order to find out the persons inhabiting.

These were the subjects of the first night's cogitations, after I was come home again, while the apprehensions which had so overrun my mind were fresh upon me, and my head was full of vapors as above. Thus, fear of danger is ten thousand times more terrifying than danger itself, when apparent to the eyes; and we find the burden of anxiety greater, by much, than the evil which we are anxious about; but, which was worse than all this, I had not that relief in this trouble, from the resignation I used to practice, that I hoped to have. I looked, I thought, like Saul, who complained not only that the Philistines were upon him, but that God had forsaken him; for I did not now take due ways to compose my mind, by crying to God in my distress, and resting upon his providence, as I had done before, for my defence and deliverance; which if I had done, I had at least been more cheerfully supported under this new surprise, and perhaps carried through it with more resolution.

This confusion of my thoughts kept me waking all night; but in the morning I fell asleep; and having by the amusement of my mind been, as it were, tired, and my spirits exhausted, I slept very soundly, and awaked much better composed than I had ever been before. And now I began to think sedately; and, upon the utmost debate with myself, I concluded that this island (which was so exceeding pleasant, fruitful, and no farther from the mainland than as I had seen) was not so entirely abandoned as I might imagine; that although there were no stated inhabitants who lived on the spot, yet that there might sometimes come boats off from the shore, who either with design, or perhaps never but when they were driven by cross winds, might come to this place; that I had lived here fifteen years now and had not met with the least shadow or figure of any people yet; and that, if at any time they should be driven here, it was probable they went away again as soon as ever they could, seeing they had never thought fit to fix here upon any occasion to this time; that the most I could suggest any danger from was, from any casual accidental landing of straggling people from the main, who, as it was likely, if they were driven hither, were here against their wills; so they made no stay here, but went off again, with all possible speed, seldom staying one night on shore, lest they should not have the help of the tides and daylight back again; and that, therefore, I had nothing to do but to consider of some safe retreat, in case I should see any savages land upon the spot.

Now I began sorely to repent that I had dug my cave so large as to bring a door through again, which door, as I said, came out beyond where my fortification joined to the rock. Upon maturely considering this, therefore, I resolved to draw me a second fortification, in the same manner of a semicircle, at a distance from my wall, just where I had planted a double row of trees about twelve years before, of which I made mention; these trees having been planted so thick before, there wanted but few piles to be driven between them, that they should be thicker and stronger, and my wall would be soon finished. So that I had now a double wall; and my outer wall was thickened with pieces of timber, old cables, and everything I could think of to make it strong, having in it seven little holes, about as big as I might put my arm out at. In the inside of this, I thickened my wall to about ten feet thick, continually bringing earth out of my cave, and laying it at the foot of the wall, and walking upon it; and through the seven holes I contrived to plant the muskets, of which I took notice that I got seven on shore out of the ship; these I say, I planted like my cannon, and fitted them into frames, that held them like a carriage, that so I could fire all the seven guns in two minutes' time. This wall I was many a weary month in finishing, and yet never thought myself safe till it was done.

When this was done, I stuck all the ground without my wall, for a great way every way, as full with stakes or sticks to the osier-like wood, which I found so apt to grow, as they could well stand; insomuch that I believe I might set in near twenty thousand of them, leaving a pretty large space between them and my wall, that I might have room to see an enemy, and they might have no shelter from the young trees, if they attempted to approach my outer wall.

Thus, in two years' time, I had a thick grove; and in five or six years' time I had a wood before my dwelling grown so monstrous thick and strong that it was indeed perfectly impassable; and no man, of what kind soever, would ever imagine that there was anything beyond it, much less a habitation. As for the way which I proposed to myself to go in or out (for I left no avenue), it was by setting two ladders, one to a part of the rock which was low, and then broke in, and left room to place another ladder upon that; so when the two ladders were taken down, no man living could come down to me without mischiefing himself; and if they had come down, they were still on the outside of my outer wall.

Thus I took all the measures human prudence could suggest for my own preservation; and it will be seen, at length, that they were not altogether without just reason; though I foresaw nothing at that time more than my mere fear suggested to me.

While this was doing, I was not altogether careless of my other affairs; for I had a great concern upon me for my little herd of goats; they were not only a present supply to me upon every occasion, and began to be sufficient for me, without the expense of powder and shot, but also abated the fatigue of my hunting after the wild ones; and I was loath to lose the advantage of them, and to have them all to nurse up over again.

For this purpose, after long consideration, I could think of but two ways to preserve them: one was to find another convenient place to dig a cave under ground, and to drive them into it every night; and the other was to inclose two or three little bits of land, remote one from another, and as much concealed as I could, where I might keep about half a dozen young goats in each place; so that if any disaster happened to the flock in general, I might be able to raise them again with a little trouble and time: and this, though it would require a good deal of time and labour, I thought was the most rational design.

Accordingly, I spent some time to find out the most retired parts of the island; and I pitched upon one which was as private indeed as my heart could wish; it was a little damp piece of ground, in the middle of the hollow and thick woods, where, as is observed, I almost lost myself once before, endeavouring to come back that way from the eastern part of the island. Here I found a clear piece of land, near three acres, so surrounded with woods, that it was almost an inclosure by Nature; at least, it did not want near so much labour to make it so as the other pieces of ground I had worked so hard at.

CHAPTER X

IMMEDIATELY went to work with this piece of ground; and, in less than a month's time, I had so fenced it round that my flock or herd, call it which you please, which were not so wild now as at first they might be supposed to be, were well enough secured in it. So, without any further delay, I removed ten she-goats, and two he-goats, to this piece; and, when they were there, I continued to perfect the fence, till I had made it as secure as the other; which, however, I did at more leisure, and it took me up more time by a great deal. All this labour I was at the expense of, purely from my apprehensions on the account of the print of a man's foot which I had seen: for, as yet, I had never seen any human creature come near the island; and I had now lived two years under this uneasiness, which, indeed, made my life much less comfortable than it was before, as may well be imagined by any who know what it is to live in the constant snare of the fear of man. And this I must observe, with grief, too, that the discomposure of my mind had too great impressions also upon the religious part of my thoughts; for the dread and terror of falling into the hands of savages and cannibals lay so upon my spirits that I seldom found myself in a due temper for application to my Maker; at least, not with the sedate calmness and resignation of soul which I was wont to do; I rather prayed to God as under great affliction and pressure of mind, surrounded with danger, and in expectation every night of being murdered and devoured before morning; and I must testify, from my experience, that a temper of peace, thankfulness, love and affection, is much the more proper frame for prayer than that of terror and discomposure; and that under the dread of mischief impending, a man is no more fit for a comforting performance of the duty of praying to God than he is for repentance on a sick bed; for these discomposures affect the mind, as the others do the body: and the discomposure of the mind must necessarily be as great a disability as that of the body, and much greater; praying to God being properly an act of the mind, not of the body.

But to go on: after I had thus secured one part of my little living stock, I went about the whole island, searching for another private place to make such another deposit; when, wandering more to the west point of the island than I had ever done yet, and looking out to sea, I thought I saw a boat upon the sea, at a great distance. I had found a perspective glass or two in one of the seamen's chests, which I saved out of our ship, but I had it not about me; and this was so remote that I could not tell what to make of it, though I looked at it till my eyes were not able to hold to look any longer: whether it was a boat or not, I do not know; but as I descended from the hill I could see no more of it, so I gave it over; only I resolved to go no more out without a perspective glass in my pocket.

When I was come down the hill to the end of the island, where, indeed, I had never been before, I was presently convinced that the seeing the print of a man's foot was not such a strange thing in the island as I imagined; and, but that it was a special providence that I was cast upon the side of the island where the savages never came, I should easily have known that nothing was more frequent than for the canoes from the main, when they happened to be a little too far out at sea, to shoot over to that side of the island for harbour: likewise, as they often met and fought in their canoes, the victors, having taken any prisoners, would bring them over to this shore, where, according to their dreadful customs, being all cannibals, they would kill and eat them; of which hereafter.

When I was come down the hill to the shore, as I said above, being the S.W. point of the island, I was perfectly confounded and amazed; nor is it possible for me to express the horror of my mind, at seeing the shore spread with skulls, hands, feet, and other bones of human bodies; and particularly, I observed a place where there had been a fire made, and a circle dug in the earth, like a cockpit, where I supposed the savage wretches had sat down to their inhuman feastings upon the bodies of their fellow-creatures.

I was so astonished with the sight of these things that I entertained no notions of any danger to myself from it for a long while: all my apprehensions were buried in the thoughts of such a pitch of inhuman, hellish brutality, and the horror of the degeneracy of human nature, which, though I had heard of often, yet I never had so near a view of before; in short, I turned away my face from the horrid spectacle; my stomach grew sick, and I was just at the point of fainting, when nature discharged the disorder from my stomach; and having vomited with uncommon violence, I was a little relieved, but could not bear to stay in the place a moment; so I got up the hill again with all the speed I could, and walked on towards my own habitation.

When I came a little out of that part of the island, I stood still awhile, as amazed, and then, recovering myself, I looked up with the utmost affection of my soul, and, with a flood of tears in my eyes, gave God thanks, that had cast my first lot in a part of the world where I was distinguished from such dreadful creatures as these; and that, though I had esteemed my present condition very miserable, had yet given me so many comforts in it that I had still more to give thanks for than to complain of: and this, above all, that I had, even in this miserable condition, been comforted with the knowledge of himself, and the hope of his blessing: which was a felicity more than sufficiently equivalent to all the misery which I had suffered, or could suffer.

In this frame of thankfulness, I went home to my castle, and began to be much easier now, as to the safety of my circumstances than ever I was before: for I observed that these wretches never came to this island in search of what they could get; perhaps not seeking, not wanting, or not expecting, anything here; and having often, no doubt, been up in the covered, woody part of it, without finding anything to their purpose. I knew I had been here almost eighteen years, and never saw the least footsteps of human creature there before; and I might be eighteen years more as entirely concealed as I was now, if I did not discover myself to them, which I had no manner of occasion to do; it being my only business to keep myself entirely concealed where I was, unless I found a better sort of creatures than cannibals to make myself known to. Yet I entertained such an abhorrence of the savage wretches that I have been speaking of, and of the wretched inhuman custom of their devouring and eating one another up, that I continued pensive and sad, and kept close within my own circle for almost two years after this: when I say my own circle, I mean by it my three plantations, viz., my castle, my country-seat (which I called my bower) and my inclosure in the woods: nor did I look after this for any other use than as an inclosure for my goats; for the aversion which nature gave me to these hellish wretches was such that I was as fearful of seeing them as of seeing the devil himself, nor did I so much as go to look after my boat in all this time, but began rather to think of making me another; for I could not think of ever making any more attempts to bring the other boat round the island to me, lest I should meet with some of those creatures at sea; in which case, if I had happened to have fallen into their hands, I knew what would have been my lot.

Time, however, and the satisfaction I had that I was in no danger of being discovered by these people, began to wear off my uneasiness about them; and I began to live just in the same composed manner as before, only with this difference, that I used more caution, and kept my eyes more about me than I did before, lest I should happen to be seen by any of them; and particularly, I was more cautious in firing my gun, lest any of them, being on the

island, should happen to hear it; and it was, therefore, a
very good providence to me that I had furnished myself with
a tame breed of goats, and that I had no need to hunt
any more about the woods, or shoot at them; and if I
did catch any of them after this, it was by traps and snares,
as I had done before: so that for two years after this, I
believe I never fired my gun once off, though I never went
out without it; and which was more, as I had saved three
pistols out of the ship, I always carried them out with me,
or at least two of them, sticking them in my goat-skin belt.
I likewise furbished up one of the great cutlasses that
I had out of the ship, and made me a belt to put it on also;
so that I was now a most formidable fellow to look at when
I went abroad, if you add to the former description of myself,
the particular of two pistols, and a great broadsword hanging at my side in a belt, but without a scabbard.

Things going on thus, as I have said, for some time
I seemed, excepting these cautions, to be reduced to my
former calm, sedate way of living. All these things tended
to show me, more and more, how far my condition was from
being miserable, compared to some others; nay, to many
other particulars of life, which it might have pleased God to
have made my lot. It put me upon reflecting how little
repining there would be among mankind at any condition
of life, if people would rather compare their condition with
those that are worse, in order to be thankful, than be always
comparing them with those which are better, to assist
their murmurings and complainings.

As in my present condition there were not really many
things which I wanted, so, indeed, I thought that the frights
I had been in about these savage wretches, and the concern
I had been in for my own preservation, had taken off the
edge of my invention for my own conveniences; and I had
dropped a good design, which I had once bent my thoughts
upon, and that was to try if I could not make some of my
barley into malt, and then to try to brew myself some beer.
This was really a whimsical thought, and I reproved myself

often for the simplicity of it: for I presently saw there would be the want of several things necessary to the making my beer, that it would be impossible for me to supply; as, first, casks to preserve it in, which was a thing that, as I have observed already, I could never compass; no, though I spent not many days, but weeks, nay, months, in attempting it, but to no purpose. In the next place, I had no hops to make it keep, no yeast to make it work, no copper or kettle to make it boil; and yet had not all these things intervened—I mean, the frights and terrors I was in about the savages—I had undertaken it, and perhaps brought it to pass, too; for I seldom gave anything over without accomplishing it, when I once had hit in my head enough to begin it. But my invention now ran quite another way; for, night and day, I could think of nothing but how I might destroy some of these monsters in their cruel, bloody entertainment; and, if possible, save the victim they should bring hither to destroy. It would take up a larger volume than this whole work is intended to be, to set down all the contrivances I hatched, or rather brooded upon, in my thoughts, for the destroying these creatures, or at least frightening them so as to prevent their coming hither any more: but all was abortive; nothing could be possible to take effect, unless I was to be there to do it myself; and what could one man do among them, when perhaps there might be twenty or thirty of them together with their darts, or their bows and arrows, with which they could shoot as true to a mark as I could with my gun?

Sometimes I thought of digging a hole under the place where they made their fire, and putting in five or six pounds of gunpowder, which, when they kindled their fire, would consequently take fire, and blow up all that was near it: but as, in the first place, I should be unwilling to waste so much powder upon them, my store being now within the quantity of one barrel, so neither could I be sure of its going off at any certain time, when it might surprise them and, at best, that it would do little more than just blow the fire

about their ears and frighten them, but not sufficient to
make them forsake the place: so I laid it aside; and then
proposed that I would place myself in ambush in some
convenient place with my three guns all double loaded,
and in the middle of their bloody ceremony let fly at them,
when I should be sure to kill or wound perhaps two or three
at every shot; and then falling in upon them with my three
pistols and my sword, I made no doubt but that, if there
were twenty, I should kill them all. This fancy pleased
my thoughts for some weeks, and I was so full of it that I
often dreamed of it, and sometimes, that I was just going
to let fly at them in my sleep. I went so far with it in my
imagination, that I employed myself several days to find
out proper places to put myself in ambuscade, as I said, to
watch for them, and I went frequently to the place itself,
which was now grown more familiar to me; but while
my mind was thus filled with thoughts of revenge and of a
bloody putting twenty or thirty of them to the sword, as
I may call it, the horror I had at the place, and at the signals
of the barbarous wretches devouring one another, abetted
my malice. Well, at length I found a place in the side of
the hill, where I was satisfied I might securely wait till I
saw any of their boats coming; and might then, even before
they would be ready to come on shore, convey myself
unseen into some thickets of trees, in one of which there
was a hollow large enough to conceal me entirely; and
there I might sit and observe all their bloody doings, and
take my full aim at their heads when they were so close
together as that it would be next to impossible that I should
miss my shot, or that I could fail wounding three or four
of them at the first shot. In this place, then, I resolved to
fix my design; and accordingly, I prepared two muskets
and my ordinary fowling-piece. The two muskets I loaded
with a brace of slugs each, and four or five smaller bullets,
about the size of pistol bullets; and the fowling-piece I
loaded with near a handful of swan-shot of the largest size;
I also loaded my pistols with about four bullets each;

and in this posture, well provided with ammunition for a second and third charge, I prepared myself for my expedition.

After I had thus laid the scheme of my design, and in my imagination put it in practice, I continually made my tour every morning to the top of the hill, which was from my castle, as I called it, about three miles, or more, to see if I could observe any boats upon the sea, coming near the island, or standing over towards it; but I began to tire of this hard duty, after I had for two or three months constantly kept my watch, but came always back without any discovery; there having not, in all that time, been the least appearance, not only on or near the shore, but on the whole ocean, as far as my eyes or glass could reach every way.

As long as I kept my daily tour to the hill to look out, so long also I kept up the vigour of my design, and my spirits seemed to be all the while in a suitable frame for so outrageous an execution as the killing twenty or thirty naked savages for an offence which I had not at all entered into a discussion of in my thoughts, any farther than my passions were at first fired by the horror I conceived at the unnatural custom of the people of that country; who, it seems, had been suffered by Providence, in his wise disposition of the world, to have no other guide than that of their own abominable and vitiated passions; and, consequently, were left, and perhaps had been so for some ages, to act such horrid things, and receive such dreadful customs, as nothing but nature, entirely abandoned by Heaven, and actuated by some hellish degeneracy, could have run them into. But now, when, as I have said, I began to be weary of the fruitless excursion which I had made so long and so far every morning in vain, so my opinion of the action itself began to alter; and I began, with cooler and calmer thoughts, to consider what I was going to engage in; what authority or call I had to pretend to be judge and executioner upon these men as criminals, whom Heaven had thought fit, for so many ages, to suffer, unpunished, to go on, and to be, as it were, the executioners of his judgments, one upon another; how far these people were offenders against me, and what right I had to engage in the quarrel of that blood which they shed promiscuously upon one another. I debated this very often with myself thus, "How do I know what God himself judges in this particular case? It is certain these people do not commit this as a crime; it is not against their own conscience reproving, or their light reproaching them; they do not know it to be an offence, and then commit it in defiance of Divine justice, as we do in almost all the sins we commit. They think it no more a crime to kill a captive taken in war than we do to kill an ox; or to eat human flesh than we do to eat mutton."

When I considered this a little, it followed necessarily that I was certainly in the wrong in it; that these people were not murderers, in the sense that I had before condemned them in my thoughts, any more than those Christians were murderers who often put to death the prisoners taken in battle; or more frequently, upon many occasions, put whole troops of men to the sword, without giving quarter, though they threw down their arms and submitted. In the next place, it occurred to me, that albeit the usage they gave one another was thus brutish and inhuman, yet it was really nothing to me. These people had done me no injury; that if they attempted me, or I saw it necessary, for my immediate preservation, to fall upon them, something might be said for it: but that I was yet out of their power, and they really had no knowledge of me, and consequently no design upon me; and, therefore, it could not be just for me to fall upon them. That this would justify the conduct of the Spaniards in all their barbarities practised in America, where they destroyed millions of these people; who, however they were idolators and barbarians, and had several bloody and barbarous rites in their customs, such as sacrificing human bodies to their idols, were yet, as to the Spaniards, very innocent people; and that the rooting them out of the country is spoken of with the utmost abhorrence and detestation by even the Spaniards themselves, at this time, and by all other Christian nations in Europe, as a mere butchery, a bloody and unnatural piece of cruelty, unjustifiable either to God or man; and such as for which the very name of a Spaniard is reckoned to be frightful and terrible to all people of humanity or of Christian compassion; as if the kingdom of Spain were particularly eminent for the product of a race of men who were without principles of tenderness, or the common bowels of pity to the miserable, which is reckoned to be a mark of a generous temper in the mind.

These considerations really put me to a pause, and to a kind of a full stop: and I began, by little and little, to be off my design, and to conclude I had taken wrong measures in my resolution to attack the savages; and that it was not my business to meddle with them, unless they first attacked me; and this it was my business, if possible, to prevent; but that, if I were discovered and attacked by them, then I knew my duty. On the other hand, I argued with myself that this really was the way not to deliver myself, but entirely to ruin and destroy myself; for, unless I was sure to kill every one that not only should be on shore at that time, but that should ever come on shore afterwards, if but one of them escaped to tell their country-people what had happened, they would come over again by thousands to revenge the death of their fellows, and I should only bring upon myself a certain destruction, which, at present, I had no manner of occasion for. Upon the whole, I concluded that I ought, neither in principle nor in policy, one way or other, to concern myself in this affair; that my business was, by all possible means, to conceal myself from them, and not to leave the least sign for them to guess by that there were any living creatures upon the island—I mean of human shape. Religion joined in with this prudential resolution; and I was convinced now, many ways, that I was perfectly out of my duty when I was laying all my bloody schemes for the destruction of innocent creatures—I mean innocent as to me. As to the crimes they were guilty of towards one another, I had nothing to do with them; these were national punishments, to make a just retribution for national offence, and to bring public judgment upon those who offend in a public manner, by such ways as best please God. This appeared so clear to me now, that nothing was a greater satisfaction to me than that I had not been suffered to do a thing which I now saw so much reason to believe would have been no less a sin than that of wilful murder, if I had committed it; and I gave most humble thanks, on my knees, to God, that he had thus delivered me from blood-guiltiness; beseeching him to grant me the protection of his providence, that I might not fall into the hands of the barbarians, or that I might not lay my hands upon them, unless I had a more clear call from Heaven to do it, in defence of my own life.

In this disposition I continued for near a year after this; and so far was I from desiring an occasion for falling upon these wretches, that in all that time I never once went up the hill to see whether there were any of them in sight, or to know whether any of them had been on shore there or not, that I might not be tempted to renew any of my contrivances against them, or be provoked by any advantage that might present itself, to fall upon them: only this I did; I went and removed my boat, which I had on the other side of the island, and carried it down to the east end of the whole island, where I ran it into a little cove, which I found under some high rocks, and where I knew, by reason of the currents, the savages durst not, at least would not, come with their boats upon any account whatever. With my boat I carried away everything that I had left there belonging to her, though not necessary for the bare going thither, viz., a mast and sail which I had made for her, and a thing like an anchor, but which indeed could not be called either anchor or grapnel; however, it was the best I could make of its kind: all these I removed, that there might not be the least shadow for discovery, or any appearance of any boat, or of any habitation upon the island. Besides this, I kept myself, as I said, more retired than ever, and seldom went from my cell, except upon my constant employment, viz., to milk my she-goats, and manage my little flock in the wood, which, as it was quite on the other part of the island, was out of danger; for certain it is that these savage people, who sometimes haunted this island, never came with any thoughts of finding anything here, and consequently never wandered off from the coast, and I doubt not but they might have been several times on shore after my apprehensions of them had made me cautious, as well as before. Indeed, I looked back with some horror upon the thoughts of what my condition would have been, if I had chopped upon them and been discovered before that; when, naked, and unarmed, except with one gun, and that loaded often only with small shot, I walked everywhere, peeping and peering about the island to see what I could get; what a surprise should I have been in, if, when I discovered the print of a man's foot, I had instead of that seen fifteen or twenty savages, and found them pursuing me, and by the swiftness of their running, no possibility of my escaping them! The thoughts of this sometimes sunk my very soul within me, and distressed my mind so much that I could not soon recover it, to think what I should have done, and how I should not only have been unable to resist them, but even should not have had presence of mind enough to do what I might have done; much less what now, after so much consideration and preparation, I might be able to do. Indeed, after serious thinking of these things I would be very melancholy, and sometimes, it would last a great while: but I resolved it all, at last, into thankfulness to that Providence which had delivered me from so many unseen dangers, and had kept me from those mischiefs which I could have no way been the agent in delivering myself from, because I had not the least notion of any such thing depending, or the least supposition of its being possible.

This renewed a contemplation which often had come

into my thoughts in former times, when first I began to see the merciful dispositions of Heaven, in the dangers we run through in this life; how wonderfully we are delivered when we know nothing of it; how, when we are in a quandary (as we call it), a doubt or hesitation whether to go this way or that way, a secret hint shall direct us this way when we intended to go that way: nay, when sense, our own inclination, and perhaps business, have called us to go the other way, yet a strange impression upon the mind, from we know not what springs, and by we know not what power, shall overrule us to go this way; and it shall afterwards appear that had we gone that way which we should have gone, and even to our imagination ought to have gone, we should have been ruined and lost. Upon these, and many like reflections, I afterwards made it a certain rule with me, that whenever I found these secret hints or pressings of mind, to doing or not doing anything that presented, or going this way or that way, I never failed to obey the secret dictate; though I knew no other reason for it than that such a pressure, or such a hint, hung upon my mind. I could give many examples of the success of this conduct in the course of my life, but more especially in the latter part of my inhabiting this unhappy island; besides many occasions which it is very likely I might have taken notice of if I had seen with the same eyes then that I see with now. But it is never too late to be wise; and I cannot but advise all considering men, whose lives are attended with such extraordinary incidents as mine, or even though not so extraordinary, not to slight such secret intimations of Providence, let them come from what invisible intelligence they will. That I shall not discuss, and perhaps cannot account for; but certainly they are a proof of the converse of spirits, and a secret communication between those embodied and those unembodied, and such a proof as can never be withstood; of which I shall have occasion to give some very remarkable instances in the remainder of my solitary residence in this dismal place.

I believe the reader of this will not think it strange if I confess that these anxieties, these constant dangers I lived in, and the concern that was now upon me, put an end to all invention, and to all the contrivances that I had laid for my future accommodations and conveniences. I had the care of my safety more now upon hand than that of my food. I cared not to drive a nail, or chop a stick of wood now, for fear the noise I should make should be heard; much less would I fire a gun for the same reason; and, above all, I was intolerably uneasy at making any fire, lest the smoke which is visible at a great distance in the day, should betray me. For this reason, I removed that part of my business which required fire, such as burning of pots and pipes, etc., into my new apartment in the woods, where, after I had been some time, I found, to my unspeakable consolation, a mere natural cave in the earth, which went in a vast way, and where, I dare say, no savage, had he been at the mouth of it, would be so hardy as to venture in; nor, indeed, would any man else, but one who, like me, wanted nothing so much as a safe retreat.

The mouth of this hollow was at the bottom of a great rock, where, by mere accident (I would say, if I did not see abundant reason to ascribe all such things now to Providence), I was cutting down some thick branches of trees to make charcoal; and before I go on I must observe the reason of my making this charcoal, which was thus: I was afraid of making a smoke about my habitation, as I said before; and yet I could not live there without baking my bread, cooking my meat, etc.; so I contrived to burn some wood here, as I had seen done in England, under turf, till it became chark, or dry coal; and then putting the fire out, I preserved the coal to carry home and perform the other services for which fire was wanting, without danger of smoke. But this is by the bye. While I was cutting down some wood here, I perceived that, behind a very thick branch of low brushwood or underwood, there was a kind of hollow place: I was curious to look in it; and getting with difficulty into the mouth of it, I found it was pretty large, that is to say, sufficient for me to stand upright in it, and perhaps another with me: but I must confess to you that I made more haste out than I did in, when looking farther into the place, which was perfectly dark, I saw there two broad shining eyes of some creature—whether devil or man I knew not—which twinkled like two stars; the dim light from the cave's mouth shining directly in, and making the reflection. However, after some pause, I recovered myself, and began to call myself a thousand fools, and to think that he that was afraid to see the devil was not fit to live twenty years in an island all alone; and that I might well think there was nothing in this cave that was more frightful than myself. Upon this, plucking up my courage, I took up a firebrand, and in I rushed again, with the stick flaming in my hand: I had not gone three steps in, before I was almost as much frightened as before; for I heard a very loud sigh, like that of a man in some pain, and it was followed by a broken noise, as of words half expressed, and then a deep sigh again. I stepped back, and was indeed struck with such a surprise that it put me into a cold sweat, and if I had had a hat on my head, I will not answer for it that my hair might not have lifted it off. But still plucking up my spirits as well as I could, and encouraging myself a little with considering that the power and presence of God was everywhere, and was able to protect me, I stepped forward again and by the dim light of the firebrand, holding it up a little over my head, I saw lying on the ground a monstrous, frightful old he-goat, just making his will, as we say, and gasping for life, and dying indeed of mere old age. I stirred him a little to see if I could get him out, and he essayed to get up, but was not able to raise himself; and I thought with myself he might even lie there; for if he had frightened me, so he would certainly fright any of the savages, if any one of them should be so hardy as to come in there while he had any life in him.

I was now recovered from my surprise, and began to

look round me, when I found the cave was but very small, that is to say, it might be about twelve feet over, but in no manner of shape, neither round nor square, no hands having ever been employed in making it but those of mere Nature. I observed also that there was a place at the further side of it that went in farther, but was so low that it required me to creep upon my hands and knees to go into it, and whither it went I knew not; so, having no candle, I gave it over for that time, but resolved to come again the next day provided with candles and a tinder-box, which I had made of the lock of one of the muskets, with some wildfire in the pan.

Accordingly, the next day, I came provided with six large candles of my own making (for I made very good candles now of goats' tallow, but was hard set for candle-wick, using sometimes rags or rope-yarn, and sometimes the dried rind of a weed like nettles); and going into this low place I was obliged to creep upon all fours, as I have said, almost ten yards—which, by the way, I thought was a venture bold enough, considering that I knew not how far it might go, nor what was beyond it. When I had got through the strait, I found the roof rose higher up, I believe near twenty feet; but never was such a glorious sight seen in the island, I dare say, as it was to look round the sides and roof of this vault or cave; the wall reflected a hundred thousand lights to me from my two candles. What it was in the rock—whether diamonds, or any other precious stones, or gold—which I rather supposed it to be—I knew not. The place I was in was a most delightful cavity, or grotto, though perfectly dark; the floor was dry and level, and had a sort of a small loose gravel upon it, so that there was no nauseous or venomous creature to be seen, neither was there any damp or wet on the sides or roof; the only difficulty in it was the entrance—which, however, as it was a place of security, and such a retreat as I wanted, I thought was a convenience—so that I was really rejoiced at the discovery, and resolved, without any delay, to bring some of those things which I was most anxious about to this place! particularly, I resolved to bring hither my magazine of powder, and all my spare arms; viz., two fowling-pieces— for I had three in all—and three muskets—for of them I had eight in all; so I kept in my castle only five, which stood ready mounted like pieces of cannon on my outmost defense, and were ready also to take out upon any expedition. Upon this occasion of removing my ammunition, I happened to open the barrel of powder which I took up out of the sea, and which had been wet, and I found that the water had penetrated about three or four inches into the powder on every side, which caking and growing hard, had preserved the inside like a kernel in the shell, so that I had near sixty pounds of very good powder in the centre of the cask; and this was a very agreeable discovery to me at that time; so I carried all away thither, never keeping above two or three pounds of powder with me in my castle, for fear of a surprise of any kind; I also carried thither all the lead I had left for bullets.

I fancied myself now like one of the ancient giants who were said to live in caves and holes in the rocks, where none could come at them; for I persuaded myself, while I was here, that if five hundred savages were to hunt me, they could never find me out—or if they did, they would not venture to attack me here. The old goat whom I found expiring died in the mouth of the cave the next day after I made this discovery; and I found it much easier to dig a great hole there, and throw him in and cover him with earth, than to drag him out; so I interred him there, to prevent offence to my nose.

I was now in the twenty-third year of residence in this island, and was so naturalized to the place and the manner of living, that, could I but have enjoyed the certainty that no savages would come to the place to disturb me, I could have been content to have capitulated for spending the rest of my time there, even to the last moment, till I had laid me down and died, like the old goat in the cave. I had also arrived to some little diversions and amusements, which made the time pass more pleasantly with me a great deal than it did before; first, I had taught my Poll, as I noted before, to speak, and he did it so familiarly, and talk so articulately and plain, that it was very pleasant to me, and he lived with me no less than six-and-twenty years. How long he might have lived afterwards I know not, though I know they have a notion in the Brazils that they live a hundred years. Perhaps some of my Polls may be alive there still, calling after poor Robinson Crusoe to this day; I wish no Englishman the ill-luck to come there and hear them; but if he did he would certainly believe it was the devil. My dog was a pleasant and loving companion to me for no less than sixteen years of my time, and then died of mere old age. As for my cats, they multiplied, as I have observed, to that degree, that I was obliged to shoot several of them at first, to keep them from devouring me and all I had; but, at length, when the old ones I brought with me were gone, and after some time continually driving them from me, and letting them have no provision with me, they all ran wild into the woods, except two or three favourites, which I kept tame, and whose young, when they had any, I always drowned; and these were part of my family. Besides these I always kept two or three household kids about me, whom I taught to feed out of my hand; and I had two more parrots, which talked pretty well, and would all call "Robin Crusoe," but none like my first; nor, indeed, did I take the pains with any of them that I had done with him. I had also several tame sea-fowls, whose name I knew not, that I caught upon the shore, and cut their wings; and the little stakes which I had planted before my castle-wall being now grown up to a good thick grove, these fowls all lived among these low trees, and bred there, which was very agreeable to me; so that, as I said above, I began to be very well contented with the life I led, if I could have been secured from the dread of the savages. But it was otherwise directed; and it may not be amiss for all people who shall meet with my story to make this just observation from it; viz., how frequently, in the course of our lives, the evil which in itself we seek most to shun, and which, when we are fallen into, is the most dreadful to us, is oftentimes the very means or door of our deliverance, by which alone we can be raised again from the affliction we are fallen into. I could give many examples of this in the course of my unaccountable life, but in nothing was it more particularly remarkable than in the circumstances of my last years of solitary residence in this island.

CHAPTER XI

IT was now the month of December, as I said above, in my twenty-third year; and this, being the southern solstice (for winter I cannot call it), was the particular time of my harvest, and required me to be pretty much abroad in the fields, when, going out pretty early in the morning, even before it was thorough daylight, I was surprised with seeing a light of some fire upon the shore, at a distance from me of about two miles towards the end of the island where I had observed some savages had been, as before, and not on the other side, but, to my great affliction, it was on my side of the island.

I was indeed terribly surprised at the sight, and stopped short within my grove, not daring to go out, lest I might be surprised; and yet I had no more peace within, from the apprehensions I had that if these savages, in rambling over the island, should find my corn standing or cut, or any of my works and improvements, they would immediately conclude there were people in the place, and would then never rest till they had found me out. In this extremity I went back directly to my castle, pulled up the ladder after me, having made all things without look as wild and natural as I could.

Then I prepared myself within, putting myself in a posture of defence; I loaded all my cannon, as I called them—that is to say, my muskets, which were mounted upon my new fortification, and all my pistols, and resolved to defend myself to the last gasp—not forgetting seriously to commend myself to the Divine protection, and earnestly to pray to God to deliver me out of the hands of the barbarians. And in this posture I continued about two hours, and began to be impatient for intelligence abroad, for I had no spies to send out. After sitting a while longer and musing what I should do in this case, I was not able to bear sitting in ignorance any longer; so setting up my ladder to the side of the hill, where there was a flat place, as I observed before, and then pulling the ladder after me, I set it up again, and mounted to the top of the hill, and pulling out my perspective-glass, which I had taken on purpose, I laid me down flat on my belly on the ground, and began to look for the place. I presently found there were no less than nine naked savages sitting round a small fire they had made, not to warm them, for they had no need of that, the weather being extremely hot, but, as I supposed, to dress some of their barbarous diet of human flesh which they had brought with them, whether alive or dead I could not know.

They had two canoes with them, which they had hauled up upon the shore; and as it was then ebb of tide, they seemed to me to wait the return of the flood to go away again. It is not easy to imagine what confusion this sight put me into, especially seeing them come on my side of the island, and so near me, too; but when I considered their coming must be always with the current of the ebb, I began afterwards to be more sedate in my mind, being satisfied that I might go abroad with safety all the time of the flood of tide, if they were not on shore before; and having made this observation, I went abroad about my harvest work with the more composure.

As I expected, so it proved; for, as soon as the tide made to the westward, I saw them all take boat and row (or paddle, as we call it) away. I should have observed, that for an hour or more before they went off they were dancing, and I could easily discern their postures and gestures by my glass. I could not perceive, by my nicest observation, but that they were stark naked, and had not the least covering upon them; but whether they were men or women I could not distinguish.

As soon as I saw them shipped and gone, I took two

guns upon my shoulders, and two pistols in my girdle, and my great sword by my side, without a scabbard, and with all the speed I was able to make went away to the hill where I had discovered the first appearance of all; and as soon as I got thither, which was not less than two hours (for I could not go apace, being so loaded with arms as I was), I perceived there had been three canoes more of savages at that place; and, looking out farther I saw they were all at sea together, making over for the main. This was a dreadful sight to me, especially when, going down to the shore, I could see the marks of horror which the dismal work they had been about had left behind it, vix., the blood, the bones, and part of the flesh of human bodies eaten and devoured by those wretches with merriment and sport. I was so filled with indignation at the sight, that I now began to premeditate the destruction of the next that I saw there, let them be whom or how many soever. It seemed evident to me that the visits which they made thus to this island were not very frequent, for it was above fifteen months before any more of them came on shore there again—that is to say, I neither saw them nor any footsteps or signals of them in all that time; for as to the rainy seasons, then they are sure not to come abroad, at least not so far: yet all this while I lived uncomfortably, by reason of the constant apprehensions of their coming upon me by surprise—from whence I observe that the expectation of evil is more bitter than the suffering, especially if there is no room to shake off that expectation or those apprehensions.

During all this time I was in the murdering humour, and spent most of my hours, which should have been better employed, in contriving how to circumvent and fall upon them the very next time I should see them—especially if they should be divided, as they were the last time, into two parties; nor did I consider at all that if I killed one party—suppose ten or a dozen—I was still the next day, or week, or month, to kill another, and so another, even *ad infinitum*, till I should be, at length, no less a murderer than they were in being man-eaters—and perhaps much more so. I spent my days now in great perplexity and anxiety of mind, expecting that I should one day or other fall into the hands of these merciless creatures; and if I did at any time venture abroad, it was not without looking around me with the greatest care and caution imaginable. And now I found, to my great comfort, how happy it was that I had provided a tame flock, or herd, of goats; for I durst not upon any account fire my gun, especially near that side of the island where they usually came, lest I should alarm the savages; and if they had fled from me now, I was sure to have them come again with perhaps two or three hundred canoes with them in a few days, and then I knew what to expect. However, I wore out a year and three months more before I ever saw any more of the savages, and then I found them again, as I shall soon observe. It is true they might have been there once or twice, but either they made no stay, or at least I did not hear them; but, in the month of May, as near as I could calculate, and in my four-and-twentieth year, I had a very strange encounter with them; of which in its place.

The perturbation of my mind, during this fifteen or sixteen months' interval was very great; I slept unquietly, dreamed always frightful dreams, and often started out of my sleep in the night. In the day, great troubles overwhelmed my mind; and in the night, I dreamed often of killing the savages, and of the reasons why I might justify the doing of it. But to waive all this for a while. It was in the middle of May, on the sixteenth day, I think, as well as my poor wooden calendar would reckon, for I marked all upon the post still; I say, it was on the sixteenth of May that it blew a very great storm of wind all day, with a great deal of lightning and thunder, and a very foul night it was after it. I knew not what was the particular occasion of it; but as I was reading the Bible, and taken up with very serious thoughts about my present condition,

I was surprised with the noise of a gun, as I thought, fired
at sea. This was, to be sure, a surprise of a quite different
nature from any I had met with before; for the notions
this put into my thoughts were quite of another kind. I
started up in the greatest haste imaginable; and, in a
trice, clapped my ladder to the middle place of the rock,
and pulled it after me; and, mounting it the second time,
got to the top of the hill the very moment that a flash of
fire bid me listen for a second gun, which accordingly, in
about half a minute, I heard; and by the sound, knew that
it was from that part of the sea where I was driven out with
the current in my boat. I immediately considered that
this must be some ship in distress, and that they had some
comrade, or some other ship in company, and fired these
for signals of distress, and to obtain help. I had the presence
of mind, at that minute, to think, that though I could not
help them, it might be they might help me; so I brought
together all the dry wood I could get at hand, and, making
a good handsome pile, I set it on fire upon the hill. The
wood was dry, and blazed freely; and though the wind
blew very hard, yet it burned fairly out, so that I was certain
if there was any such thing as a ship, they must need see
it, and no doubt they did; for as soon as ever my fire
blazed up, I heard another gun, and after that several
others, all from the same quarter. I plied my fire all night
long, till daybreak; and when it was broad day, and the
air cleared up, I saw something at a great distance at sea,
full east of the island, whether a sail or a hull I could not
distinguish—no, not with my glass; the distance was so
great, and the weather still something hazy also—at least,
it was so out at sea.

I looked frequently at it all that day, and soon perceived
that it did not move; so I presently concluded that it
was a ship at anchor; and being eager, you may be sure,
to be satisfied, I took my gun in my hand, and ran towards
the south side of the island, to the rocks where I had formerly
been carried away with the current; and getting up there,

the weather by this time being perfectly clear, I could plainly see, to my great sorrow, the wreck of a ship, cast away in the night upon those concealed rocks which I found when I was out in my boat; and which rocks, as they checked the violence of the stream, and made a kind of counter-stream, or eddy, were the occasion of my recovering from the most desperate, hopeless condition that ever I had been in in all my life. Thus, what is one man's safety is another man's destruction; for it seems these men, whoever they were, being out of their knowledge, and the rocks being wholly under water, had been driven upon them in the night, the wind blowing hard at E. and E.N.E. Had they seen the island, as I must necessarily suppose they did not, they must, as I thought, have endeavoured to have saved themselves on shore by the help of their boat; but their firing of their guns for help, especially when they saw, as I imagined, my fire, filled me with many thoughts. First, I imagined that upon seeing my light, they might have put themselves into their boat, and endeavoured to make the shore; but that the sea running very high, they might have been cast away. Other times, I imagined that they might have lost their boat before, as might be the case many ways; as particularly, by the breaking of the sea upon their ship, which many times obliged men to stave, or take in pieces, their boat, and sometimes to throw it overboard with their own hands. Other times, I imagined they had some other ship or ships in company, who, upon the signals of distress they made, had taken them up and carried them off. Other times, I fancied they were all gone off to sea in their boat, and being carried away by the current that I had been formerly in, were carried out into the great ocean, where there was nothing but misery and perishing; and that, perhaps, they might by this time think of starving, and of being in a condition to eat one another.

As all these were but conjectures at best, so, in the condition I was in, I could do no more than look on upon the misery of the poor men, and pity them; which had still this good effect upon my side, that it gave me more and more cause to give thanks to God, who had so happily and comfortably provided for me in my desolate condition; and that of two ships' companies, who were now cast away upon this part of the world, not one life should be spared but mine. I learned here again to observe, that it is very rare that the providence of God casts us into any condition of life so low, or any misery so great, but we may see something or other to be thankful for, and may see others in worse circumstances than our own. Such certainly was the case of these men, of whom I could not so much as see room to suppose any of them were saved; nothing could make it rational so much as to wish or expect that they did not all perish there, except the possibility only of their being taken up by another ship in company; and this was but mere possibility indeed, for I saw not the least signal or appearance of any such thing. I cannot explain, by any possible energy of words, what a strange longing I felt in my soul upon this sight, breaking out sometimes thus: "Oh, that there had been but one or two, nay, or but one soul, saved out of this ship, to have escaped to me, that I might but have one companion, one fellow-creature, to have spoken to me and to have conversed with!" In all the time of my solitary life, I never felt so earnest, so strong a desire after the society of my fellow-creatures, or so deep a regret at the want of it.

There are some secret moving springs in the affections, and, when they are set a-going by some object in view, or, though not in view, yet rendered present to the mind by the power of imagination, that motion carries out the soul, by its impetuosity, to such violent, eager, embracings of the object, that the absence of it is unsupportable. Such were these earnest wishings that but one man had been saved. I believe I repeated the words, "Oh, that it had been but one!" a thousand times; and my desires were so moved by it that when I spoke the words my hands would clinch

together, and my fingers would press the palms of my
hands, so that if I had had any soft thing in my hand, I
would have crushed it involuntarily; and my teeth in
my head would strike together, and set against one another
so strong, that for some time I could not part them again.
Let the naturalists explain these things, and the reason
and manner of them. All I can say of them is to describe
the fact, which was ever surprising to me, when I found it,
though I knew not from what it should proceed; it was,
doubtless, the effect of ardent wishes, and of strong ideas
formed in my mind, realizing the comfort which the conversation of one of my fellow-Christians would have been to
me. But it was not to be; either their fate, or mine, or
both, forbade it, for till the last year of my being on this
island, I never knew whether any were saved out of that
ship or no; and had only the affliction, some days after
to see the corpse of a drowned boy come on shore at the
end of the island which was next the shipwreck. He had no
clothes on but a seaman's waistcoat, a pair of open-kneed
linen drawers, and a blue linen shirt; nothing to direct me
so much as to guess what nation he was of. He had nothing
in his pockets but two pieces of eight and a tobacco-pipe—
the last was to me of ten times more value than the first.

It was now calm, and I had a great mind to venture out
in my boat to this wreck, not doubting but I might find
something on board that might be useful to me. But that
did not altogether press me so much as the possibility
that there might be yet some living creature on board,
whose life I might not only save, but might, by saving
that life, comfort my own to the last degree; and this
thought clung so to my heart that I could not be quiet
night or day, but I must venture out in my boat on board
this wreck; and committing the rest to God's providence,
I thought the impression was so strong upon my mind that it
could not be resisted, that it must come from some invisible
direction, and that I should be wanting to myself if I did
not go.

Under the power of this impression, I hastened back to my castle, prepared everything for my voyage, took a quantity of bread, a great pot for fresh water, a compass to steer by, a bottle of rum (for I had still a great deal of that left), and a basket of raisins; and thus loading myself with everything necessary, I went down to my boat, got the water out of her, got her afloat, loaded all my cargo in her, and then went home again for more. My second cargo was a great bag full of rice, the umbrella to set up over my head for a shade, another large pot full of fresh water, and about two dozen of small loaves, or barley-cakes, more than before, with a bottle of goat's-milk, and a cheese; all of which, with great labour and sweat, I brought to my boat; and praying to God to direct my voyage, I put out, and, rowing or paddling the canoe along the shore, came at last to the utmost point of the island on the north-east side. And now I was to launch out into the ocean, and either to venture or not to venture. I looked on the rapid currents which ran constantly on both sides of the island at a distance, and which were very terrible to me, from the remembrance of the hazard I had been in before, and my heart began to fail me; for I foresaw that if I was driven into either of those currents, I should be carried a great way out to sea, and perhaps out of my reach, or sight of the island again; and that then, as my boat was but small if any little gale of wind should rise, I should be inevitably lost.

These thoughts so oppressed my mind, that I began to give over my enterprise; and having hauled my boat into a little creek on the shore, I stepped out, and sat down upon a rising bit of ground, very pensive and anxious, between fear and desire about my voyage; when, as I was musing, I could perceive that the tide was turned, and the flood came on; upon which, my going was impracticable for so many hours. Upon this, presently it occurred to me that I should go up to the highest piece of ground I could find, and observe, if I could, how the sets of the tide, or currents lay, when the flood came in, that I might judge whether, if I was driven one way out, I might not expect to be driven another way home, with the same rapidity of the currents. This thought was no sooner in my head then I cast my eye upon a little hill, which sufficiently overlooked the sea both ways, and from whence I had a clear view of the currents, or sets of the tide, and which way I was to guide myself in my return. Here I found that as the current of ebb set out close by the south point of the island, so the current of the flood set in close by the shore of the north side ; and that I had nothing to do but to keep to the north of the island in my return, and I should do well enough.

Encouraged with this observation, I resolved, the next morning, to set out with the first of the tide ; and reposing myself for the night in my canoe, under the great watch-coat I mentioned, I launched out. I first made a little out to sea, full north, till I began to feel the benefit of the current, which set eastward, and which carried me at a great rate, and yet did not so hurry me as the current on the south side had done before, so as to take from me all government of the boat ; but having a strong steerage with my paddle, I went, at a great rate, directly for the wreck, and in less than two hours I came up to it. It was a dismal sight to look at : the ship, which, by its building, was Spanish, stuck fast, jammed in between two rocks ; all the stern and quarter of her were beaten to pieces by the sea ; and as her forecastle, which stuck in the rocks, had run on with great violence, her mainmast and foremast were brought by the board—that is to say, broken short off ; but her bowsprit was sound, and the head and bow appeared firm. When I came close to her, a dog appeared upon her, who, seeing me coming, yelped and cried ; and, as soon as I called him jumped into the sea to come to me. I took him into the boat, and found him almost dead with hunger and thirst. I gave him a cake of my bread, and he devoured it like a ravenous wolf that had been starving a fortnight in the snow ; I then gave the poor creature some

fresh water, with which, if I would have let him, he would
have burst himself. After this I went on board; but the
first sight I met with was two men drowned in the cook-
room, or forecastle, of the ship, with their arms fast about
one another. I concluded, as is indeed probable, that when
the ship struck, it being in a storm, the sea broke so high
and so continually over her, that the men were not able to
bear it, and were strangled with the constant rushing in
of the water, as much as if they had been under water.
Besides the dog, there was nothing left in the ship that
had life; nor any goods, that I could see, but what were
spoiled by the water. There were some casks of liquor,
whether wine or brandy, I knew not, which lay lower in
the hold, and which, the water being ebbed out, I could
see; but they were too big to meddle with. I saw several
chests, which I believed belonged to some of the seamen;
and I got two of them into the boat, without examining
what was in them. Had the stern of the ship been fixed,
and the forepart broken off, I am persuaded I might have
made a good voyage; for, by what I found in these two
chests, I had room to suppose the ship had a great deal of
wealth on board; and, if I may guess from the course
she steered, she must have been bound from Buenos Ayres,
or the Rio de la Plata, in the south part of America, beyond
the Brazils to the Havannah, in the Gulf of Mexico, and so
perhaps to Spain. She had, no doubt, a great treasure in
her, but of no use, at that time, to anybody, but what
became of the crew I then knew not.

I found, besides these chests, a little cask full of liquor,
of about twenty gallons, which I got into my boat with
much difficulty. There were several muskets in the cabin,
and a great powder horn, with about four pounds of powder
in it; as for the muskets, I had no occasion for them, so
I left them, but took the powder horn. I took a fire-shovel
and tongs, which I wanted extremely; as also two little
brass kettles, a copper pot to make chocolate, and a gridiron;
and with this cargo, and the dog, I came away, the tide

beginning to make home again; and the same evening, about an hour within night, I reached the island again, weary and fatigued to the last degree. I reposed that night in the boat; and in the morning I resolved to harbour what I had got in my new cave, and not carry it home to my castle. After refreshing myself, I got all my cargo on shore, and began to examine the particulars. The cask of liquor I found to be a kind of rum, but not such as we had in the Brazils; and, in a word, not at all good: but when I came to open the chests, I found several things of great use to me; for example, I found in one a fine case of bottles, of an extraordinary kind, and filled with cordial waters, fine and very good; the bottles held about three pints each, and were tipped with silver. I found two pots of very good succades, or sweetmeats, so fastened also on the top that the salt water had not hurt them; and two more of the same which the water had spoiled I found some very good shirts, which were very welcome to me; and about a dozen and a half of white linen handkerchiefs and coloured neckcloths; the former were also very welcome, being exceedingly refreshing to wipe my face in a hot day. Besides this, when I came to the till in the chest, I found there three great bags of pieces of eight, which held about eleven hundred pieces in all; and in one of them, wrapped up in a paper, six dubloons of gold, and some small bars or wedges of gold; I suppose they might all weigh near a pound. In the other chest were some clothes, but of little value; but, by circumstances, it must have belonged to the gunner's mate; though there was no powder in it, except two pounds of fine glazed powder, in three small flasks, kept, I suppose, for charging their fowling-pieces on occasion. Upon the whole, I got very little by this voyage that was of any use to me; for as to the money, I had no manner of occasion for it: it was to me as the dirt under my feet, and I would have given it all for three or four pair of English shoes and stockings, which were things I greatly wanted, but had none on my feet for many years.

I had, indeed, got two pairs of shoes now, which I took off the feet of the two drowned men whom I saw in the wreck, and I found two pair more in one of the chests, which were very welcome to me; but they were not like our English shoes, either for ease or service, being rather what we call pumps than shoes. I found in this seaman's chest about fifty pieces of eight, in reals, but no gold. I supposed this belonged to a poorer man than the other, which seemed to belong to some officer. Well, however, I lugged this money home to my cave, and laid it up, as I had done that before which I had brought from our own ship; but it was a great pity, as I said, that the other part of this ship had not come to my share; for I am satisfied I might have loaded my canoe several times over with money; which, if I had ever escaped to England, would have lain here safe enough till I might have come again and fetched it.

Having now brought all my things on shore and secured them, I went back to my boat, and rowed or paddled her along the shore to her old harbour where I laid her up, and made the best of my way to my old habitation, where I found everything safe and quiet. I began now to repose myself, live after my own fashion, and take care after my family affairs; and for a while I lived easy enough, only that I was more vigilant than I used to be, looked out oftener, and did not go abroad so much; and if, at any time, I did stir with any freedom, it was always to the east part of the island, where I was pretty well satisfied the savages never came, and where I could go without so many precautions, and such a load of arms and ammunition as I always carried with me if I went the other way. I lived in this condition near two years more; but my unlucky head, that was always to let me know it was born to make my body miserable, was all these two years filled with projects and designs, how, if it were possible, I might get away from this island; for sometimes I was for making another voyage to the wreck, though my reason told me

that there was nothing left there worth the hazard of my
voyage; sometimes for a ramble one way, sometimes
another; and I believe verily, if I had had the boat that I
went from Salee in, I should have ventured to sea, bound
anywhere, I knew not whither. I have been in all my
circumstances, a *memento* to those who are touched with
the general plague of mankind, whence, for aught I know,
one half of their miseries flow; I mean that of not being
satisfied with the station wherein God and Nature have
placed them: for, not to look back upon my primitive
condition, and the excellent advice of my father, the
opposition to which was, as I may call it, my *original sin*,
my subsequent mistakes of the same kind had been the
means of my coming into this miserable condition; for
had that Providence, which so happily seated me at the
Brazils as a planter, blessed me with confined desires, and
I could have been contented to have gone on gradually, I
might have been by this time, I mean in the time of my
being in this island, one of the most considerable planters
in the Brazils; nay, I am persuaded that by the improvements I had made in that little time I lived there, and the
increase I should probably have made if I had remained,
I might have been worth a hundred thousand moidores:
and what business had I to leave a settled fortune, a well-
stocked plantation, improving and increasing, to turn
supercargo to Guinea to fetch negroes, when patience and
time would have so increased our stock at home, that we
could have bought them at our own door from those whose
business it was to fetch them? and though it had cost us
something more, yet the difference of that price was by no
means worth saving at so great a hazard. But as this is
ordinarily the fate of young heads, so reflection upon the
folly of it is as commonly the exercise of more years, or
of the dear-bought experience of time; so it was with me
now; and yet so deep had the mistake taken root in my
temper, that I could not satisfy myself in my station, but
was continually poring upon the means and possibility of

my escape from this place; and that I may, with the greater pleasure to the reader, bring on the remaining part of my story, it may not be improper to give some account of my first conceptions on the subject of this foolish scheme for my escape, and how, and upon what foundation, I acted.

I am now to be supposed retired into my castle, after my late voyage to the wreck, my frigate laid up and secured under water, as usual, and my condition restored to what it was before. I had more wealth, indeed than I had before, but was not at all the richer; for I had no more use for it than the Indians of Peru had before the Spaniards came there.

It was one of the nights in the rainy season in March, the four-and-twentieth year of my first setting foot in this island of solitude. I was lying in my bed or hammock, awake, very well in health, had no pain, no distemper, no uneasiness of body nor any uneasiness of mind more than ordinary, but could by no means close my eyes, that is so as to sleep; no, not a wink all night long, otherwise than as follows: It is impossible and needless to set down the innumerable crowd of thoughts that whirled through that great thoroughfare of the brain—the memory—in this night's time. I ran over the whole history of my life in miniature, or by abridgment, as I may call it, to my coming to this island, and also of that part of my life since I came to this island. In my reflections upon the state of my case since I came on shore on this island, I was comparing the happy posture of my affairs in the first years of my habitation here, with the life of anxiety, fear, and care which I had lived in ever since I had seen the print of a foot in the sand; not that I did not believe the savages had frequented the island even all the while, and might have been several hundreds of them at times on shore there, but I had never known it, and was incapable of any apprehensions about it; my satisfaction was perfect, though any danger was the same, and I was as happy in not knowing my danger as if I had never really been exposed to it. This furnished my thoughts with many very profitable reflections, and particularly this one: How infinitely good that providence is which has provided, in its government of mankind, such narrow bounds to his sight and knowledge of things; and though he walks in the midst of so many thousand dangers, the sight of which, if discovered to him, would distract his mind and sink his spirits, he is kept serene and calm, by having the events of things hid from his eyes, and knowing nothing of the dangers which surround him.

After these thoughts had for some time entertained me, I came to reflect seriously upon the real danger I had been in for so many years in this very island, and how I had walked about in the greatest security, and with all possible tranquillity, even when perhaps nothing but the brow of a hill, a great tree, or the casual approach of night, had been between me and the worst kind of destruction, viz., that of falling into the hands of cannibals and savages, who would have seized on me with the same view as I would on a goat or a turtle; and have thought it no more crime to kill and devour me than I did of a pigeon or a curlew. I would unjustly slander myself, if I should say I was not sincerely thankful to my great Preserver, to whose singular protection I acknowledged, with great humility, all these unknown deliverances were due, and without which I must inevitably have fallen into their merciless hands.

When these thoughts were over, my head was for some time taken up in considering the nature of these wretched creatures, I mean the savages, and how it came to pass, in the world, that the wise Governor of all things should give up any of his creatures to such inhumanity, nay, to something so much below even brutality itself, as to devour its own kind; but as this ended in some (at that time) fruitless speculations, it occurred to me to inquire what part of the world these wretches lived in? how far off the coast was from whence they came? what they ventured over so far from home for? what kind of boats they had? and why I might not order myself and my business so, that I might be as able to go over thither, as they were to come to me.

I never so much as troubled myself to consider what I should do with myself when I went thither; what would become of me if I fell into the hands of these savages; or how I should escape them if they attacked me; no, nor so much as how it was possible for me to reach the coast, and not be attacked by some or other of them, without any possibility of delivering myself: and if I should not fall into their hands, what I should do for provision, or whither I should bend my course; none of these thoughts I say, so much as came in my way; but my mind was wholly bent upon the notion of my passing over in my boat to the mainland. I looked upon my present condition as the most miserable that could possibly be; that I was not able to throw myself into anything but death, that could be called worse; and if I reached the shore of the main, I might perhaps meet with relief, or I might coast along, as I did on the African shore, till I came to some inhabited country, and where I might find some relief; and, after all, perhaps I might fall in with some Christian ship that might take me in; and if the worst came to the worst, I could but die, which would put an end to all these miseries at once. Pray note, all this was the fruit of a disturbed mind, an impatient temper, made, as it were, desperate by the long continuance of my troubles, and the disappointments I had met with in the wreck I had been on board of, and where I had been so near the obtaining what I so earnestly longed for, namely, somebody to speak to, and to learn some knowledge of the place where I was, and of the probable means of my deliverance. I say I was agitated wholly by these thoughts; all my calm of mind, in my resignation to Providence, and waiting the issue of the dispositions of Heaven, seemed to be suspended; and I had, as it were, no power to turn my thoughts to anything but the project of a voyage to the main, which came upon me with such force, and such an impetuosity of desire, that it was not to be resisted.

When this had agitated my thoughts for two hours or more, with such violence that it set my very blood into a ferment, and my pulse beat as if I had been in a fever, merely with the extraordinary fervour of my mind about it, Nature, as if I had been fatigued and exhausted with the very thoughts of it, threw me into a sound sleep. One would have thought I should have dreamed of it, but I did not, nor of anything relating to it; but I dreamed that as I was going out in the morning, as usual, from my castle, I saw upon the shore two canoes and eleven savages, coming to land, and that they brought with them another savage, whom they were going to kill, in order to eat him; when, on a sudden, the savage that they were going to kill jumped away, and ran for his life; then I thought, in my sleep, that he came running into my little thick grove before my fortification to hide himself; and that I, seeing him alone, and not perceiving that the others sought him that way, showed myself to him, and, smiling upon him, encouraged him; that he kneeled down to me, seeming to pray me to assist him; upon which I showed him my ladder, made him go up it, and carried him into my cave, and he became my servant; and that as soon as I had got this man, I said to myself, "Now I may certainly venture to the mainland, for this fellow will serve me as a pilot, and will tell me what to do, and whither to go for provisions, and whither not to go for fear of being devoured; what places to venture into and what to escape." I waked with this thought; and was under such inexpressible impressions of joy at the prospect of my escape in my dream, that the disappointments which I felt upon coming to myself, and finding that it was no more than a dream, were equally extravagant the other way, and threw me into a good dejection of spirits.

Upon this, however, I made this conclusion; that my only way to go about an attempt for an escape was, if possible, to get a savage into my possession; and, if possible, it should be one of their prisoners, whom they had condemned to be eaten, and should bring hither to kill. But these thoughts still were attended with this difficulty, that it was impossible to effect this without attacking a whole caravan of them, and killing them all; and this was not only a very desperate attempt, and might miscarry, but, on the other hand, I had greatly scrupled the lawfulness of it to me; and my heart trembled at the thoughts of shedding so much blood, though it was for my deliverance. I need not repeat the arguments which occurred to me against this, they being the same mentioned before; but though I had other reasons to offer now—viz., that those men were enemies to my life, and would devour me if they could; that it was self-preservation, in the highest degree, to deliver myself from this death of a life, and was acting in my own defence as much as if they were actually assaulting me, and the like; I say, though these things argued for it, yet the thoughts of shedding human blood for my deliverance were very terrible to me, and such as I could by no means reconcile myself to for a great while. However, at last, after many secret disputes with myself, and after great perplexities about it (for all these arguments, one way and another, struggled in my head a long time), the eager prevailing desire of deliverance at length mastered all the rest; and I resolved, if possible, to get one of these savages into my hands, cost what it would. My next thing was to contrive how to do it, and this indeed was very difficult to resolve on; but as I could pitch upon no probable means for it, so I resolved to put myself upon the watch, to see them when they came on shore, and leave the rest to the event; taking such measures as the opportunity should present, let be what would be.

With these resolutions in my thoughts, I set myself upon the scout as often as possible, and indeed so often that I was heartily tired of it; for it was above a year and a half that I waited; and for a great part of that time went out to the west end, and to the southwest corner of the island almost every day, to look for canoes, but none appeared. This was very discouraging, and began to trouble me much, though I cannot say that it did in this case (as it had done some time before) wear off the edge of my desire to the thing; but the longer it seemed to be delayed, the more eager I was for it; in a word, I was not at first so careful to shun the sight of these savages, and avoid being seen by them, as I was now eager to be upon them. Besides, I fancied myself able to manage one, nay, two or three savages, if I had them, so as to make them entirely slaves to me, to do whatever I should direct them, and to prevent their being able at any time to do me any hurt. It was a great while that I pleased myself with this affair; but nothing still presented; all my fancies and schemes came to nothing, for no savages came near me for a great while.

CHAPTER XII

ABOUT a year and a half after I entertained these notions (and by long musing had, as it were, resolved them all into nothing, for want of an occasion to put them in execution), I was surprised one morning early by seeing no less than five canoes all on shore together on my side the island, and the people who belonged to them all landed and out of my sight. The number of them broke all my measures; for seeing so many, and knowing that they always came four or six, or sometimes more, in a boat, I could not tell what to think of it, or how to take my measures to attack twenty or thirty men single-handed; so lay still in my castle, perplexed and discomforted. However, I put myself into all the same postures for an attack that I had formerly provided, and was just ready for action, if anything had presented. Having waited a good while, listening to hear if they made any noise, at length, being very impatient, I set my guns at the foot of my ladder, and clambered up to the top of the hill, by my two stages, as usual; standing so, however, that my head did not appear above the hill, so that they could not perceive me by any means. Here I observed, by the help of my perspective glass, that they were no less than thirty in number; that they had a fire kindled, and that they had meat dressed. How they had cooked it, I know not, or what it was; but they were all dancing, in I know not how many barbarous gestures and figures, their own way, round the fire.

While I was thus looking on them, I perceived, by my perspective, two miserable wretches dragged from the boats, where, it seems, they were laid by, and were now brought out for slaughter. I perceived one of them immediately fall; being knocked down, I suppose, with a club or wooden sword, for that was their way; and two or three others were at work immediately, cutting him open for their cookery, while the other victim was left standing by himself, till they should be ready for him. In that very moment, this poor wretch, seeing himself a little at liberty, and unbound, Nature inspired him with hopes of life and he started away from them, and ran with incredible swiftness along the sands, directly towards me; I mean towards that part of the coast where my habitation was. I was dreadfully frightened, that I must acknowledge, when I perceived him run my way; and especially when, as I thought, I saw him pursued by the whole body; and now I expected that part of my dream was coming to pass, and that he would certainly take shelter in my grove; but I could not depend, by any means, upon my dream, that the other savages would not pursue him thither, and find him there. However, I kept my station, and my spirits began to recover when I found that there were not above three men that followed him; and still more was encouraged, when I found that he outstripped them exceedingly in running, and gained ground on them; so that, if he could but hold it for half an hour, I saw easily he would fairly get away from them all.

There was, between them and my castle, the creek, which I mentioned often in the first part of my story, where I landed my cargoes out of the ship; and this I saw plainly he must necessarily swim over, or the poor wretch would be taken there; but when the savage escaping came thither, he made nothing of it, though the tide was then up; but, plunging in, swam through in about thirty strokes, or thereabouts, landed, and ran with exceeding strength and swiftness. When the three persons came to the creek, I found that two of them could swim, but the third could not, and that, standing on the other side, he looked at the others, but went no farther, and soon after went softly back again; which, as it happened, was very well for him in the end. I observed that the two who swam were yet more than twice as long swimming over the creek then the fellow was that fled from them. It came very warmly upon my thoughts, and indeed irresistibly, that now was the time to get me a servant, and perhaps a companion or assistant; and that I was plainly called by Providence to save this poor creature's life. I immediately ran down the ladder with all possible expedition, fetched my two guns, for they were both at the foot of the ladder, as I observed before, and getting up again with the same haste to the top of the hill, I crossed towards the sea; and having a very short cut, and all down hill, placed myself in the way between the pursuers and the pursued, hallooing aloud to him that fled, who, looking back, was at first perhaps as much frightened at me as at them; but I beckoned with my hand to him to come back; and, in the mean time, I slowly advanced towards the two that followed; then rushing at once upon the foremost, I knocked him down with the stock of my piece. I was loath to fire, because I would not have the rest hear; though at that distance, it would not have been easily heard, and being out of sight of the smoke, too, they would not have known what to make of it. Having knocked this fellow down, the other who pursued him stopped, as if he had been frightened, and I advanced towards him; but as I came nearer, I perceived presently he had a bow and arrow, and was fitting it to shoot at me; so I was then obliged to shoot at him first, which I did, and killed him at the first shot. The poor savage who fled, but had stopped, though he saw both his enemies fallen and killed, as he thought, yet was so frightened with the fire and noise of my piece that he stood stock still, and neither came forward nor went backward, though he seemed rather inclined still to fly than to come on. I hallooed again to him, and made signs to come forward, which he easily understood, and came a little way; then stopped again, and then a little farther, and stopped again; and I could then perceive that he stood trembling, as if he had been taken prisoner, and had just been to be killed as his two enemies were. I beckoned to him again to come to me, and gave him all the signs of encouragement that I could think of; and he came nearer and nearer, kneeling down every ten or twelve steps, in token of acknowledgment for saving his life. I smiled at him, and looked pleasantly, and beckoned to him to come still nearer; at length, he came close to me; and then he kneeled down again, kissed the ground, and laid his head upon the ground, and, taking me by the foot, set my foot upon his head; this, it seems, was in token of swearing to be my slave forever. I took him up, and made much of him, and encouraged him all I could. But there was more work to do yet; for I perceived the savage whom I had knocked down was not killed, but stunned with the blow, and began to come to himself. So I pointed to him, and showed him the savage, that he was not dead; upon this he spoke some words to me, and though I could not understand them, yet I thought they were pleasant to hear; for they were the first sound of a man's voice that I had heard, my own excepted, for above twenty-five years. But there was no time for such reflections now; the savage who was knocked down recovered himself so far as to sit up upon the ground, and I perceived that my savage began to be afraid; but when I saw that, I presented my other piece at the man, as if I would shoot him; upon this my savage, for so I call him now, made a motion to me to lend him my sword, which hung naked in a belt by my side, which I did. He no sooner had it, but he ran to his enemy, and at one blow cut off his head as cleverly, no executioner in Germany could have done it sooner or better; which I thought very strange for one who, I had reason to believe, never saw a sword in his life before, except their own wooden swords: however, it seems, as I learned afterwards, they make their wooden swords so sharp, so heavy, and the wood is so hard, that they will even cut off heads with them, ay, and arms, and that at one blow, too. When he had done this, he came laughing to me in sign of triumph, and brought me the sword again, and with abundance of gestures which I did not understand, laid it down, with the head of the savage that he had killed just before me. But that which astonished him most, was to know how I killed the other Indian so far off; so pointing to him, he made signs to me to let him go to him; and I bade him go, as well as I could. When he came to him, he stood like one amazed, looking at him, turning him first on one side, then on the other; looked at the wound the bullet had made, which it seems was just in his breast, where it had made a hole, and no great quantity of blood had followed; but he had bled inwardly, for he was quite dead. He took up his bow and arrows, and came back; so I turned to go away, and beckoned him to follow me, making signs to him that more might come after them.

Upon this he made signs to me, that he should bury them with sand, that they might not be seen by the rest, if they followed; and so I made signs to him again to do so. He fell to work; and in an instant he had scraped a hole in the sands with his hands, big enough to bury the first in, and then dragged him into it, and covered him; and did so by the other also; I believe he had buried them both in a quarter of an hour. Then calling him away, I carried him, not to my castle, but quite away to my cave, on the farther part of the island; so I did not let my dream come to pass in that part, that he came into my grove for shelter. Here I gave him bread and a bunch of raisins to eat, and a draught of water, which I found he was indeed in great distress for from his running; and having refreshed him, I made signs for him to go and lie down to sleep, showing him a place where I had laid some rice straw, and a blanket upon it, which I used to sleep upon myself sometimes; so the poor creature lay down, and went to sleep.

He was a comely, handsome fellow, perfectly well made, with straight, strong limbs, not too large, tall and well shaped; and, as I reckon, about twenty-six years of age. He had a very good countenance, not a fierce and surly aspect, but seemed to have something very manly in his face; and yet he had all the sweetness and softness of a European in his countenance, too, especially when he smiled. His hair was long and black, not curled like wool; his forehead very high and large; and a great vivacity and sparkling sharpness in his eyes. The colour of his skin was not quite black, but very tawny; and yet not an ugly, yellow, nauseous tawny, as the Brazilians and Virginians, and other natives of America are, but of a bright kind of a dun olive-colour, that had in it something very agreeable, though not very easy to describe. His face was round and plump; his nose small, not flat like the negroes; a very good mouth, thin lips, and his fine teeth well set, and as white as ivory.

After he had slumbered, rather than slept, about half-an-hour, he awoke again, and came out of the cave to me, for I had been milking my goats, which I had in the inclosure just by: when he espied me, he came running to me, laying himself down again upon the ground, with all the possible signs of an humble, thankful disposition, making a great many antic gestures to show it. At last he lays his head flat upon the ground, close to my foot, and sets my other foot upon his head, as he had done before; and after this, made all the signs to me of subjection, servitude, and submission imaginable, to let me know how he would serve me so long as he lived. I understood him in many things, and let him know I was very well pleased with him. In a little time I began to speak to him, and teach him to speak to me; and, first, I let him know his name should be FRIDAY, which was the day I saved his life; I called him so for the memory of the time. I likewise taught him to say Master, and then let him know that was to be my name; I likewise taught him to say Yes and No, and to know the meaning of them. I gave him some milk in an earthen pot, and let him see me drink it before him, and sop my bread in it; and gave him a cake of bread to do the like, which he quickly complied with, and made signs that it was very good for him. I kept there with him all that night; but, as soon as it was day, I beckoned to him to come with me, and let him know I would give him some clothes; at which he seemed very glad, for he was stark naked. As we went by the place where he had buried the two men, he pointed exactly to the place, and showed me the marks that he had made to find them again, making signs to me that we should dig them up again and eat them. At this I appeared very angry, expressed my abhorrence of it, made as if I would vomit at the thoughts of it, and beckoned with my hand to him to come away, which he did immediately, with great submission. I then led him up to the top of the hill, to see if his enemies were gone, and pulling out my glass, I looked and saw plainly the place where they had been, but no appearance of them or their canoes; so that it was plain they were gone, and had left their two comrades behind them without any search after them.

But I was not content with this discovery; but, having now took more courage, and consequently more curiosity, I took my man Friday with me, giving him the sword in his hand, with the bow and arrows at his back, which I found he could use very dexterously, making him carry one gun for me, and I two for myself; and away we marched to the place where these creatures had been—for I had a mind now to get some fuller intelligence of them. When I came to the place, my very blood ran chill in my veins, and my heart sank within me at the horror of the spectacle; indeed, it was a dreadful sight; at least it was so to me, though Friday made nothing of it. The place was covered with human bones, the ground dyed with the blood, and great pieces of flesh left here and there, half-eaten, mangled, and scorched; and, in short, all the tokens of the triumphant feast they had been making there, after a victory over their enemies. I saw three skulls, five hands, and the bones of three or four legs and feet, and abundance of other parts of the bodies; and Friday, by his signs, made me understand that they brought over four prisoners to feast upon; that three of them were eaten up and that he, pointing to himself was the fourth; that there had been a great battle between them and their next king, of whose subjects, it seems, he had been one, and that they had taken a great number of prisoners; all which were carried to several places by those who had taken them in the fight, in order to feast upon them, as was done here by these wretches upon those they brought hither.

I caused Friday to gather all the skulls, bones, flesh, and whatever remained, and lay them together on a heap, and make a great fire upon it, and burn them all to ashes. I found Friday had still a hankering stomach after some of the flesh, and was still a cannibal in his nature; but I discovered so much abhorrence at the very thought of it, and at the least appearance of it, that he durst not discover it—for I had, by some means let him know that I would kill him if he offered it.

When he had done this we came back to our castle, and there I fell to work for my man Friday; and, first of all, I gave him a pair of linen drawers, which I had out of the poor gunner's chest I mentioned, which I found in the wreck, and which, with a little alteration, fitted him very well; and then I made him a jerkin of goat's skin, as well as my skill would allow (for I was now grown a tolerably good tailor); and I gave him a cap which I made of hare's skin, very convenient, and fashionable enough, and thus he was clothed, for the present, tolerably well, and was mighty well pleased to see himself almost as well clothed as his master, It is true, he went awkwardly in these clothes at first; wearing the drawers was very awkward to him, and the sleeves of the waistcoat galled his shoulders and the inside of his arms—but with easing them where he complained they hurt him, and using himself to them, at length he took to them very well.

The next day, after I came home to my hutch with him, I began to consider where I should lodge him; and, that I might do well for him, and yet be perfectly easy myself,

I made a little tent for him in the vacant place between
my two fortifications, in the inside of the last, and in the
outside of the first. As there was a door or entrance there
into my cave, I made a formal framed door-case, and door
to it of boards, and set it up in the passage, a little within
the entrance; and, causing the door to open in the inside,
I barred it up in the night, taking in my ladders, too;
so that Friday could no way come at me in the inside of
my innermost wall, without making so much noise in
getting over that it must needs awaken me; for my first
wall had now a complete roof over it of long poles, covering
all my tent, and leaning up to the side of the hill; which was
again laid across with smaller sticks, instead of laths, and
then thatched over a great thickness with the rice-straw,
which was strong, like reeds; and at the hole or place
which was left to go in or out by the ladder, I had placed
a kind of trap-door, which, if it had been attempted on the
outside, would not have opened at all, but would have
fallen down and made a great noise; as to weapons, I took
them all into my side every night. But I needed none of
all this precaution; for never man had a more faithful,
loving, sincere servant than Friday was to me; without
passions, sullenness, or designs, perfectly obliged and
engaged; his very affections were tied to me like those of a
child to a father; and I dare say he would have sacrificed
his life for saving mine, upon any occasion whatsoever:
the many testimonies he gave me of this put it out of doubt,
and soon convinced me that I needed no precautions for
my safety on his account.

This frequently gave me occasion to observe, and that
with wonder, that however it had pleased God in his
Providence, and in the government of the works of his
hands, to take from so great a part of the world of
his creatures the best uses to which their faculties and
the powers of their souls are adapted, yet that he has
bestowed upon them the same powers, the same reason,
the same affections; the same sentiments of kindness and

obligation; the same passions and resentments of wrongs; the same sense of gratitude, sincerity, fidelity, and all the capacities of doing good and receiving good, that he has given to us; and that when he pleases to offer them occasions of exerting these, they are as ready, nay, more ready, to apply them to the right uses for which they were bestowed than we are. This made me very melancholy sometimes, in reflecting, as the several occasions presented, how mean a use we make of all these, even though we have these powers enlightened by the great lamp of instruction, the spirit of God, and by the knowledge of his word added to our understanding; and why it has pleased God to hide the like saving knowledge from so many millions of souls, who, if I might judge by this poor savage, would make a much better use of it than we did. From hence, I sometimes was led too far, to invade the sovereignty of Providence, and, as it were, arraign the justice of so arbitrary a disposition of things, that should hide that sight from some, and reveal it to others, and yet expect a little duty from both; but I shut it up, and checked my thoughts with this conclusion: first, That we did not know by what light and law these should be condemned; but that as God was necessarily, and, by the nature of his being, infinitely holy and just, so it could not be; but if these creatures were all sentenced to absence from himself, it was on account of sinning against that light, which, as the Scripture says, was a law to themselves, and by such rules as their conscience would acknowledge to be just, though the foundation was not discovered to us; and, secondly, That still, as we are all the clay in the hand of the Potter, no vessel could say to him, "Why hast thou formed me thus?"

But to return to my new companion: I was greatly delighted with him, and made it my business to teach him everything that was proper to make him useful, handy, and helpful; but especially to make him speak, and understand me when I spoke; and he was the aptest scholar that ever was; and particularly was so merry, so constantly diligent, and so pleased when he could but understand me, or make me understand him, that it was very pleasant to me to talk to him. And now my life became so easy that I began to say to myself, that could I but have been safe from more savages, I cared not if I was never to remove from the place while I lived.

After I had been two or three days returned to my castle, I thought that, in order to bring Friday off from his horrid way of feeding, and from the relish of a cannibal's stomach, I ought to let him taste other flesh; so I took him out with me one morning to the woods. I went, indeed, intending to kill a kid out of my own flock, and bring it home and dress it; but as I was going, I saw a she-goat lying down in the shade, and two young kids sitting by her. I catched hold of Friday. "Hold," said I, "stand still"; and made signs to him not to stir; immediately I presented my piece, shot and killed one of the kids. The poor creature, who had, at a distance, indeed, seen me kill the savage, his enemy, but did not know, nor could imagine, how it was done, was sensibly surprised; trembled, and shook, and looked so amazed that I thought he would have sunk down. He did not see the kid I shot at, or perceive I had killed it, but ripped up his waistcoat to feel whether he was not wounded; and, as I found presently, thought I was resolved to kill him: for he came and kneeled down to me, and, embracing my knees, said a great many things I did not understand; but I could easily see the meaning was to pray me not to kill him.

I soon found a way to convince him that I would do him no harm; and taking him up by the hand, laughed at him, and pointing to the kid which I had killed, beckoned to him to run and fetch it, which he did: and while he was wondering, and looking to see how the creature was killed, I loaded my gun again. By and by I saw a great fowl, like a hawk, sitting upon a tree within shot; so, to let Friday understand a little what I would do, I called him to me again, pointed at the fowl, which was indeed a parrot, though I thought it had been a hawk; I say, pointing to the parrot, and to my gun, and to the ground under the parrot, to let him see I would make it fall, I made him understand that I would shoot and kill that bird; accordingly, I fired, and bade him look, and immediately he saw the parrot fall. He stood like one frightened again, notwithstanding all I had said to him; and I found he was the more amazed, because he did not see me put anything into the gun, but thought that there must be some wonderful fund of death and destruction in that thing, able to kill man, beast, bird, or anything near or far off; and the astonishment this created in him was such as could not wear off for a long time; and I believe, if I would have let him, he would have worshipped me and my gun. As for the gun itself, he would not so much as touch it for several days after; but he would speak to it and talk to it, as if it had answered him, when he was by himself; which, as I afterwards learned of him, was to desire it not to kill him. Well, after his astonishment was a little over at this, I pointed to him to run and fetch the bird I had shot, which he did, but stayed some time; for the parrot, not being quite dead, had fluttered away a good distance from the place where she fell: however, he found her, took her up, and brought her to me; and as I had perceived his ignorance about the gun before, I took this advantage to charge the gun again, and to let him see me do it, that I might be ready for any other mark that might present; but nothing more offered at that time: so I brought home the kid, and the same evening I took the skin off, and cut it out as well as I could; and having a pot fit for that purpose, I boiled or stewed some of the flesh, and made some very good broth. After I had begun to eat some, I gave some to my man, who seemed very glad of it, and liked it very well; but that which was strangest to him was to see me eat salt with it. He made a sign to me that the salt was not good to eat; and putting a little into his own mouth, he seemed nauseated and would spit and sputter at it, washing his mouth with fresh water after it; on the other hand, I took some meat into my mouth without salt, and I pretended to spit and sputter for want of salt, as fast as he had done at the salt; but it would not do; he would never care for salt with his meat, or in his broth; at least, not for a great while, and then but a very little.

Having thus fed him boiled meat and broth, I was resolved to feast him the next day with roasting a piece of the kid; this I did by hanging it before the fire on a string, as I had seen many people do in England, setting two poles up, one on each side of the fire, and one across on the top, and tying the string to the cross stick, letting the meat turn continually. This Friday admired very much; and when he came to taste the flesh, he took so many ways to tell me how well he liked it, that I could not but understand him; and at last he told me, as well as he could, he would never eat man's flesh any more, which I was very glad to hear.

The next day I set him to work to beating some corn out, and sifting it in the manner I used to do, as I observed before; and he soon understood how to do it as well as I, especially after he had seen what the meaning of it was, and that it was to make bread of; for after that, I let him see me make my bread, and bake it, too: and in a little time Friday was able to do all the work for me, as well as I could do it myself.

I began now to consider that having two mouths to feed instead of one, I must provide more ground for my harvest, and plant a larger quantity of corn than I used to do; so I marked out a larger piece of land, and began the fence in the same manner as before, in which Friday worked not only very willingly and very hard, but did it very cheerfully; and I told him what it was for; that it was for corn to make more bread, because he was now with me, and that I might have enough for him and myself too. He appeared very sensible of that part, and let me know that he thought I had much more labour upon me on his account, than I had for myself; and that he would work the harder for me, if I would tell him what to do.

This was the pleasantest year of all the life I led in this place. Friday began to talk pretty well, and understand the names of almost everything I had occasion to call for, and of every place I had to send him to, and talk a great deal to me; so that, in short, I began now to have some use for my tongue again, which, indeed, I had very little occasion for before; that is to say about speech. Besides the pleasure of talking to him, I had a singular satisfaction in the fellow himself: his simple, unfeigned honesty appeared to me more and more every day, and I began really to love the creature; and on his side I believe he loved me more than it was possible for him ever to love anything before.

I had a mind once to try if he had any hankering inclination to his own country again; and having taught him English so well that he could answer me almost any question, I asked him whether the nation that he belonged to never conquered in battle. At which he smiled, and said, "Yes, yes, we always fight the better"; that is, he meant, always get the better in fight; and so we began the following discourse:

Master.—You always fight the better; how came you to be taken prisoner then, Friday?

Friday.—My nation beat much, for all that.

Master.—How beat? If your nation beat them, how came you to be taken?

Friday.—They more many than my nation, in the place where me was; they take one, two, three, and me; my nation overbeat them in the yonder place, where me no was; there my nation take one, two, great thousand.

Master.—But why did not your side recover you from the hands of your enemies then?

Friday.—They run, one, two, three, and me, and make me go in the canoe; my nation have no canoe that time.

Master.—Well, Friday, and what does your nation do with the men they take? Do they carry them away and eat them, as these did?

Friday.—Yes, my nation eat mans too; eat all up.

Master.—Where do they carry them?

Friday.—Go to other place, where they think.

Master.—Do they come hither?

Friday.—Yes, yes, they come hither; come other else place.

Master.—Have you been here with them?

Friday.—Yes, I been here (points to the N. W. side of the island, which, it seems, was their side).

By this I understood that my man Friday had formerly been among the savages who used to come on shore on the farther part of the island, on the said man-eating occasions that he was now brought for; and, some time after, when I took the courage to carry him to that side, being the same I formerly mentioned, he presently knew the place, and told me he was there once, when they eat up twenty men, two women, and one child; he could not tell twenty in English, but he numbered them by laying so many stones in a row, and pointing to me to tell them over.

I have told this passage, because it introduces what follows; that after this discourse I had with him, I asked him how far it was from our island to the shore, and whether the canoes were not often lost. He told me there was no danger, no canoes ever lost; but that after a little way out to sea, there was a current and wind, always one way in the morning, the other in the afternoon. This I understood to be no more than the sets of the tide, as going out or coming in; but I afterwards understood it was occasioned by the great draft and reflux of the mighty river Orinoco, in the mouth of which river, as I thought afterwards, our island lay; and that this land which I perceived to the

W. and N.W. was the great island Trinidad, on the north point of the mouth of the river. I asked Friday a thousand questions about the country, the inhabitants, the sea, the coast, and what nations were near; he told me all he knew, with the greatest openness imaginable. I asked him the names of the several nations of his sort of people, but could get no other name than Caribs; from whence easily understood that these were the Caribbees, which our maps place on the part of America which reaches from the mouth of the river Orinoco to Guiana, and onwards to St. Martha. He told me, that up a great way beyond the moon (that was, beyond the setting of the moon, which must be west from their country), there dwelt white-bearded men like me, and pointed to my great whiskers, which I mentioned before; and that they had killed much mans, that was his word; by all which I understood he meant the Spaniards, whose cruelties in America had been spread over the whole country and were remembered by all the nations, from father to son.

I inquired if he could tell me how I might come from this island, and get among those white men: he told me, "Yes, yes, I might go in two canoe." I could not understand what he meant by two canoe, till at last with great difficulty, I found he meant it must be in a large, great boat, as big as two canoes. This part of Friday's discourse began to relish with me very well; and from this time I entertained some hopes that, one time or other, I might find an opportunity to make my escape from this place, and that this poor savage might be a means to help me to do it.

During the long time that Friday had now been with me, and that he began to speak to me, and understand me, I was not wanting to lay a foundation of religious knowledge in his mind; particularly I asked him one time who made him. The poor creature did not understand me at all, but thought I had asked him who was his father: but I took it by another handle, and asked him who made the sea, the ground we walked on, and the hills and woods. He told me, "It was one Benamuckee, that lived beyond all"; he could describe nothing of this great person, but that he was very old, "much older," he said, "than the sea or the land, than the moon or the stars." I asked him then, if this old person had made all things, why did not all things worship him? He looked very grave, and, with a perfect look of innocence, said, "All things said O! to him." I asked him if the people who die in his country went away anywhere. He said, "Yes; they all went to Benamuckee." Then I asked him whether those they ate up went thither too. He said, "Yes."

From these things I began to instruct him in the knowledge of the true God: I told him that the great Maker of all things lived there, pointing up towards heaven; that he governed the world by the same power and providence by which he made it; that he was omnipotent, and could do everything for us, give everything to us, take everything from us; and thus, by degrees, I opened his eyes. He listened with great attention, and received with pleasure the notion of Jesus Christ being sent to redeem us, and of the manner of making our prayers to God, and his being able to hear us, even into heaven. He told me one day, that if our God could hear us, up beyond the sun, he must needs be a greater God than their Benamuckee, who lived but a little way off, and yet could not hear till they went up to the great mountains where he dwelt to speak to him. I asked him if ever he went thither to speak to him. He said, "No; they never went that were young men; none went thither but the old men," whom he called their Oowokakee; that is, as I made him explain it to me, their religious, or clergy and that they went to say O! (so he called saying prayers) and then came back and told them what Benamuckee said. By this I observed, that there is priestcraft even among the most blinded, ignorant pagans in the world; and the policy of making a secret of religion, in order to preserve the veneration of the people to the clergy, is not only to be found in the Roman, but, perhaps, among all religions in the world, even among the most brutish and barbarous savages.

I endeavoured to clear up this fraud to my man Friday, and told him that the pretence of their old men going up to the mountains to say O! to their god Benamuckee was a cheat; and their bringing word from thence what he said was much more so; that if they met with any answer, or spoke with any one there, it must be with an evil spirit; and then I entered into a long discourse with him about the devil, the original of him, his rebellion against God, his enmity to man, the reason of it, his setting himself up in the dark parts of the world to be worshipped instead of God, and as God, and the many stratagems he made use of to delude mankind to their ruin; how he had a secret access to our passions and to our affections, and to adapt his snares to our inclinations, so as to cause us even to be our own tempters, and run upon our own destruction by our own choice.

I found it was not so easy to imprint right notions in his mind about the devil as it was about the being of a God: nature assisted all my arguments to evidence to him even the necessity of a great First Cause—an overruling, governing Power—a secret directing Providence; and of the equity and justice of paying homage to him that made us, and the like: but there appeared nothing of this kind in the notion of an evil spirit; of his original, his being, his nature; and, above all, of his inclination to do evil, and to draw us in to do so too: and the poor creature puzzled me once in such a manner, by a question merely natural and innocent, that I scarce knew what to say to him. I had been talking a great deal to him of the power of God, his omnipotence, his aversion to sin, his being a consuming fire to the workers of iniquity; how, as he had made us all, he could destroy us and all the world in a moment; and he listened with great seriousness to me all the while. After this, I had been telling him how the devil was God's enemy in the hearts of men, and used all his malice and skill to defeat the good designs of Providence, and to ruin the kingdom of Christ in the world, and the like. "Well," says Friday; "but you say God is so strong, so great; is he not much strong, much might as the devil?" "Yes, yes," says I, "Friday; God is stronger than the devil: God is above the devil, and therefore we pray to God to tread him down under our feet, and to enable us to resist his temptations and quench his fiery darts." "But," says he again, "if God much strong, much might as the devil, why God no kill the devil, so make him no more do wicked?" I was strangely surprised at this question; and after all though I was now an old man, yet I was but a young doctor, and ill qualified for a casuist, or solver of difficulties; and at first I could not tell what to say; so I pretended not to hear him, and asked him what he said; but he was too earnest for an answer to forget his question, so that he repeated it in the very same broken words as above. By this time I had recovered myself a little, and I said, "God will at last punish him severely; he is reserved for the judgment, and he is to be cast into the bottomless pit, to dwell with everlasting fire." This did not satisfy Friday; but he returns upon me, repeating my own words, "'Reserve at last!' me no understand: but why not kill the devil now, not kill great ago?" "You may as well ask me," said I, "why God does not kill you or me, when we do wicked things here that offend him: we are preserved to repent and be pardoned." He muses awhile on this: "Well, well," says he, mighty affectionately, "that well: so you, I, devil, all wicked, all preserve, repent, God pardon all." Here I was run down by him to the last degree: and it was a testimony to me, how the mere notions of nature, though they will guide reasonable creatures to the knowledge of a God, and of a worship or homage due to the supreme being of God, as the consequence of our nature, yet nothing but Divine revelation can form the knowledge of Jesus Christ, and of redemption purchased for us: of a

Mediator of the new covenant, and of an Intercessor at the footstool of God's throne; I say, nothing but a revelation from heaven can form these in the soul; and that, therefore, the gospel of our Lord and Saviour Jesus Christ, I mean the Word of God, and the Spirit of God, promised for the guide and sanctifier of his people, are the absolutely necessary instructors of the souls of men in the saving knowledge of God and the means of salvation.

I therefore diverted the present discourse between me and my man, rising up hastily as upon some sudden occasion of going out; then sending him for something a good way off, I seriously prayed to God that he would enable me to instruct savingly this poor savage; assisting by his Spirit the heart of the poor ignorant creature to receive the light of the knowledge of God in Christ, reconciling him to himself, and would guide me to speak so to him from the Word of God, that his conscience might be convinced, his eyes opened, and his soul saved. When he came again to me, I entered into a long discourse with him upon the subject of the redemption of man by the Saviour of the world, and of the doctrine of the gospel preached from heaven—viz., of repentance towards God, and faith in our blessed Lord Jesus. I then explained to him as well as I could why our blessed Redeemer took not on him the nature of angels, but the seed of Abraham; and how, for that reason, the fallen angels had no share in the redemption; that he came only to the lost sheep of the house of Israel, and the like.

I had, God knows, more sincerity than knowledge in all the methods I took for this poor creature's instruction, and must acknowledge, what I believe all that act upon the same principle will find, that, in laying things open to him, I really informed and instructed myself in many things that I either did not know, or had not fully considered before, but which occurred naturally to my mind upon searching into them, for the information of this poor savage; and I had more affection in my inquiry after things upon this occasion than ever I felt before; so that, whether this poor wild wretch was the better for me or no, I had reason to be thankful that ever he came to me; my grief sat lighter upon me; my habitation grew comfortable to me beyond measure; and when I reflected that in this solitary life which I had been confined to, I had not only been moved to look up to heaven myself, and to seek the hand that had brought me here, but was now to be made an instrument, under Providence, to save the life, and, for aught I know, the soul of a poor savage, and bring him to the true knowledge of religion, and of the Christian doctrine, that he might know Christ Jesus, to know whom is life eternal; I say, when I reflected upon all these things, a secret joy ran through every part of my soul, and I frequently rejoiced that ever I was brought to this place, which I had so often thought the most dreadful of all afflictions that could possibly have befallen me.

In this thankful frame I continued all the remainder of my time; and the conversations which employed the hours between Friday and me were such as made the three years which we lived there together perfectly and completely happy, if any such thing as complete happiness can be found in a sublunary state. This savage was now a good Christian, a much better than I; though I have reason to hope, and bless God for it, that we were equally penitent, and comforted, restored penitents. We had here the Word of God to read, and no farther off from His Spirit to instruct, than if we had been in England. I always applied myself, in reading the Scriptures, to let him know, as well as I could, the meaning of what I read; and he again, by his serious inquiries and questionings, made me, as I said before, a much better scholar in the Scripture knowledge than I should ever have been by my own mere private reading. Another thing I cannot refrain from observing here also, from experience in this retired part of my life— viz., how infinite and inexpressible a blessing it is that the knowledge of God, and of the doctrine of salvation by

Christ Jesus, is so plainly laid down in the Word of God, so easy to be received and understood, that, as the bare reading the Scripture made me capable of understanding enough of my duty to carry me directly on to the great work of sincere repentance for my sins, and of laying hold of a Saviour for life and salvation, to a stated reformation in practice, and obedience to all God's commands, and this without any teacher or instructor, I mean human; so the same plain instruction sufficiently served to the enlightening this savage creature, and bringing him to be such a Christian as I have known few equal to him in my life.

As to the disputes, wrangling, strife, and contention which happened in the world about religion, whether niceties in doctrines or schemes of church government, they were all perfectly useless to us, and, for aught I can yet see, they have been to the rest of the world. We had the sure guide to heaven, viz., the Word of God; and we had, blessed be God, comfortable views of the Spirit of God teaching and instructing us by his word, leading us into all truth, and making us both willing and obedient to the instruction of his word. And I cannot see the least use that the greatest knowledge of the disputed points of religion, which have made such confusions in the world, would have been to us, if we could have obtained it; but I must go on with the historical part of things, and take every part in its order.

CHAPTER XIII

AFTER Friday and I became more intimately acquainted, and that he could understand almost all I said to him, and speak fluently, though in broken English, to me, I acquainted him with my own story, or at least so much of it as related to my coming into this place; how I had lived there, and how long: I let him into the mystery, for such it was to him, of gunpowder and bullet, and taught him how to shoot. I gave him a knife, with which he was wonderfully delighted; and I made him a belt, with a frog hanging to it, such as in England we wear hangers in; and in the frog, instead of a hanger, I gave him a hatchet, which was not only as good a weapon in some cases, but much more useful upon many occasions.

I described to him the countries of Europe, particularly England, which I came from; how we lived, how we worshipped God, how we behaved to one another, and how we traded in ships to all parts of the world. I gave him an account of the wreck which I had been on board of, and showed him, as near as I could, the place where she lay: but she was all beaten in pieces long before, and quite gone. I showed him the ruins of our boat, which we lost when we escaped, and which I could not stir with my whole strength then; but was now fallen almost all to pieces. Upon seeing this boat, Friday stood musing a great while, and said nothing. I asked him what it was he studied upon. At last, says he, "Me see such boat like come to place at my nation." I did not understand him a good while; but, at last, when I had examined further into it, I understood from him, that a boat, such as that had been, came on shore upon the country where he lived; that is, as he explained it, was driven thither by stress of weather.

I presently imagined that some European ship must have been cast away upon their coast, the boat getting loose and driving ashore; but was so dull that I never once thought of men making their escape from a wreck thither, much less whence they might come: so I only inquired after the description of the boat.

Friday described the boat to me well enough; but brought me better to understand him when he added with some warmth, "We save the white mans from drown." Then I presently asked if there were any white mans, as he called them, in the boat. "Yes," he said; "the boat full of white mans." I asked him how many. He told upon his fingers seventeen. I asked him then what became of them. He told me, "They live, they dwell at my nation."

This put new thoughts into my head; for I presently imagined that these might be the men belonging to the ship that was cast away in the sight of my island, as I now called it; and who, after the ship was struck on the rock and they saw her inevitably lost, had saved themselves in their boat, and were landed upon that wild shore among the savages. Upon this I inquired of him more critically what was become of them. He assured me they lived still there; that they had been there about four years; that the savages left them alone, and gave them victuals to live. I asked him how it came to pass that they did not kill them and eat them. He said, "No, they make brother with them"; that is, as I understood him, a truce; and then he added, "They no eat mans but when make the war fight"; that is to say, they never eat any men but such as come to fight with them, and are taken in battle.

It was after this some considerable time, that being upon the top of the hill, at the east side of the island, from whence, as I have said, I had, in a clear day, discovered the main or continent of America, Friday, the weather being very serene, looks very earnestly towards the mainland, and, in a kind of surprise, falls a-jumping and dancing, and calls out to me, for I was at some distance from him. I asked him what was the matter. "Oh, joy!" says he; "oh, glad! there see my country, there my nation!" I observed an extraordinary sense of pleasure appeared in his face and his eyes sparkled, and his countenance discovered a strange eagerness, as if he had a mind to be in his own country again. This observation of mine put a great many thoughts into me, which made me at first not so easy about my new man Friday as I was before; and I made no doubt but that, if Friday could get back to his own nation again, he would not only forget all his religion, but all his obligation to me, and would be forward enough to give his countrymen an account of me, and come back, perhaps, with a hundred or two of them, and make a feast upon me, at which he might be as merry as he used to be with those of his enemies, when they were taken in war. But I wronged the poor honest creature very much, for which I was very sorry afterwards. However, as my jealousy increased, and held me some weeks, I was a little more circumspect, and not so familiar and kind to him as before: in which I was certainly in the wrong too: the honest, grateful creature having no thought about it, but what consisted with the best principles both as a religious Christian, and as a grateful friend; as appeared afterwards to my full satisfaction.

While my jealousy of him lasted, you may be sure I was every day pumping him, to see if he would discover any of the new thoughts, which I suspected were in him; but I found everything he said was so honest and so innocent, that I could find nothing to nourish my suspicion; and, in spite of all my uneasiness, he made me at last entirely his own again; nor did he in the least perceive that I was uneasy, and therefore I could not suspect him of deceit.

One day, walking up the same hill, but the weather being hazy at sea, so that we could not see the continent, I called to him, and said, "Friday, do not you wish yourself in your own country, your own nation?" "Yes," he said, "I be much O glad to be at my own nation." "What would you do there?" said I: "would you turn wild again, eat men's flesh again, and be a savage, as you were before?" He looked full of concern, and shaking his head, said, "No, no; Friday tell them to live good; tell them to pray God: tell them to eat corn-bread, cattle-flesh, milk; no eat man again." "Why, then," said I to him, "they will kill you." He looked grave at that, and then said, "No, no; they no kill me, they willing love learn." He meant by this, they would be willing to learn. He added, they learned much of the bearded mans that came in the boat. Then I asked him if he would go back to them. He smiled at that, and told me he could not swim so far. I told him I would make a canoe for him. He told me he would go if I would go with him. "I go!" says I; "why they will eat me if I come there." "No, no," says he, "me make them no eat you; me make them much love you." He meant, he would tell them how I had killed his enemies, and saved his life, and so he would make them love me. Then he told me, as well as he could, how kind they were to seventeen white men, or bearded men as he called them, who came on shore in distress.

From this time, I confess, I had a mind to venture over, and see if I could possibly join with those bearded men, who, I made no doubt, were Spaniards or Portuguese; not doubting but, if I could, we might find some method to escape from thence, being upon the continent, and a good company together, better than I could from an island forty miles off the shore, alone, and without help. So, after some days, I took Friday to work again, by way of discourse, and told him I would give him a boat to go back to his own nation; and, accordingly, I carried him to my frigate, which lay on the other side of the island, and having cleared it of water (for I always kept it sunk in the water) I brought it out, showed it him, and we both went into it. I found he was a most dexterous fellow at managing it and would make it go almost as swift and fast again as I could. So when he was in, I said to him, "Well, now,

ROBINSON CRUSOE

Friday, shall we go to your nation?" He looked very dull at my saying so; which it seems was because he thought the boat too small to go so far. I then told him I had a bigger; so the next day I went to the place where the first boat lay which I had made, but which I could not get into the water. He said that was big enough; but then, as I had taken no care of it, and it had lain two or three and twenty years there, the sun had split and dried it, that it was rotten. Friday told me that such a boat would do very well, and would carry "much enough vittle, drink, bread;"—that was his way of talking.

Upon the whole, I was by this time so fixed upon my design of going over with him to the continent, that I told him we would go and make one as big as that, and he should go home in it. He answered not one word, but looked very grave and sad. I asked him what was the matter with him. He asked me again, "Why you angry mad with Friday?—what me done?" I asked him what he meant. I told him I was not angry with him at all. "No angry?" says he, repeating the words several times; "why send Friday home away to my nation?" "Why," says I, "Friday, did not you say you wished you were there?" "Yes, yes," says he, "wish we both there; no wish Friday there, no master there." In a word, he would not think of going there without me. "I go there, Friday?" says I: "what shall I do there?" He turned very quick upon me at this. "You do great deal much good," says he; "you teach wild mans be good, sober, tame mans; you tell them know God, pray God, and live new life." "Alas, Friday!" says I, "thou knowest not what thou sayest; I am but an ignorant man myself." "Yes, yes," says he, "you teachee me good, you teachee them good." "No, no, Friday," says I, "you shall go without me; leave me here to live by myself, as I did before." He looked confused again at that word; and running to one of his hatchets which he used to wear, he takes it up hastily, and gives it to me. "What must I do with this?" says I to him. "You take kill Friday," says

he. "What must I kill you for?" said I again. He returns
very quick: "What you send Friday away for? Take
kill Friday, no send Friday away." This he spoke so
earnestly that I saw tears stand in his eyes. In a word,
I so plainly discovered the utmost affection in him to me,
and a firm resolution in him, that I told him then, and
often after, that I would never send him away from me,
if he was willing to stay with me.

Upon the whole, as I found by all his discourse a settled
affection to me, and that nothing could part him from
me, so I found all the foundation of his desire to go to his
own country was laid in his ardent affection to the people,
and his hopes of my doing them good; a thing which, as
I had no notion of myself, so I had not the least thought,
or intention, or desire of undertaking it. But still I found
a strong inclination to my attempting an escape, founded
on the supposition gathered from the former discourse,
that there were seventeen bearded men there; and therefore, without any more delay, I went to work with Friday
to find out a great tree proper to fell, and make a large
periagua, or canoe, to undertake the voyage. There were
trees enough in the island to have built a little fleet, not
of periaguas or canoes, but even of good large vessels;
but the main thing I looked at was, to get one so near
the water that we might launch it when it was made,
to avoid the mistake I committed at first. At last, Friday
pitched upon a tree; for I found he knew much better
than I what kind of wood was fittest for it; nor can I tell,
to this day, what wood to call the tree we cut down, except
that it was very like the tree we call fustic, or between
that and the Nicaragua wood, for it was much of the same
colour and smell. Friday was for burning the hollow or
cavity of this tree out, to make it into a boat, but I showed
him how rather to cut it with tools; which, after I had
showed him how to use, he did very handily; and in about
a month's hard labour, we finished it and made it very
handsome; especially, when, with our axes, which I showed

him how to handle, we cut and hewed the outside into the true shape of a boat. After this, however, it cost us near a fortnight's time to get her along, as it were, inch by inch, upon great rollers into the water; but when she was in, she would have carried twenty men with great ease.

When she was in the water, though she was so big, it amazed me to see with what dexterity and how swift my man Friday could manage her, turn her, and paddle her along. So I asked him if we would, and if we might venture over in her. "Yes," he said; "we venture over in her very well, though great blow wind." However, I had a farther design that he knew nothing of, and that was to make a mast and a sail, and to fit her with an anchor and cable. As to a mast, that was easy enough to get; so I pitched upon a straight young cedar tree, which I found near the place, and which there was great plenty of in the island, and I set Friday to work to cut it down, and gave him directions how to shape and order it. But as to the sail, that was my particular care. I knew I had old sails, or rather pieces of old sails, enough; but as I had had them now six-and-twenty years by me, and had not been very careful to preserve them, not imagining that I should ever have this kind of use for them, I did not doubt but they were all rotten; and, indeed, most of them were so. However, I found two pieces, which appeared pretty good, and with these I went to work; and with a great deal of pains, and awkward, tedious stitching, you may be sure, for want of needles, I at length made a three-cornered ugly thing, like what we call in England a shoulder-of-mutton sail, to go with a boom at bottom, and a little short sprit at the top, such as usually our ships' longboats sail with, and such as I best knew how to manage, because it was such a one as I used in the boat in which I made my escape from Barbary, as related in the first part of my story.

I was near two months performing this last work—viz., rigging and fitting my mast and sails; for I finished them very complete, making a small stay, and a sail or foresail to it, to assist if we should turn to windward; and, which was more than all, I fixed a rudder to the stern of her to steer with. And though I was but a bungling shipwright, yet as I knew the usefulness, and even the necessity of such a thing, I applied myself with so much pains to do it, that at last I brought it to pass; though, considering the many dull contrivances I had for it that failed, I think it cost me almost as much labour as making the boat.

After all this was done, I had my man Friday to teach as to what belonged to the navigation of my boat; for, though he knew very well how to paddle the canoe, he knew nothing of what belonged to a sail and a rudder; and was the most amazed when he saw me work the boat to and again in the sea by the rudder, and how the sail gibbed, and filled this way or that way, as the course we sailed changed; I say, when he saw this, he stood like one astonished and amazed. However, with a little use, I made all these things familiar to him, and he became an expert sailor, except that as to the compass I could make him understand very little of that. On the other hand, as there was very little cloudy weather, and seldom or never any fogs in those parts, there was the less occasion for the compass, seeing the stars were always to be seen by night, and the shore by day, except in the rainy seasons, and then nobody cared to stir abroad either by land or sea.

I was now entered on the seven-and-twentieth year of my captivity in this place; though the three last years that I had this creature with me ought rather to be left out of the account, my habitation being quite of another kind than in all the rest of my time. I kept the anniversary of my landing here with the same thankfulness to God for his mercies as at first: and if I had such cause of acknowledgment at first, I had much more so now, having such additional testimonies of the care of Providence over me and the great hopes I had of being effectually and speedily delivered; for I had an invincible impression upon my thoughts that my deliverance was at hand, and that I should not be another year in this place. However, I went on with my husbandry; digging, planting, and fencing, as usual. I gathered and cured my grapes, and did every necessary thing as before.

The rainy season was in the meantime upon me, when I kept more within doors than at other times. I had stowed our new vessel as secure as we could, bringing her up into the creek, where, as I said in the beginning, I landed my rafts from the ship; and hauling her up to the shore at high-water mark, I made my man Friday dig a little dock, just big enough to hold her, and just deep enough to give her water enough to float in; and then, when the tide was out, we made a strong dam across the end of it, to keep the water out; and so she lay dry as to the tide from the sea: and to keep the rain off, we laid a great many boughs of trees, so thick that she was as well thatched as a house; and thus we waited for the months of November and December, in which I designed to make my adventure.

When the settled season began to come in, as the thought of my design returned with the fair weather, I was preparing daily for the voyage. And the first thing I did was to lay by a certain quantity of provisions, being the stores for our voyage; and intended, in a week or a fortnight's time, to open the dock, and launch out our boat. I was busy one morning upon something of this kind, when I called to Friday, and bid him go to the seashore, and see if he could find a turtle or tortoise, a thing which we generally got once a week, for the sake of the eggs, as well as the flesh. Friday had not been gone long when he came running back, and flew over my outer wall, or fence, like one that felt not the ground, or the steps he set his feet on; and before I had time to speak to him, he cries out to me, "O master! O master! O sorrow! O bad!" "What's the matter, Friday?" said I. "Oh! yonder, there," says he; "one, two, three canoes; one, two, three!" By this way of speaking, I concluded there were six; but on inquiry

I found there were but three. "Well, Friday," says I, "do not be frightened." So I heartened him up as well as I could. However, I saw the poor fellow was most terribly scared, for nothing ran in his head but that they were come back to look for him, and would cut him in pieces and eat him; and the poor fellow trembled so that I scarcely knew what to do with him. I comforted him as well as I could, and told him I was in as much danger as he, and that they would eat me as well as him. "But," said I, "Friday, we must resolve to fight them. Can you fight, Friday?" "Me shoot," says he; "but there come many great number." "No matter for that," said I, again; "our guns will fright them that we do not kill." So I asked him whether, if I resolved to defend him, he would defend me, and stand by me, and do just as I bid him. He said, "Me die, when you bid die, master." So I went and fetched a good dram of rum and gave him; for I had been so good a husband of my rum, that I had a great deal left. When he had drunk it, I made him take the two fowling-pieces, which we always carried, and load them with large swanshot, as big as small pistol-bullets. Then I took four muskets, and loaded them with two slugs, and five small bullets each; and my two pistols I loaded with a brace of bullets each. I hung my great sword, as usual, naked by my side, and gave Friday his hatchet. When I had thus prepared myself, I took my perspective-glass, and went up to the side of the hill, to see what I could discover; and I found quickly by my glass that there were one-and-twenty savages, three prisoners, and three canoes; and that their whole business seemed to be the triumphant banquet upon these three human bodies; a barbarous feast indeed, but nothing more than, as I had observed, was usual with them. I observed also that they landed, not where they had done when Friday made his escape, but nearer to my creek, where the shore was low, and where a thick wood came close almost down to the sea. This, with the abhorrence of the inhuman errand these wretches came upon, filled me with such indignation that I came down again to Friday, and told him I was resolved to go down to them, and kill them all; and asked him if he would stand by me. He had now got over his fright, and his spirits being a little raised with the dram I had given him, he was very cheerful, and told me, as before, he would die when I bid him die.

In this fit of fury I took first and divided the arms which I had charged, as before, between us; I gave Friday one pistol to stick in his girdle, and three guns upon his shoulder, and I took one pistol and the other three myself; and in this posture we marched out. I took a small bottle of rum in my pocket, and gave Friday a large bag with more powder and bullets; and as to orders, I charged him to keep close behind me, and not to stir, or shoot, or do anything till I bid him, and in the meantime not to speak a word. In this posture I fetched a compass to my right hand of near a mile, as well to get over the creek as to get into the wood so that I might come within shot of them before I should be discovered, which I had seen by my glass it was easy to do.

While I was making this march, my former thoughts returning, I began to abate my resolution—I do not mean that I entertained any fear of their number, for, as they were naked, unarmed wretches, it is certain I was superior to them—nay, though I had been alone. But it occurred to my thoughts, what call, what occasion, much less what necessity, I was in to go and dip my hands in blood, to attack people who had neither done nor intended me any wrong?— who, as to me, were innocent, and whose barbarous customs were their own disaster, being in them a token, indeed, of God's having left them, with the other nations of that part of the world, to such stupidity, and to such inhuman courses, but did not call me to take upon me to be a judge of their actions, much less an executioner of his justice— that whenever he thought fit to would take the cause into his own hands, and by national vengeance punish them for national crimes; but that, in the meantime, it was none of my business—that it was true Friday might justify it, because he was a declared enemy, and in a state of war with those very particular people, and it was lawful for him to attack them; but I could not say the same with regard to myself. These things were so warmly pressed upon my thoughts all the way as I went, that I resolved I would only go and place myself near them that I might observe their barbarous feast, and that I would act then as God should direct; and that unless something offered that was more a call to me than yet I knew of, I would not meddle with them.

With this resolution I entered the wood, and with all possible wariness and silence, Friday following close at my heels, I marched till I came to the skirt of the wood on the side which was next to them, only that one corner of the wood lay between me and them. Here I called softly to Friday, and showing him a great tree, which was just at the corner of the wood, I bade him go to the tree, and bring me word if he could see there plainly what they were doing. He did so, and came immediately back to me, and told me they might be plainly viewed there—that they were all about their fire eating the flesh of one of their prisoners, and that another lay bound upon the sand a little from them, whom he said they would kill next; and this fired the very soul within me. He told me it was not one of their nation but one of the bearded men whom he had told me of, that came to their country in a boat. I was filled with horror at the very naming of the white, bearded man; and going to the tree, I saw plainly by my glass a white man, who lay upon the beach of the sea with his hands and feet tied with flags, or things like rushes and that he was a European and had clothes on.

There was another tree, and a little thicket beyond it, about fifty yards nearer to them than the place where I was, which by going a little way about, I saw I might come at undiscovered, and that then I should be within half a shot of them; so I withheld my passion, though I was indeed enraged to the highest degree; and going back about twenty paces, I got behind some bushes, which held all the way till I came to the other tree, and then came to a little rising ground, which gave me a full view of them at the distance of about eighty yards.

I had now not a moment to lose, for nineteen of the dreadful wretches sat upon the ground, all close huddled together, and had just sent the other two to butcher the poor Christian, and bring him perhaps limb by limb to their fire, and they were stooping down to untie the bands at his feet. I turned to Friday. "Now, Friday," said I, "do as I bid thee." Friday said he would. "Then, Friday," said I, "do exactly as you see me do; fail in nothing." So I set down one of the muskets and the fowling-piece upon the ground, and Friday did the like by his, and with the other musket I took my aim at the savages, bidding him do the like; then asking him if he was ready, he said, "Yes." "Then fire at them," said I; and at the same moment I fired also.

Friday took his aim so much better than I, that on the side that he shot he killed two of them, and wounded three more; and on my side I killed one, and wounded two. They were, you may be sure, in a dreadful consternation; and all of them that were not hurt jumped upon their feet, but did not immediately know which way to run, or which way to look, for they knew not from whence their destruction came. Friday kept his eyes close upon me that, as I had bid him, he might observe what I did; so, as soon as the first shot was made, I threw down the piece, and took up the fowling-piece, and Friday did the like; he saw me cock and present; he did the same again. "Are you ready, Friday?" said I. "Yes," says he. "Let fly, then," said I, "in the name of God!" and with that I fired again among the amazed wretches, and so did Friday; and as our pieces were now loaded with what I call swan-shot, or small pistol-bullets, we found only two drop;

but so many were wounded, that they ran about yelling and screaming like mad creatures, all bloody, and most of them miserably wounded; whereof three more fell quickly after, though not quite dead.

"Now, Friday," said I, laying down the discharged pieces, and taking up the musket which was yet loaded, "follow me," which he did with a great deal of courage; upon which I rushed out of the wood and showed myself, and Friday close at my foot. As soon as I perceived they saw me, I shouted as loud as I could, and bade Friday do so too, and running as fast as I could, which by the way was not very fast, being loaded with arms as I was, I made directly toward the poor victim, who was, as I said, lying upon the beach or shore, between the place where they sat and the sea. The two butchers who were just going to work with him had left him at the surprise of our first fire, and fled in a terrible fright to the seaside, and jumped into a canoe, and three more of the rest made the same way. I turned to Friday, and bade him step forward and fire at them; he understood me immediately, and running about forty yards to be nearer them, he shot at them; and I thought he killed them all, for I saw them all fall of a heap into the boat, though I saw two of them up again quickly; however, he killed two of them, and wounded the third so that he lay down in the bottom of the boat as if he had been dead.

While my man Friday fired at them, I pulled out my knife and cut the flags that bound the poor victim; and loosing his hands and feet, I lifted him up, and asked him, in the Portuguese tongue, what he was. He answered, in Latin, Christianus; but was so weak and faint that he could scarce stand or speak. I took my bottle out of my pocket, and gave it him, making signs that he should drink, which he did; and I gave him a piece of bread, which he ate. Then I asked him what countryman he was, and he said Espagnole; and being a little recovered, let me know, by all the signs he could possibly make, how much he was in my debt for his deliverance. "Seignior," said I, with as much Spanish as I could make up, "we will talk afterwards, but we must fight now; if you have any strength left, take this pistol and sword, and lay about you." He took them very thankfully; and no sooner had he the arms in his hands, but, as if they had put new vigour into him, he flew upon his murderers like a fury, and had cut two of them in pieces in an instant; for the truth is, as the whole was a surprise to them, so the poor creatures were so much frightened with the noise of our pieces that they fell down for mere amazement and fear, and had no more power to attempt their own escape, than their flesh had to resist our shot: and that was the case of those five that Friday shot at in the boat; for as three of them fell with the hurt they received, so the other two fell with the fright.

I kept my piece in my hand still without firing, being willing to keep my charge ready, because I had given the Spaniard my pistol and sword; so I called to Friday, and bade him run up to the tree from whence we first fired, and fetch the arms which lay there that had been discharged, which he did with great swiftness; and then giving him my musket, I sat down myself to load all the rest again, and bade them come to me when they wanted. While I was loading these pieces, there happened a fierce engagement between the Spaniard and one of the savages, who made at him with one of their great wooden swords, the same weapon that was to have killed him before, if I had not prevented it. The Spaniard, who was as bold and brave as could be imagined, though weak, had fought this Indian a good while, and had cut two great wounds on his head; but the savage being a stout lusty fellow, closing in with him, had thrown him down, being faint, and was wringing my sword out of his hand; when the Spaniard, though undermost, wisely quitted the sword, drew the pistol from his girdle, shot the savage through the body, and killed him upon the spot, before I, who was running to help him, could come near him.

Friday, being now left to his liberty, pursued the flying wretches, with no weapon in his hand but his hatchet; and with that he dispatched those three who, as I said before, were wounded at first, and fallen, and all the rest he could come up with: and the Spaniard coming to me for a gun, I gave him one of the fowling-pieces, with which he pursued two of the savages, and wounded them both; but, as he was not able to run, they both got from him into the wood, where Friday pursued them, and killed one of them, but the other was too nimble for him; and though he was wounded, yet had plunged himself into the sea, and swam with all his might off to those two who were left in the canoe; which three in the canoe, with one wounded, that we knew not whether he died or no, were all that escaped our hands, of one-and-twenty. The account of the whole is as follows: Three killed at our first shot from the tree; two killed at the next shot; two killed by Friday in the boat; two killed by Friday, of those at first wounded; one killed by Friday in the wood; three killed by the Spaniard; four killed, being found dropped here and there, of the wounds, or killed by Friday in his chase of them; four escaped in the boat, whereof one wounded if not dead—twenty-one, in all.

Those that were in the canoe worked hard to get out of gunshot, and though Friday made two or three shots at them, I did not find that he hit any of them. Friday would fain have had me take one of their canoes, and pursue them; and, indeed, I was very anxious about their escape, lest carrying the news home to their people, they should come back perhaps with two or three hundred of the canoes, and devour us by mere multitude; so I consented to pursue them by sea, and running to one of their canoes, I jumped in, and bade Friday follow me; but when I was in the canoe, I was surprised to find another poor creature lie there bound hand and foot, as the Spaniard was, for the slaughter, and almost dead with fear, not knowing what was the matter; for he had not been able to look up over the side of the boat, he was tied so hard, neck and heels, and had been tied so long, that he had really little life in him.

I immediately cut the twisted flags or rushes, which they had bound him with, and would have helped him up, but he could not stand or speak, but groaned most piteously, believing, it seems, still, that he was only unbound in order to be killed. When Friday came to him, I bade him speak to him, and tell him of his deliverance; and pulling out my bottle, made him give the poor wretch a dram; which, with the news of his being delivered, revived him, and he sat up in the boat. But when Friday came to hear him speak, and look in his face, it would have moved any one to tears to have seen how Friday kissed him, embraced him, hugged him, cried, laughed, hallooed, jumped about, danced, sung; then cried again, wrung his hands, beat his own face and head; and then sung and jumped about again like a distracted creature. It was a good while before I could make him speak to me, or tell me what was the matter; but when he came a little to himself, he told me that it was his father.

It is not easy for me to express how it moved me to see what ecstasy and filial affection had worked in this poor savage at the sight of his father, and of his being delivered from death; nor, indeed, can I describe half the extravagances of his affection after this; for he went into the boat, and out of the boat, a great many times: when he went in to him, he would sit down by him, open his breast, and hold his father's head close to his bosom half an hour together, to nourish it; then he took his arms and ankles, which were numbed and stiff with the binding, and chafed and rubbed them with his hands; and I, perceiving what the case was, gave him some rum out of my bottle to rub them with, which did them a great deal of good.

This action put an end to our pursuit of the canoe with the other savages, who were now gotten almost out of sight; and it was happy for us that we did not, for it blew so hard within two hours after, and before they could be got a quarter of their way, and continued blowing so hard all night, and that from the northwest, which was against them, that I could not suppose their boat could live, or that they ever reached their own coast.

But to return to Friday; he was so busy about his father, that I could not find in my heart to take him off for some time; but after I thought he could leave him a little I called him to me, and he came jumping and laughing, and pleased to the highest extreme; then I asked him if he had given his father any bread. He shook his head, and said, "None; ugly dog eat all up self." I then gave him a cake of bread, out of a little pouch I carried on purpose; I also gave him a dram for himself; but he would not taste it, but carried it to his father. I had in my pocket also two or three bunches of raisins, so I gave him a handful of them for his father. He had no sooner given his father these raisins, but I saw him come out of the boat, and run away as if he had been bewitched, for he was the swiftest fellow on his feet that ever I saw; I say, he ran at such a rate that he was out of sight, as it were, in an instant; and though I called, and hallooed out, too, after him, it was all one—away he went; and in a quarter of an hour I saw him come back again, though not so fast as he went; and, as he came nearer, I found his pace slacker, because he had something in his hand. When he came up to me, I found he had been quite home for an earthen jug or pot, to bring his father some fresh water, and that he had got two more cakes or loaves of bread: the bread he gave me, but the water he carried to his father; however, as I was very thirsty, too, I took a little sup of it. This water revived his father more than all the rum or spirits I had given him, for he was just fainting with thirst.

When his father had drunk, I called to him to know if there was any water left; he said "Yes"; and I bade him give to the poor Spaniard, who was in as much want of it as his father; and I sent one of the cakes, that Friday brought, to the Spaniard too, who was indeed very weak, and was reposing himself upon a green place under the shade of a tree; and whose limbs were also very stiff, and very much swelled with the rude bandage he had been tied with. When I saw that upon Friday's coming to him with the water he sat up and drank, and took the bread and began to eat, I went to him and gave him a handful of raisins; he looked up in my face with all the tokens of gratitude and thankfulness that could appear in any countenance; but was so weak, notwithstanding he had so exerted himself in the fight, that he could not stand up upon his feet; he tried to do it two or three times, but was really not able, his ankles were so swelled and so painful to him; so I bade him sit still, and caused Friday to rub his ankles, and bathe them with rum, as he had done his father's.

I observed the poor affectionate creature every two minutes, or perhaps less, all the while he was here, turned his head about, to see if his father was in the same place and posture as he left him sitting; and at last he found he was not to be seen; at which he started up, and, without speaking a word, flew with that swiftness to him that one could scarce perceive his feet to touch the ground as he went : but when he came, he only found he had lain himself down to ease his limbs, so Friday came back to me presently; and I then spoke to the Spaniard to let Friday help him up, if he could, and lead him to the boat, and then he should carry him to our dwelling, where I would take care of him. But Friday, a lusty young fellow, took the Spaniard quite up upon his back, and carried him away to the boat, and set him down softly upon the side or gunnel of the canoe, with his feet in the inside of it; and then lifted him quite in, and set him close to his father; and presently stepping out again, launched the boat off, and paddled it along the shore faster than I could walk, though the wind blew pretty hard too; so he brought them both safe into our creek, and, leaving them in the boat, ran away to fetch the other canoe. As he passed me I spoke to him, and asked him

whither he went. He told me, "Go fetch more boat";
so away he went like the wind, for sure never man or horse
ran like him; and he had the other canoe in the creek
almost as soon as I got to it by land; so he wafted me over,
and then went to help our new guests out of the boat,
which he did; but they were neither of them able to walk;
so that poor Friday knew not what to do.

To remedy this, I went to work in my thoughts, and
calling to Friday to bid them sit down on the bank while
he came to me, I soon made a kind of hand-barrow to lay
them on, and Friday and I carried them up both together
upon it between us.

But when we got them to the outside of our wall, or
fortification, we were at a worse loss than before, for it
was impossible to get them over, and I was resolved not
to break it down; so I set to work again, and Friday and
I, in about two hours' time, made a very handsome tent,
covered with old sails, and above that with boughs of trees,
being in the space without our outward fence, and between
that and the grove of young wood which I had planted;
and here we made them two beds of such things as I had,
viz., of good rice straw, with blankets laid upon it, to lie
on, and another to cover them, on each bed.

CHAPTER XIV

MY island was now peopled, and I thought myself very rich in subjects; and it was a merry reflection, which I frequently made, how like a king I looked. First of all, the whole country was my own mere property, so that I had an undoubted right of dominion. Secondly, my people were perfectly subjected; I was absolutely lord and lawgiver; they all owed their lives to me, and were ready to lay down their lives, if there had been occasion for it, for me. It was remarkable, too, I had but three subjects, and they were of three different religions: my man Friday was a Protestant, his father was a Pagan and a cannibal, and the Spaniard was a Papist. However, I allowed liberty of conscience throughout my dominion. But this is by the way.

As soon as I had secured my two weak rescued prisoners, and given them shelter, and a place to rest them upon, I began to think of making some provisions for them; and the first thing I did, I ordered Friday to take a yearling goat, betwixt a kid and a goat, out of my particular flock, to be killed; then I cut off the hinder quarter, and chopping it into small pieces, I set Friday to work to boiling and stewing, and made them a very good dish, I assure you, of flesh and broth, having put some barley and rice also into the broth; and as I cooked it without doors, for I made no fire within my inner wall, so I carried it all into the new tent, and having set a table there for them, I sat down, and ate my own dinner also with them, and, as well as I could, cheered them and encouraged them. Friday was my interpreter, especially to his father, and, indeed, to the Spaniard too; for the Spaniard spoke the language of the savages pretty well.

After we had dined, or rather supped, I ordered Friday to take one of the canoes and go and fetch our muskets and other firearms, which, for want of time, we had left upon the place of battle; and, the next day, I ordered him to go and bury the dead bodies of the savages, which lay open to the sun and would presently be offensive. I also ordered him to bury the horrid remains of their barbarous feast, which I could not think of doing myself; nay, I could not bear to see them, if I went that way; all which he punctually performed, and defaced the very appearance of the savages being there; so that when I went again, I could scarce know where it was, otherwise than by the corner of the wood pointing to the place.

I then began to enter into a little conversation with my two new subjects; and, first, I set Friday to inquire of his father what he thought of the escape of the savages in that canoe, and whether we might expect a return of them, with a power too great for us to resist. His first opinion was, that the savages in the boat never could live out the storm which blew that night they went off, but must, of necessity, be drowned, or driven south to those other shores, where they were as sure to be devoured as they were to be drowned if they were cast away; but, as to what they would do if they came safe on shore, he said he knew not; but it was his opinion that they were so dreadfully frightened with the manner of their being attacked, the noise, and the fire, that he believed they would tell the people they were all killed by thunder and lightning, not by the hand of men; and that the two which appeared, viz., Friday and I, were two heavenly spirits, or furies, come down to destroy them, and not men with weapons. This he said he knew because he heard them all cry out so, in their language, one to another; for it was impossible for them to conceive that a man could dart fire, and speak thunder, and kill at a distance without lifting up the hand as was done now; and this old savage was in the right; for, as I understood since, by other hands, the savages never attempted to go over to the island afterwards; they were so terrified with the accounts given by those four men (for it seems they did escape the sea), that they believed whoever went to that enchanted island would be destroyed with fire from the gods. This, however, I knew not, and therefore was under continual apprehension for a good while, and kept always upon my guard, I and all my army; for, as we were now four of us, I would have ventured upon a hundred of them, fairly in the open field, at any time.

In a little time, however, no more canoes appearing, the fear of their coming wore off; and I began to take my former thoughts of a voyage to the main into consideration; being likewise assured by Friday's father that I might depend upon good usage from their nation, on his account, if I would go. But my thoughts were a little suspended when I had a serious discourse with the Spaniard, and when I understood that there were sixteen more of his countrymen and Portuguese, who, having been cast away and made their escape to that side, lived there at peace, indeed, with the savages, but were very sore put to it for necessaries, and, indeed, for life. I asked him all the particulars of their voyage, and found they were a Spanish ship, bound from the Rio de la Plata to the Havanna, being directed to leave their loading there, which was chiefly hides and silver, and to bring back what European goods they could meet with there; that they had five Portuguese seamen on board, whom they took out of another wreck; that five of their own men were drowned, when first the ship was lost, and that these escaped through infinite danger and hazards, and arrived, almost starved, on the cannibal coast, where they expected to have been devoured every moment. He told me they had some arms with them, but they were perfectly useless, for that they had neither powder nor ball, the washing of the sea having spoiled all their powder but a little, which they used, at their first landing, to provide themselves with food.

I asked him what he thought would become of them there, and if they had formed no design of making any escape. He said they had many consultations about it; but that having neither vessel, nor tools to build one, nor provisions of any kind, their councils always ended in tears and despair. I asked him how he thought they would receive a proposal from me, which might tend towards an escape; and whether, if they were all here, it might not be done. I told him with freedom, I feared mostly their treachery and ill-usage of me, if I put my life in their hands; for that gratitude was no inherent virtue in the nature of man, nor did men always square their dealings by the obligations they had received so much as they did by the advantages they expected. I told him it would be very hard that I should be the instrument of their deliverance, and that they should afterwards make me their prisoner in New Spain, where an Englishman was certain to be made a sacrifice, what necessity, or what accident soever brought him thither; and that I had rather be delivered up to the savages, and be devoured alive, than fall into the merciless claws of the priests, and be carried into the Inquisition. I added that, otherwise, I was persuaded, if they were all here, we might, with so many hands, build a bark large enough to carry us all away, either to the Brazils southward, or to the islands or Spanish coast northward; but that if, in requital, they should, when I had put weapons into their hands, carry me by force among their own people, I might be ill used for my kindness to them, and make my case worse than it was before.

He answered, with a great deal of candour and ingenuousness, that their condition was so miserable, and that they were so sensible of it, that he believed they would abhor the thought of using any man unkindly that should contribute to their deliverance; and that, if I pleased, he would go to them, with the old man, and discourse with them about it and return again, and bring me their answer:

that he would make conditions with them upon their solemn oath, that they should be absolutely under my direction, as their commander and captain; and they should swear upon the holy sacrament and gospel, to be true to me, and go to such Christian country as I should agree to, and no other; and to be directed wholly and absolutely by my orders, till they were landed safely in such country as I intended; and that he would bring a contract from them, under their hands, for that purpose. Then he told me he would first swear to me himself, that he would never stir from me as long as he lived, till I gave him orders; and that he would take my side to the last drop of his blood, if there should happen the least breach of faith among his countrymen. He told me they were all of them very civil, honest men, and they were under the greatest distress imaginable, having neither weapons nor clothes, nor any food, but at the mercy and discretion of the savages; out of all hopes of ever returning to their own country; and that he was sure, if I would undertake their relief, they would live and die by me.

Upon these assurances, I resolved to venture to relieve them, if possible, and to send the old savage and this Spaniard over to them to treat. But when we had got all things in readiness to go, the Spaniard himself started an objection, which had so much prudence in it on one hand, and so much sincerity on the other hand, that I could not but be very well satisfied in it; and, by his advice, put off the deliverance of his comrades for at least half a year. The case was thus: he had been with us now about a month, during which time I had let him see in what manner I had provided, with the assistance of Providence, for my support; and he saw evidently what stock of corn and rice I had laid up; which, though it was more than sufficient for myself, yet it was not sufficient, without good husbandry, for my family, now it was increased to four; but much less would it be sufficient if his countrymen, who were, as he said, fourteen, still alive, should come over; and, least of all would it be sufficient to victual our vessel, if we should build one, for a voyage to any of the Christian colonies of America; so he told me he thought it would be more advisable to let him and the other two dig and cultivate some more land, as much as I could spare seed to sow, and that we should wait another harvest, that we might have a supply of corn for his countrymen, when they should come; for want might be a temptation to them to disagree, or not to think themselves delivered, otherwise than out of one difficulty into another. "You know," says he, "the children of Israel, though they rejoiced at first for their being delivered out of Egypt, yet rebelled even against God himself, that delivered them, when they came to want bread in the wilderness."

His caution was so seasonable, and his advice so good, that I could not but be very well pleased with his proposal, as well as I was satisfied with his fidelity; so we fell to digging, all four of us, as well as the wooden tools we were furnished with permitted; and in about a month's time, by the end of which it was seed-time, we had got as much land cured and trimmed up, as we sowed two-and-twenty bushels of barley on, and sixteen jars of rice, which was, in short, all the seed we had to spare; indeed, we left ourselves barely sufficient for our own food for the six months that we had to expect our crop; that is to say, reckoning from the time we set our seed aside for sowing; for it is not to be supposed it is six months in the ground in that country.

Having now society enough, and our number being sufficient to put us out of fear of the savages, if they had come, unless their number had been very great, we went freely all over the island, whenever we found occasion; and as we had our escape or deliverance upon our thoughts, it was impossible, at least for me, to have the means of it out of mind. For this purpose, I marked out several trees which I thought fit for our work, and I set Friday and his father to cut them down; and then I caused the Spaniard, to whom I imparted my thoughts on that affair, to oversee and direct their work. I showed them with what indefatigable pains I had hewed a large tree into single planks, and I caused them to do the like, till they had made about a dozen large planks of good oak, near two feet broad, thirty-five feet long, and from two inches to four inches thick; what prodigious labour it took up, any one may imagine.

At the same time, I contrived to increase my little stock of tame goats as much as I could; and for this purpose I made Friday and the Spaniard go out one day, and myself with Friday the next day (for we took our turns), and by this means we got about twenty young kids to breed up with the rest; for whenever we shot the dam, we saved the kids and added them to our flock. But, above all, the season for curing the grapes coming on, I caused such a prodigious quantity to be hung up in the sun, that, I believe, had we been at Alicant, where the raisins of the sun are cured, we could have filled sixty or eighty barrels; and these, with our bread, formed a great part of our food— very good living, too, I assure you, for they are exceedingly nourishing.

It was now harvest, and our crop in good order; it was not the most plentiful increase I had seen in the island, but, however, it was enough to answer our end; for, from twenty-two bushels of barley, we brought in and thrashed out above two hundred and twenty bushels; and the like in proportion of the rice; which was store enough for our food to the next harvest, though all the sixteen Spaniards had been on shore with me; or, if we had been ready for a voyage, it would very plentifully have victualed our ship to have carried us to any part of the world, that is to say, of America. When we had thus housed and secured our magazine of corn, we fell to work to make more wicker-work, viz., great baskets, in which we kept it; and the Spaniard was very handy and dexterous at this part, and often blamed me that I did not make some things for defence of this kind of work; but I saw no need of it.

And now, having a full supply of food for all the guests expected, I gave the Spaniard leave to go over the main, to see what he could do with those he had left behind him there. I gave him a strict charge not to bring any man with him who would not first swear, in the presence of himself and the old savage, that he would no way injure, fight with, or attack the person he should find in the island, who was so kind as to send for them in order to their deliverance; but that they would stand by him and defend him against all such attempts, and wherever they went, would be entirely under and subjected to his command; and that this should be put in writing, and signed with their hands. How they were to have done this, when I knew they had neither pen nor ink—that, indeed, was a question which we never asked. Under these instructions, the Spaniard and the old savage, the father of Friday, went away in one of the canoes which they might be said to have come in, or rather were brought in, when they came as prisoners to be devoured by the savages. I gave each of them a musket, with a firelock on it, and about eight charges of powder and ball, charging them to be very good husbands of both, and not to use either of them but upon urgent occasion.

This was a cheerful work, being the first measures used by me, in view of my deliverance, for now twenty-seven years and some days. I gave them provisions of bread, and of dried grapes, sufficient for themselves for many days, and sufficient for all the Spaniards for about eight days' time; and wishing them a good voyage, I saw them go, agreeing with them about a signal they should hang out at their return, by which I should know them again, when they came back, at a distance, before they came on shore. They went away, with a fair gale, on the day the moon was at full, by my account, in the month of October; but as for an exact reckoning of days, after I had once lost it,

I could never recover it again; nor had I kept even the number of years so punctually as to be sure I was right, though, as it proved, when I afterwards examined my account, I found I had kept a true reckoning of years.

It was no less than eight days I had waited for them, when a strange and unforeseen accident intervened, of which the like has not, perhaps, been heard of in history. I was fast asleep in my hutch one morning, when my man Friday came running in to me, and called aloud, "Master, master, they are come, they are come!" I jumped up, and, regardless of danger, I went out as soon as I could get my clothes on, through my little grove, which, by the way, was by this time grown to be a very thick wood; I say, regardless of danger, I went without my arms, which was not my custom to do: but I was surprised, when, turning my eyes to the sea, I presently saw a boat at about a league and a half distance, standing in for the shore, with a shoulder-of-mutton sail, as they call it, and the wind blowing pretty fair to bring them in: also I observed presently, that they did not come from that side which the shore lay on, but from the southernmost end of the island. Upon this I called Friday in, and bade him lie close, for these were not the people we looked for, and that we might not know yet whether they were friends or enemies. In the next place, I went in to fetch my perspective-glass, to see what I could make of them; and, having taken the ladder out, I climbed up to the top of the hill, as I used to do when I was apprehensive of anything, and to take my view plainer, without being discovered. I had scarce set my foot upon the hill, when my eye plainly discovered a ship lying at an anchor, at about two leagues and a half distance from me, S.S.E., but not above a league and a half from the shore. By my observation, it appeared plainly to be an English ship, and the boat appeared to be an English longboat.

I cannot express the confusion I was in, though the joy of seeing a ship, and one that I had reason to believe was manned by my own countrymen, and consequently friends, was such as I cannot describe; but yet I had some secret doubts hung about me—I cannot tell from whence they came—bidding me keep upon my guard. In the first place, it occurred to me to consider what business an English ship could have in that part of the world, since it was not the way to or from any part of the world where the English had any traffic; and I knew there had been no storms to drive them in there, in distress; and that if they were really English, it was most probable that they were here upon no good designs; and that I had better continue as I was, than fall into the hands of thieves and murderers.

Let no man despise the secret hints and notices of danger which sometimes are given him when he may think there is no possibility of its being real. That such hints and notices are given us, I believe few that have made any observations of things can deny; that they are certain discoveries of an invisible world, and a converse of spirits, we cannot doubt; and if the tendency of them seems to be to warn us of danger, why should we not suppose they are from some friendly agent (whether supreme, or inferior and subordinate, is not the question), and that they are given for our good?

The present question abundantly confirms me in the justice of this reasoning; for had I not been made cautious by this secret admonition, come from whence it will, I had been undone inevitably, and in a far worse condition than before, as you will see presently. I had not kept myself long in this posture, till I saw the boat draw near the shore, as if they looked for a creek to thrust it in at, for convenience of landing; however, as they did not come quite far enough, they did not see the little inlet where I formerly landed my rafts, but ran their boat on shore upon the beach, at about half a mile from me; which was very happy for me; for otherwise they would have landed just at my door, as I may say, and would soon have beaten me out of my castle, and perhaps have plundered me of all I had. When they were on shore, I was fully satisfied they were Englishmen, at least most of them; one or two I thought were Dutch, but it did not prove so; there were in all eleven men, whereof three of them I found were un-armed, and, as I thought, bound; and when the first four or five of them were jumped on shore, they took those three out of the boat, as prisoners: one of the three I could perceive using the most passionate gestures of entreaty, affliction, and despair, even to a kind of extravagance; the other two, I could perceive, lifted up their hands some-times, and appeared concerned, indeed, but not to such a degree as the first. I was perfectly confounded at the sight, and knew not what the meaning of it should be. Friday called out to me in English, as well as he could, "O master! you see English mans eat prisoner as well as savage mans." "Why, Friday," says I, "do you think they are going to eat them, then?" "Yes," says Friday, "they will eat them." "No, no," says I, "Friday; I am afraid they will murder them, indeed; but you may be sure they will not eat them."

All this while I had no thought of what the matter really was, but stood trembling with the horror of the sight, expecting every moment when the three prisoners should be killed; nay, once I saw one of the villains lift up his arm with a great cutlass, as the seamen call it, or sword, to strike one of the poor men; and I expected to see him fall every moment; at which all the blood in my body seemed to run chill in my veins. I wished heartily now for my Spaniard, and the savage that was gone with him, or that I had any way to have come undiscovered within shot of them, that I might have secured the three men, for I saw no fire-arms they had among them; but it fell out to my mind another way. After I had observed the outrageous usage of the three men by the insolent seamen, I observed the fellows run scattering about the land, as if they wanted to see the country. I observed also that the three other men had liberty to go where they pleased;

but they sat down all three upon the ground, very pensive, and looked like men in despair. This put me in mind of the first time when I came on shore, and began to look about me; how I gave myself over for lost; how wildly I looked round me; what dreadful apprehensions I had; and how I lodged in the tree all night, for fear of being devoured by wild beasts. As I knew nothing that night of the supply I was to receive by the providential driving of the ship nearer the land by the storms and tide, by which I have since been so long nourished and supported; so these three poor desolate men knew nothing how certain of deliverance and supply they were, how near it was to them, and how effectually and really they were in a condition of safety, at the same time they thought themselves lost, and their case desperate. So little do we see before us in the world, and so much reason have we to depend cheerfully upon the great Maker of the world, that he does not leave his creatures so absolutely destitute, but that, in the worst circumstances, they have always something to be thankful for, and sometimes are nearer their deliverance than they imagine; nay, are even brought to their deliverance by the means by which they seem to be brought to their destruction.

CHAPTER XV

IT was just at the top of high water when these people came on shore; and while they rambled about to see what kind of a place they were in, they had carelessly stayed till the tide was spent, and the water was ebbed considerably away, leaving their boat aground. They had left two men in the boat who, as I found afterwards, having drunk a little too much brandy, fell asleep; however, one of them waking a little sooner than the other, and finding the boat too fast aground for him to stir it, hallooed out for the rest, who were straggling about; upon which they all soon came to the boat; but it was past all their strength to launch her, the boat being very heavy, and the shore on that side being a soft oozy sand, almost like a quicksand. In this condition, like true seamen, who are, perhaps, the least of all mankind given to forethought, they gave it over, and away they strolled about the country again; and I heard one of them say aloud to another, calling them off from the boat, "Why, let her alone, Jack, can't you? she'll float next tide"; by which I was fully confirmed in the main inquiry of what countrymen they were. All this while I kept myself close, not once daring to stir out of my castle, any farther than to my place of observation, near the top of the hill; and very glad I was to think how well it was fortified. I knew it was no less than ten hours before the boat could float again, and by that time it would be dark, and I might be at more liberty to see their motions, and to hear their discourse, if they had any. In the meantime, I fitted myself up for a battle, as before, though with more caution, knowing I had to do with another kind of enemy than I had at first. I ordered Friday, also, whom I had made an excellent marksman with his gun, to load himself with arms. I took myself two fowling-pieces, and I gave him three muskets. My figure, indeed, was very fierce; I had my formidable goatskin coat on, with the great cap I have mentioned, a naked sword, two pistols in my belt, and a gun upon each shoulder.

It was my design, as I said above, not to have made any attempt till it was dark; but about two o'clock, being the heat of the day, I found, in short, they were all gone straggling into the woods, and, as I thought, were all laid down to sleep. The three poor distressed men, too anxious for their condition to get any sleep, had, however, sat down under the shelter of a great tree, at about a quarter of a mile from me, and, as I thought, out of sight of any of the rest. Upon this I resolved to discover myself to them, and learn something of their condition; immediately I marched as above, my man Friday at a good distance behind me, as formidable for his arms as I, but not making quite so staring a spectre-like figure as I did. I came as near them undiscovered as I could, and then, before any of them saw me, I called aloud to them in Spanish, "What are ye, gentlemen?" They started up at the noise, but were ten times more confounded when they saw me, and the uncouth figure that I made. They made no answer at all, but I thought I perceived them just going to fly from me, when I spoke to them in English: "Gentlemen," said I, "do not be surprised at me: perhaps you may have a friend near, when you did not expect it." "He must be sent directly from heaven, then," said one of them very gravely to me, and pulling off his hat at the same time; "for our condition is past the help of man." "All help is from heaven, sir," said I: "but can you put a stranger in the way to help you? for you seem to be in some great distress. I saw you when you landed; and when you seemed to make application to the brutes that came with you, I saw one of them lift up his sword to kill you."

The poor man, with tears running down his face, and trembling like one greatly astonished, returned, "Am I

talking to God, or man? Is it a real man, or an angel?"
"Be in no fear about that, sir," said I; "if God had sent
an angel to relieve you, he would have come better clothed,
and armed after another manner than you see me in;
pray lay aside your fears; I am a man, an Englishman,
and disposed to assist you; you see I have one servant
only; we have arms and ammunition; tell us freely, can
we serve you? What is your case?" "Our case, sir," said
he, "is too long to tell you, while our murderers are so
near us; but, in short, sir, I was commander of that ship;
my men have mutinied against me; they have been hardly
prevailed on not to murder me, and, at last, have set me
on shore in this desolate place, with these two men with
me—one my mate, the other a passenger, where we expected
to perish, believing the place to be uninhabited, and know
not yet what to think of it." "Where are these brutes,
your enemies?" said I; "do you know where they are
gone?" "There they lie, sir," said he, pointing to a thicket
of trees; "my heart trembles for fear they have seen us,
and heard you speak; if they have, they will certainly
murder us all." "Have they any firearms?" said I. He
answered, "They had only two pieces, one of which they
left in the boat." "Well, then," said I, "leave the rest to
me; I see they are all asleep; it is an easy thing to kill them
all; but shall we rather take them prisoners?" He told
me there were two desperate villains among them that it
was scarce safe to show any mercy to; but if they were
secured, he believed all the rest would return to their duty.
I asked him which they were. He told me he could not
at that distance distinguish them, but he would obey my
orders in anything I would direct. "Well," says I, "let
us retreat out of their view of hearing, lest they awake,
and we will resolve further." So they willingly went back
with me, till the woods covered us from them.

"Look you, sir," said I; "if I venture upon your deliverance, are you willing to make two conditions with me?"
He anticipated my proposals by telling me that both he

and the ship, if recovered, should be wholly directed and commanded by me in everything; and if the ship was not recovered, he would live and die with me in what part of the world soever I would send him; and the two other men said the same. "Well," said I, "my conditions are but two; first,—that while you stay on this island with me, you will not pretend to any authority here; and if I put arms in your hands, you will, upon all occasions, give them up to me, and do no prejudice to me or mine upon this island, and in the meantime be governed by my orders; secondly,—that if the ship is or may be recovered, you will carry me and my man to England passage free."

He gave me all the assurance that the invention and faith of a man could devise that he would comply with these most reasonable demands, and besides would owe his life to me, and acknowledge it upon all occasions as long as he lived. "Well, then," said I, "here are three muskets for you, with powder and ball; tell me next what you think is proper to be done." He showed all the testimony of his gratitude that he was able, but offered to be wholly guided by me. I told him I thought it was hard venturing anything; but the best method I could think of was to fire on them at once as they lay, and if any were not killed at the first volley, and offered to submit, we might save them, and so put it wholly upon God's providence to direct the shot. He said, very modestly, that he was loath to kill them, if he could help it; but that those two were incorrigible villains, and had been the authors of all the mutiny in the ship, and if they escaped, we should be undone still, for they would go on board and bring the whole ship's company, and destroy us all. "Well, then," says I, "necessity legitimates my advice, for it is the only way to save our lives." However, seeing him still cautious of shedding blood, I told him they should go themselves, and manage as they found convenient.

In the middle of this discourse we heard some of them awake, and soon after we saw two of them on their feet.

I asked him if either of them were the men who he had said were the heads of the mutiny? He said, "No." "Well, then," said I, "you may let them escape; and Providence seems to have awakened them on purpose to save themselves. Now," says I, "if the rest escape you, it is your fault." Animated with this, he took the musket I had given him in his hand, and a pistol in his belt, and his two comrades with him, with each man a piece in his hand; the two men who were with him, going first, made some noise, at which one of the seamen, who was awake, turned about, and seeing them coming, cried out to the rest; but it was too late then, for the moment he cried out they fired—I mean the two men, the captain wisely reserving his own piece. They had so well aimed their shot at the men they knew, that one of them was killed on the spot, and the other very much wounded; but not being dead, he started up on his feet, and called eagerly for help to the other; but the captain, stepping to him, told him it was too late to cry for help, he should call upon God to forgive his villainy, and with that word knocked him down with the stock of his musket, so that he never spoke more: there were three more in the company, and one of them was slightly wounded. By this time I was come; and when they saw their danger, and that it was in vain to resist, they begged for mercy. The captain told them he would spare their lives if they would give him an assurance of their abhorrence of the treachery they had been guilty of, and would swear to be faithful to him in recovering the ship, and afterwards in carrying her back to Jamaica, from whence they came. They gave him all the protestations of their sincerity that could be desired; and he was willing to believe them, and spare their lives, which I was not against, only I obliged him to keep them bound hand and foot while they were upon the island.

While this was doing, I sent Friday with the captain's mate to the boat, with orders to secure her, and bring away the oars and sails, which they did; and by and by three straggling men, that were (happily for them) separated from the rest, came back upon hearing the guns fired; and seeing the captain, who before was their prisoner, now their conqueror, they submitted to be bound also; and so our victory was complete.

It now remained that the captain and I should inquire into one another's circumstances. I began first, and told him my whole history, which he heard with an attention even to amazement—and particularly at the wonderful manner of my being furnished with provisions and ammunition; and, indeed, as my story is a whole collection of wonders, it affected him deeply.

But when he reflected from thence upon himself, and how I seemed to have been preserved there on purpose to save his life, the tears ran down his face, and he could not speak a word more. After this communication was at an end, I carried him and his two men into my apartments, leading them in just where I came out, viz., at the top of the house, where I refreshed him with such provision as I had, and showed them all the contrivances I had made during my long, long inhabiting that place.

All I showed them, all I said to them, was perfectly amazing; above all, the captain admired my fortification, and how perfectly I had concealed my retreat with a grove of trees, which, having been now planted near twenty years, and the trees growing much faster than in England, was become a little wood, so thick that it was impassable in any part of it but at that one side where I had reserved my little winding passage into it. I told him this was my castle and my residence, but that I had a seat in the country, as most princes have, whither I could retreat upon occasion, and I would show him that, too, another time; but at present our business was to consider how to recover the ship. He agreed with me as to that, but told me he was perfectly at a loss what measures to take, for that there were still six-and-twenty hands on board, who, having entered in a cursed conspiracy, by which they all forfeited their lives to the law, would be hardened in it now by desperation, and would carry it on, knowing that if they were subdued they should be brought to the gallows as soon as they came to England, or to any of the English colonies, and that, therefore, there would be no attacking them with so small a number as we were.

I mused for some time upon what he had said, and found it was a very rational conclusion, and that therefore something was to be resolved on very speedily, as well to draw the men on board into some snare for their surprise, as to prevent their landing upon us, and destroying us. Upon this, it presently occurred to me that in a little while the ship's crew, wondering what was become of their comrades and of the boat, would certainly come on shore in their other boat to look for them, and that then, perhaps, they might come armed, and be too strong for us: this he allowed to be rational. Upon this, I told him the first thing we had to do was to stave the boat, which lay upon the beach, so that they might not carry her off, and taking everything out of her, leave her so far useless as not to be fit to swim. Accordingly we went on board; took the arms which were left on board out of her, and whatever else we found there— which was a bottle of brandy, and another of rum, a few biscuit-cakes, a horn of powder, and a great lump of sugar in a piece of canvas (the sugar was five or six pounds); all which was very welcome to me, especially the brandy and sugar, of which I had had none left for many years.

When we had carried all these things on shore (the oars, mast, sail, and rudder of the boat were carried away before), we knocked a great hole in her bottom, that if they had come strong enough to master us, yet they could not carry off the boat. Indeed, it was not much in my thoughts that we could be able to recover the ship; but my view was, that if they went away without the boat, I did not much question to make her again fit to carry us to the Leeward Islands, and call upon our friends the Spaniards in my way, for I had them still in my thoughts.

While we were thus preparing our designs, and had first, by main strength, heaved the boat upon the beach, so high that the tide would not float her off at high-water mark, and besides had broken a hole in her bottom too big to be quickly stopped, and were sat down musing what we should do, we heard the ship fire a gun, and make a waft with her ensign as a signal for the boat to come on board: but no boat stirred; and they fired several times, making other signals for the boat. At last, when all their signals and firing proved fruitless, and they found the boat did not stir, we saw them, by the help of my glasses, hoist another boat out, and row towards the shore; and we found, as they approached, that there were no less than ten men in her, and that they had firearms with them.

As the ship lay almost two leagues from the shore, we had a full view of them as they came, and a plain sight even of their faces; because the tide having set them a little to the east of the other boat, they rowed up under shore, to come to the same place where the other had landed, and where the boat lay; by this means, I say, we had a full view of them, and the captain knew the persons and characters of all the men in the boat, of whom, he said, there were three very honest fellows, who, he was sure, were led into this conspiracy by the rest, being overpowered and frightened but that as for the boatswain, who it seems was the chief officer among them, and all the rest, they were as outrageous as any of the ship's crew, and were no doubt made desperate in their new enterprise; and terribly apprehensive was he that they would be too powerful for us. I smiled at him, and told him that men in our circumstances were past the operation of fear; that seeing almost every condition that could be was better than that which we were supposed to be in, we ought to expect that the consequence, whether death or life, would be sure to be a deliverance. I asked him what he thought of the circumstances of my life, and whether a deliverance were not worth venturing for. "And where, sir," said I, "is your belief of my being preserved here on purpose to save your life, which elevated you a little while ago? For my part," said I, "there seems to be but one thing amiss in all the prospect of it." "What is that?" says he. "Why," said I, "it is, that as you say there are three or four honest fellows among them, which should be spared, had they been all of the wicked part of the crew, I should have thought God's providence had singled them out to deliver them into your hands; for depend upon it, every man that comes ashore is our own, and shall die or live as they behave to us." As I spoke this with a raised voice and cheerful countenance, I found it greatly encouraged him; so we set vigorously to our business.

We had, upon the first appearance of the boat coming from the ship, considered of separating our prisoners; and had, indeed, secured them effectually. Two of them, of whom the captain was less assured than ordinary, I sent with Friday and one of the three delivered men to my cave, where they were remote enough and out of danger of being heard or discovered, or of finding their way out of the woods, if they could have delivered themselves; here they left them bound, but gave them provisions; and promised them, if they continued there quietly, to give them their liberty in a day or two; but that if they attempted their escape, they should be put to death without mercy. They promised faithfully to bear their confinement with patience, and were very thankful that they had such good usage as to have provisions and a light left them: for Friday gave them candles (such as we made ourselves) for their comfort; and they did not know but that he stood sentinel over them at the entrance.

The other prisoners had better usage; two of them were kept pinioned, indeed, because the captain was not free to trust them; but the other two were taken into my service, upon the captain's recommendation, and upon their solemnly engaging to live and die with us; so with them and the three honest men we were seven men, well armed; and I made no doubt we should be able to deal well enough with the ten that were coming, considering that the captain had said there were three or four honest men among them also. As soon as they got to the place where their other boat lay, they ran their boat into the beach and came all on shore, hauling the boat up after them, which I was glad to see, for I was afraid they would rather have left the boat at anchor some distance from the shore, with some hands in her, to guard her, and so we should not be able to seize the boat. Being on shore, the first thing they did, they ran all to their other boat; and it was easy to see they were under a great surprise to find her stripped, as above, of all that was in her, and a great hole in her bottom. After they had mused awhile upon this, they set up two or three great shouts, hallooing with all their might, to try if they could make their companions hear; but all was to no purpose: then they came all close in a ring, and fired a volley of their small-arms, which, indeed, we heard, and the echoes made the woods ring; but it was all one; those in the cave, we were sure, could not hear; and those in our keeping, though they heard it well enough, yet durst give no answer to them. They were so astonished at the surprise of this, that, as they told us afterwards, they resolved to go all on board again to their ship, and let them know that the men were all murdered, and the long boat staved; accordingly, they immediately launched their boat again, and got all of them on board.

The captain was terribly amazed, and even confounded, at this, believing they would go on board the ship again, and set sail, giving their comrades over for lost, and so he should still lose the ship, which he was in hopes we should have recovered; but he was quickly as much frightened the other way.

They had not been long put off with the boat, when we perceived them all coming on shore again; but with this new measure in their conduct, which it seems they consulted together upon, viz., to leave three men in the boat, and the rest to go on shore, and go up into the country to look for their fellows. This was a great disappointment to us, for now we were at a loss what to do, as our seizing those seven men on shore would be no advantage to us if we let the boat escape; because they would row away to the ship, and then the rest of them would be sure to weigh and set sail, and so our recovering the ship would be lost. However, we had no remedy but to wait and see what the issue of things might present. The seven men came on shore, and the three who remained in the boat put her off to a good distance from the shore, and came to an anchor to wait for them; so that it was impossible for us to come at them in the boat. Those that came on shore kept close together, marching towards the top of the little hill under which my habitation lay; and we could see them plainly, though they could not perceive us. We should have been very glad if they would have come nearer to us, so that we might have fired at them, or that they would have gone farther off, that we might come abroad. But when they were come to the brow of the hill where they could see a great way into the valleys and woods, which lay towards the northeast part, and where the island lay the lowest, they shouted and hallooed till they were weary: and not caring, it seems, to venture far from the shore, nor far from one another, they sat down together, under a tree, to consider of it. Had they thought fit to have gone to sleep there as the other party of them had done, they had done the job for us; but they were too full of apprehensions of danger to venture to go to sleep, though they could not tell what the danger was they had to fear.

The captain made a very just proposal to me upon this consultation of theirs, viz., that perhaps they would all fire a volley again, to endeavour to make their fellows hear, and that we should all sally upon them just at the juncture when their pieces were all discharged, and they would certainly yield, and we should have them without bloodshed. I liked this proposal, provided it was done while we were near enough to come up to them before they could load their pieces again. But this event did not happen; and we lay still a long time, very irresolute what course to take. At length, I told them there would be nothing done, in my opinion, till night; and then if they did not return to the boat, perhaps we might find a way to get between them and the shore, and so might use some stratagem with them in the boat to get them on shore. We waited a great while, though very impatient for their removing; and were very uneasy, when, after long consultation, we saw them all start up, and march down towards the sea: it seems they had such dreadful apprehensions of the danger of the place, that they resolved to go on board the ship again, give their companions over for lost, and so go on with their intended voyage with the ship.

As soon as I perceived them go towards the shore, I imagined it to be as it really was, that they had given over their search, and were for going back again; and the captain, as soon as I told him my thoughts, was ready to sink at the apprehensions of it: but I presently thought of a stratagem to fetch them back again, which answered my end to a tittle. I ordered Friday and the captain's mate to go over the little creek westward, towards the place where the savages came on shore when Friday was rescued, and so soon as they came to a little rising ground, at about half a mile distance, I bade them halloo out, as loud as they could, and wait till they found the seamen heard them; that as soon as ever they heard the seamen answer them, they should return it again; and then keeping out of sight, take a round, always answering when the others hallooed, to draw them as far into the island, and among the woods as possible, and then wheel about again to me by such ways as I directed.

They were just going into the boat when Friday and the mate hallooed; and they presently heard them, and, answering, ran along the shore westwards, towards the voice they heard, when they were presently stopped by the creek, where, the water being up, they could not get over, and called for the boat to come up and set them over; as, indeed, I expected.

When they had set themselves over, I observed that the boat being gone up a good way into the creek, and, as it were, in a harbour within the land they took one of the three men out of her, to go along with them, and left only two in the boat, having fastened her to the stump of a little tree on the shore. This was what I wished for; and immediately leaving Friday and the captain's mate to their business, I took the rest with me, and crossing the creek out of their sight, we surprised the two men before they were aware; one of them lying on the shore, and the other being in the boat. The fellow on shore was between sleeping and waking, and going to start up; the captain, who was foremost, ran in upon him, and knocked him down; and then called out to him in the boat to yield, or he was a dead man. There needed very few arguments to persuade a single man to yield, when he saw five men upon him, and his comrade knocked down: besides, this was, it seems, one of the three who were not so hearty in the mutiny as the rest of the crew; and, therefore, was easily persuaded not only to yield, but afterwards to join very sincerely with us. In the meantime, Friday and the captain's mate so well managed their business with the rest, that they drew them, by hallooing and answering, from one hill to another, and from one wood to another, till they not only heartily tired them, but left them where they could not reach back to the boat before it was dark; and indeed, they were heartily tired themselves also, by the time they came back to us.

We had nothing now to do but to watch for them in the dark, and to fall upon them, so as to make sure work with them. It was several hours after Friday came back to me before they came back to their boat; and we could hear the foremost of them, long before they came quite up, calling to those behind to come along; and could also hear them answer, and complain how lame and tired they were, and not able to come any faster: which was very welcome news to us. At length they came up to the boat: but it is impossible to express their confusion when they found the boat fast aground in the creek, the tide ebbed out, and their two men gone. We could hear them call to one another in a most lamentable manner telling one another they were got into an enchanted island; that either there were inhabitants in it, and they should all be murdered, or else there were devils and spirits in it, and they should be all carried away and devoured. They hallooed again, and called their two comrades by their names a great many times; but no answer. After some time, we could see them, by the little light there was, run about, wringing their hands like men in despair, and sometimes they would go and sit down in the boat to rest themselves: then come ashore again, and walk about again, and so the same thing over again. My men would fain have had me give them leave to fall upon them at once in the dark; but I was willing to take them at some advantage, so as to spare them, and kill as few of them as I could; and especially I was unwilling to hazard the killing any of our men, knowing the others were very well armed. I resolved to wait, to see if they did not separate; and therefore, to make sure of them, I drew my ambuscade nearer, and ordered Friday and the captain to creep upon their hands and feet, as close to the ground as they could, that they might not be discovered, and get as near them as they could possibly, before they offered to fire.

They had not been long in that posture, when the boats-swain, who was the principal ringleader of the mutiny, and had now shown himself the most dejected and dispirited of all the rest, came walking towards them, with two more of the crew; the captain was so eager at having the principal rogue so much in his power, that he could hardly have patience to let him come so near as to be sure of him, for they only heard his tongue before; but when they came nearer, the captain and Friday, starting up on their feet,

let fly at them. The boatswain was killed upon the spot:
the next man was shot in the body, and fell just by him,
though he did not die till an hour or two after; and the
third ran for it. At the noise of the fire, I immediately
advanced with my whole army, which was now eight men;
viz., myself, generalissimo; Friday, my lieutenant-general;
the captain and his two men, and the three prisoners of
war, whom we had trusted with arms. We came upon them,
indeed, in the dark, so that they could not see our number;
and I made the man they had left in the boat, who was now
one of us, call them by name, to try if I could bring them to
a parley, and so perhaps reduce them to terms; which fell
out just as we had desired; for, indeed, it was easy to think,
as their condition then was, they would be very willing
to capitulate. So he calls out as loud as he could to one
of them, "Tom Smith! Tom Smith!" Tom Smith answered
immediately, "Who's that? Robinson?" for it seems he
knew the voice. The other answered, "Ay, ay; for God's
sake, Tom Smith, throw down your arms and yield, or
you are all dead men this moment." "Who must we yield
to? Where are they?" says Smith again. "Here they are,"
says he; "here's our captain and fifty men with him, have
been hunting you these two hours; the boatswain is killed,
Will Frye is wounded, and I am a prisoner; and if you do
not yield, you are all lost." "Will they give us quarter
then?" says Tom Smith, "and we will yield." "I'll go and
ask, if you promise to yield," said Robinson, so he asked
the captain; and the captain himself then calls out, "You,
Smith, you know my voice; if you lay down your arms
immediately, and submit, you shall have your lives, all but
Will Atkins."

Upon this Will Atkins cried out, "For God's sake,
captain, give me quarter; what have I done? They have
been all as bad as I": which, by the way, was not true;
for, it seems, this Will Atkins was the first man that laid
hold of the captain, when they first mutinied, and used
him barbarously, in tying his hands, and giving him injurious

language. However, the captain told him he must lay down his arms at discretion, and trust to the governor's mercy: by which he meant me, for they all called me governor. In a word, they all laid down their arms, and begged their lives; and I sent the man that had parleyed with them, and two more, who bound them all; and then my great army of fifty men, which with those three, were in all but eight, came up and seized upon them, and upon their boat; only that I kept myself and one more out of sight, for reasons of state.

Our next work was to repair the boat and think of seizing the ship; and as for the captain, now he had leisure to parley with them, he expostulated with them upon the villainy of their practices with him, and upon the further wickedness of their design, and how certainly it must bring them to misery and distress in the end, and perhaps to the gallows. They all appeared very penitent, and begged hard for their lives. As for that, he told them they were none of his prisoners, but the commander's of the island; that they thought they had set him on shore in a barren, uninhabited island; but it had pleased God so to direct them, that it was inhabited, and that the governor was an Englishman; that he might hang them all there, if he pleased; but as he had given them all quarter, he supposed he would send them to England, to be dealt with there as justice required, except Atkins, whom he was commanded by the governor to advise to prepare for death, that he would be hanged in the morning.

Though this was all a fiction of his own, yet it had its desired effect; Atkins fell upon his knees, to beg the captain to intercede with the governor for his life; and all the rest begged of him, for God's sake, that they might not be sent to England.

It now occurred to me that the time of our deliverance was come, and that it would be a most easy thing to bring these fellows in to be hearty in getting possession of the ship; so I retired in the dark from them, that they might not see what kind of a governor they had, and called the captain to me; when I called, as at a good distance, one of the men was ordered to speak again, and say to the captain, "Captain, the commander calls for you"; and presently the captain replied, "Tell his Excellency, I am just coming." This more perfectly amazed them, and they all believed that the commander was just by, with his fifty men. Upon the captain coming to me I told him my project for seizing the ship, which he liked wonderfully well, and resolved to put it in execution next morning. But, in order to execute it with more art, and to be secure of success, I told him we must divide the prisoners, and that he should go and take Atkins, and two more of the worst of them, and send them pinioned to the cave where the others lay. This was committed to Friday and the two men who came on shore with the captain. They conveyed them to the cave as to a prison: and it was, indeed, a dismal place, especially to men in their condition. The others I ordered to my bower, as I called it, of which I have given a full description: and as it was fenced in, and they pinioned, the place was secure enough, considering they were upon their behaviour.

To these in the morning I sent the captain, who was to enter into a parley with them; in a word, to try them, and tell me whether he thought they might be trusted or not to go on board and surprise the ship. He talked to them of the injury done him, of the condition they were brought to, and that though the governor had given them quarter for their lives as to the present action, yet that if they were sent to England they would be all hanged in chains; but that if they would join in such an attempt as to recover the ship, he would have the governor's engagement for their pardon.

Any one may guess how readily such a proposal would be accepted by men in their condition; they fell down on their knees to the captain, and promised, with the deepest imprecations, that they would be faithful to him to the last drop, and that they should owe their lives to him, and would go with him all over the world; that they would own him for a father to them as long as they lived. "Well," says the captain, "I must go and tell the governor what you say, and see what I can do to bring him to consent to it." So he brought me an account of the temper he found them in, and that he verily believed they would be faithful. However, that we might be very secure, I told him he should go back again and choose out five of them, and tell them that they might see that he did not want men, that he would take out those five to be his assistants, and that the governor would keep the other two and the three that were sent prisoners to the castle (my cave), as hostages for the fidelity of those five; and that if they proved unfaithful in the execution, the five hostages should be hanged in chains alive on the shore. This looked severe, and convinced them that the governor was in earnest, however, they had no way left them but to accept it; and it was now the business of the prisoners, as much as of the captain, to persuade the other five to do their duty.

Our strength was now thus ordered for the expedition: first, the captain, his mate, and passenger; second, then the two prisoners of the first gang, to whom, having their character from the captain, I had given their liberty, and trusted them with arms; third, the other two whom I had kept till now in my bower pinioned, but, upon the captain's motion, had now released; fourth, these five released at last; so that they were twelve in all, besides five we kept prisoners in the cave for hostages.

I asked the captain if he was willing to venture with these hands on board the ship; for as for me and my man Friday, I did not think it was proper for us to stir, having seven men left behind; and it was employment enough for us to keep them asunder, and supply them with victuals. As to the five in the cave, I resolved to keep them fast, but Friday went in twice a day to them, to supply them with necessaries; and I made the other two carry provisions to a certain distance, where Friday was to take it.

When I showed myself to the two hostages, it was with the captain, who told them I was the person the governor had ordered to look after them; and that it was the governor's pleasure they should not stir anywhere but by my direction; that if they did, they would be fetched into the castle, and be laid in irons: so that as we never suffered them to see me as governor, I now appeared as another person, and spoke of the governor, the garrison, the castle, and the like, upon all occasions.

The captain now had no difficulty before him, but to furnish his two boats, stop the breach of one, and man them. He made his passenger captain of one, with four other men; and himself, his mate, and five more, went in the other; and they contrived their business very well, for they came up to the ship about midnight. As soon as they came within call of the ship, he made Robinson hail them, and tell them they had brought off the men and the boat, but that it was a long time before they had found them, and the like; holding them in a chat till they came to the ship's side; when the captain and the mate entering first with their arms, immediately knocked down the second mate and carpenter with the butt-end of their muskets, being very faithfully seconded by their men; they secured all the rest that were upon the main and quarter decks, and began to fasten the hatches, to keep them down that were below; when the other boat and their men, entering at the forechains, secured the forecastle of the ship, and the scuttle which went down into the cook-room, making three men they found there prisoners. When this was done, and all safe upon deck, the captain ordered the mate, with three men, to break into the round-house, where the new rebel captain lay, who, having taken the alarm, had got up and with two men and a boy had got firearms in their hands; and the mate, with a crow, split open the door; the new captain and his men fired boldly among them, and wounded the mate with a musket-ball, which broke his arm, and wounded two more of the men, but killed nobody.

The mate, calling for help, rushed, however, into the round-house, wounded as he was, and with his pistol shot the new captain through the head, the bullet entering at his mouth, coming out again behind one of his ears, so that he never spoke a word more: upon which the rest yielded, and the ship was taken effectually, without any more lives lost.

As soon as the ship was thus secured, the captain ordered seven guns to be fired, which was the signal agreed upon with me to give me notice of his success, which, you may be sure, I was very glad to hear, having sat watching upon the shore for it till near two o'clock in the morning. Having thus heard the signal plainly, I laid me down; and it having been a day of great fatigue to me, I slept very sound, till I was something surprised with the noise of a gun; and presently starting up, I heard a man calling me by the name of "Governor! Governor!" and presently I knew the captain's voice; when climbing to the top of the hill, there he stood, and, pointing to the ship, he embraced me in his arms. "My dear friend and deliverer," says he, "there's your ship; for she is all yours, and so are we, and all that belongs to her." I cast my eyes to the ship, and there she rode, within little more than half a mile of the shore; for they had weighed her anchor as soon as they were masters of her, and, the weather being fair, had brought her to an anchor just against the mouth of the little creek; and, the tide being up, the captain had brought the pinnace in near the place where I first landed my rafts, so landed just at my door. I was at first ready to sink down with surprise; for I saw my deliverance, indeed, visibly put into my hands, all things easy, and a large ship just ready to carry me away whither I pleased to go. At first, for some time, I was not able to answer one word; but as he had taken me in his arms, I held fast by him, or I should have fallen to the ground. He perceived the surprise, and immediately pulled a bottle out of his pocket, and gave me a dram of cordial, which he had brought on purpose for me. After I had drunk it, I sat down upon the ground; and though it brought me to myself, yet it was a good while before I could speak a word to him. All this while the poor man was in as great an ecstasy as I, only not under any surprise as I was; and he said a thousand kind and tender things to me, to compose and bring me to myself; but such was the flood of joy in my breast that it put all my spirits into confusion: at last it broke into tears; and, in a little while after, I recovered my speech; then I took my turn, and embraced him as my deliverer, and we rejoiced together.

I told him I looked upon him as a man sent from heaven to deliver me, and that the whole transaction seemed to be a chain of wonders; that such things as these were the testimonies we had of a secret hand of Providence governing the world, and an evidence that the eye of an Infinite Power could search into the remotest corner of the world, and send help to the miserable whenever he pleased. I forgot not to lift up my heart in thankfulness to Heaven; and what heart could forbear to bless him, who had not only in a miraculous manner provided for one in such a wilderness, and in such a desolate condition, but from whom every deliverance must always be acknowledged to proceed?

When we had talked a while, the captain told me he had brought me some little refreshments, such as the ship afforded, and such as the wretches that had been so long his masters had not plundered him of. Upon this, he called aloud to the boat, and bade his men bring the things ashore that were for the governor; and, indeed, it was a present as if I had been one that was not to be carried away along with them, but as if I had been to dwell upon the island still, and they were to go without me. First, he had brought me a case of bottles full of excellent cordial waters, six large bottles of Madeira wine (the bottles held two quarts each), two pounds of excellent good tobacco, twelve good pieces of the ship's beef, and six pieces of pork, with a bag of peas, and about a hundredweight of biscuit; he also brought me a box of sugar, a box of flour, a bag full of lemons, and two bottles of lime-juice, and abundance of other things. But besides these, and what was a thousand times more useful, he brought me six new clean shirts, six very good neckcloths, two pair of gloves, one pair of shoes, a hat, and one pair of stockings, and a very good suit of clothes of his own, which had been worn but very little: in a word, he clothed me from head to foot. It was a very kind and agreeable present, as any one may imagine, to one in my circumstances; but never was anything in the world of that kind so unpleasant, awkward, and uneasy as it was to me to wear such clothes at their first putting on.

After these ceremonies were past, and after all his good things were brought into my little apartment, we began to consult what was to be done with the prisoners we had; for it was worth considering whether we might venture to take them away with us or no, especially two of them, whom he knew to be incorrigible and refractory to the last degree; and the captain said he knew they were such rogues that there was no obliging them, and if he did carry them away, it must be in irons, as malefactors, to be delivered over to justice at the first English colony he could come at: and I found that the captain himself was very anxious about it. Upon this, I told him that, if he desired it, I would undertake to bring the two men he spoke of to make it their own request that he should leave them upon the island. "I should be very glad of that," says the captain, "with all my heart." "Well," says I, "I will send for them up, and talk with them for you." So I caused Friday and the two hostages, for they were now discharged, their comrades having performed their promise; I say, I caused them to go to the cave, and bring up the five men, pinioned as they were, to the bower, and keep them there till I came. After some time I came thither dressed in my new habit; and now I was called governor again. Being all met, and the captain with me, I caused the men to be brought before me, and I told them I had got a full account of their villainous behaviour to the captain, and how they had run away with the ship, and were preparing to commit further robberies, but that Providence had ensnared them in their own ways, and that they were fallen into the pit which they had dug for others. I let them know that by my direction the ship had been seized; that she lay now in the road; and they might see by and by that their new captain had received the reward of his villainy, for that they might see him hanging at the yard-arm; that, as to them, I wanted to know what they had to say why I should not execute them as pirates, taken in the fact, as by my commission they could not doubt but I had authority to do.

One of them answered in the name of the rest, that they had nothing to say but this, that when they were taken the captain promised them their lives, and they humbly implored my mercy. But I told them I knew not what mercy to show them; for as for myself I had resolved to quit the island with all my men, and had taken passage with the captain to go to England; and as for the captain, he could not carry them to England other than as prisoners in irons, to be tried for mutiny, and running away with the ship; the consequence of which, they must needs know, would be the gallows; so that I could not tell what was the best for them, unless they had a mind to take their fate in the island. If they desired that, I did not care; as I had liberty to leave it, I had some inclination to give them their lives, if they thought they could shift on shore. They seemed very thankful for it, and said they would much rather venture to stay there than be carried to England to be hanged. So I left it on that issue.

However, the captain seemed to make some difficulty of it, as if he durst not leave them there. Upon this I seemed a little angry with the captain, and told him that they were my prisoners, not his; and, that seeing I had offered them so much favour, I would be as good as my word; and that if he did not think fit to consent to it, I would set them at liberty, as I found them; and if he did not like it, he might take them again if he could catch them. Upon this they appeared very thankful, and I accordingly set them at liberty, and bade them retire into the woods, to the place whence they came and I would leave them some firearms, some ammunition, and some directions how they should live very well, if they thought fit. Upon this I prepared to go on board the ship; but told the captain I would stay that night to prepare my things, and desired him to go on board in the meantime, and keep all right in the ship, and send the boat on shore next day for me; ordering him, in the meantime, to cause the new captain, who was killed, to be hanged at the yard-arm, that these men might see him.

When the captain was gone, I sent for the men up to me in my apartment, and entered seriously into discourse with them of their circumstances. I told them I thought they had made a right choice; but if the captain had carried them away, they would certainly be hanged. I showed them the new captain hanging at the yard-arm of the ship, and told them they had nothing less to expect.

When they had all declared their willingness to stay, I told them I would let them into the story of my living there, and put them into the way of making it easy to them. Accordingly, I gave them the whole history of the place, and of my coming to it; showed them my fortifications, the way I made my bread, planted my corn, cured my grapes, and, in a word, all that was necessary to make them easy. I told them the story also of the sixteen Spaniards, that were to be expected, for whom I left a letter, and made them promise to treat them in common with themselves.

I left them my firearms, viz., five muskets, three fowling-pieces, and three swords. I had above a barrel and a half of powder left; for after the first year or two I used but little, and wasted none. I gave them a description of the way I managed the goats, and directions to milk and fatten them, and to make both butter and cheese. In a word, I gave them every part of my story, and told them I should prevail with the captain to leave them two barrels of gunpowder more, and some garden-seeds, which I told them I would have been very glad of. Also, I gave them the bag of peas which the captain had brought me to eat, and bade them be sure to sow and increase them.

Having done all this, I left the next day, and went on board the ship. We prepared immediately to sail, but did not weigh that night. The next morning early, two of the five men came swimming to the ship's side, and made the most lamentable complaint of the other three, begged to be taken into the ship for God's sake, for they should be murdered, and begged the captain to take them on board, though he hanged them immediately. Upon this, the captain pretended to have no power without me; but after some difficulty, and after their solemn promises of amendment, they were taken on board, and were, some time after, soundly whipped and pickled; after which they proved very honest and quiet fellows.

Some time after this, I went with the boat on shore, the tide being up, with the things promised to the men; to which the captain, at my intercession, caused their chests and clothes to be added, which they took, and were very thankful for. I also encouraged them, by telling them that if it lay in my way to send any vessel to take them in I would not forget them.

When I took leave of this island, I carried on board, for relics, the great goatskin cap I had made, my umbrella, and one of my parrots; also I forgot not to take the money I formerly mentioned, which had lain by me so long useless that it was grown rusty or tarnished, and could hardly pass for silver till it had been a little rubbed and handled, and also the money I found in the wreck of the Spanish ship. And thus I left the island, the 19th of December, as I found by the ship's account, in the year 1686, after I had been upon it eight-and-twenty years, two months, and nineteen days; being delivered from this second captivity the same day of the month that I first made my escape in the longboat from among the Moors of Sallee. In this vessel, after a long voyage, I arrived in England the 11th of June, in the year 1687, having been thirty-five years absent.

CHAPTER XVI

WHEN I came to England, I was a perfect stranger to all the world, as if I had never been known there. My benefactor and faithful steward, whom I had left my money in trust with, was alive, but had had great misfortunes in the world; was become a widow the second time, and very low in the world. I made her easy as to what she owed me, assuring her I would give her no trouble; but, on the contrary, in gratitude for her former care and faithfulness to me, I relieved her as my little stock would afford; which at that time would, indeed, allow me to do but little for her: but I assured her I would never forget her former kindness to me; nor did I forget her when I had sufficient to help her, as shall be observed in its place. I went down afterwards into Yorkshire; but my father was dead, and my mother and all the family extinct, except that I found two sisters and two of the children of one of my brothers; and as I had been long ago given over for dead, there had been no provision made for me; so that, in a word, I found nothing to relieve or assist me; and that little money I had would not do much for me as to settling in the world.

I met with one piece of gratitude, indeed, which I did not expect; and this was, that the master of the ship, whom I had so happily delivered, and by the same means saved the ship and cargo, having given a very handsome account to the owners of the manner how I had saved the lives of the men and the ship, they invited me to meet them and some other merchants concerned, and altogether made me a very handsome compliment upon the subject, and a present of almost £200 sterling.

But after making several reflections upon the circumstances of my life, and how little way this would go towards settling me in the world, I resolved to go to Lisbon, and see if I might not come by some information of the state of my plantation in the Brazils, and of what was become of my partner, who, I had reason to suppose, had some years now given me over for dead. With this view I took shipping for Lisbon, where I arrived in April following; my man Friday accompanying me very honestly in all these ramblings, and proving a most faithful servant upon all occasions. When I came to Lisbon, I found out, by inquiry, and to my particular satisfaction, my old friend, the captain of the ship who first took me up at sea off the shore of Africa. He was now grown old, and had left the sea, having put his son, who was far from a young man, into his ship, and who still used the Brazil trade. The old man did not know me; and indeed, I hardly knew him. But I soon brought myself to his remembrance, when I told him who I was.

After some passionate expressions of the old acquaintance between us I inquired, you may be sure, after my plantation and my partner. The old man told me he had not been in the Brazils for about nine years; but that he could assure me, that when he came away my partner was living; but the trustees, whom I had joined with him to take cognizance of my part, were both dead; that, however, he believed that I would have a very good account of the improvement of the plantation; for that, upon the general belief of my being cast away and drowned, my trustees had given in the account of the produce of my part of the plantation to the procurator-fiscal, who had appropriated it, in case I never came to claim it, one-third to the king, two-thirds to the monastery of St. Augustine, to be expended for the benefit of the poor and for the conversion of the Indians to the Catholic faith; but that if I appeared, or any one for me, to claim the inheritance, it would be restored; only that the improvement, or annual production, being distributed to charitable uses, could not be restored; but he assured me that the steward of the king's revenue from lands, and the providore, or steward of the monastery, had taken great care all along that the incumbent, that is to say, my partner, gave every year a faithful account, of produce, of which they had received duly my moiety. I asked him if he knew to what height of improvement he had brought the plantation, and whether he thought it might be worth looking after; or whether, on my going thither, I should meet with any obstruction to my possessing my just right in the moiety. He told me he could not tell exactly to what degree the plantation was improved; but this he knew, that my partner was grown exceeding rich upon the enjoying but one half of it; and that, to the best of his remembrance, he had heard that the king's third of my part, which was, it seems, granted away to some other monastery or religious house, amounted to above two hundred moidores a year: that as to my being restored to a quiet possession of it, there was no question to be made of that, my partner being alive to witness my title, and my name being also enrolled in the register of the country, also he told me that the survivors of my two trustees were very fair, honest people, and very wealthy; and he believed I would not only have their assistance for putting me in possession, but would find a very considerable sum of money in their hands for my account, being the produce of the farm while their fathers held the trust, and before it was given up, as above; which, as he remembered, was for about twelve years.

I showed myself a little concerned and uneasy at this account and inquired of the old captain how it came to pass that the trustees should thus dispose of my effects, when he knew that I had made my will, and made him, the Portuguese captain, my universal heir, etc.

He told me that was true; but that as there was no proof of my being dead, he could not act as executor, until some certain account should come of my death; and that besides, he was not willing to intermeddle with a thing so remote; that it was true he had registered my will, and put in his claim; and could he have given any account of my being dead or alive, he would have acted by procuration, and taken possession of the ingenio (so they call the sugar-house), and have given his son, who was now at the Brazils, orders to do it. "But," says the old man, "I have one piece of news to tell you, which perhaps may not be so acceptable to you as the rest; and that is, believing you were lost, and all the world believing so also, your partner and trustees did offer to account with me, in your name, for the first six or eight years' profits, which I received. There being at that time great disbursements for increasing the works, building an ingenio, and buying slaves, it did not amount to near so much as afterwards it produced: however," says the old man, "I shall give you a true account of what I have received in all, and how I have disposed of it."

After a few days' further conference with this ancient friend, he brought me an account of the first six years' income of my plantation, signed by my partner and the merchant-trustees, being always delivered in goods, viz., tobacco in roll, and sugar in chests, besides rum, molasses, etc., which are the consequence of a sugar-works; and I found by this account, that every year the income considerably increased; but, as above, the disbursements being large, the sum at first was small; however, the old man let me see that he was debtor to me four hundred and seventy moidores of gold, besides sixty chests of sugar, and fifteen double rolls of tobacco, which were lost in his ship; he having been shipwrecked coming home to Lisbon, about eleven years after my leaving the place. The good man then began to complain of his misfortunes, and how he had been obliged to make use of my money to recover his losses, and buy him a share in a new ship. "However, my old friend," says he, "you shall not want a supply in your necessity, and as soon as my son returns you shall be fully satisfied." Upon this he pulls out an old pouch, and gives me one hundred and sixty Portugal moidores in gold; and giving me the writings of his title to the ship, which his son was gone to the Brazils in, of which he was quarter-part owner, and his son another, he puts them both in my hands for security of the rest.

I was too much moved with the honesty and kindness of the poor man to be able to bear this; and remembering what he had done for me, how he had taken me up at sea, and how generously he had used me on all occasions, and particularly how sincere a friend he was now to me, I could hardly refrain weeping at what he had said to me; therefore, first, I asked him if his circumstances admitted him to spare so much money at that time, and if it would not straiten him? He told me he could not say but it might straiten him a little; but, however, it was my money, and I might want it more than he.

Everything the good man said was full of affection, and I could hardly refrain from tears while he spoke: in short, I took one hundred of the moidores, and called for a pen and ink to give him a receipt for them; then I returned him the rest, and told him if ever I had possession of the plantation I would return the other to him also (as, indeed, I afterwards did); and that as to the bill of sale of his part in his son's ship, I would not take it by any means; but that if I wanted the money, I found he was honest enough to pay me; and if I did not, but came to receive what he gave me reason to expect, I would never have a penny more from him.

When this was past, the old man began to ask me if he should put me into a method to make claim to my plantation. I told him I thought to go over to it myself. He said I might do so if I pleased; but that, if I did not, there were ways enough to secure my right, and immediately to appropriate the profits to my use: and as there were ships in the river of Lisbon just ready to go away to Brazil, he made me enter my name in a public register, with his affidavit, affirming, upon oath, that I was alive, and that I was the same person who took up the land for the planting the said plantation at first. This being regularly attested by a notary, and a procuration affixed, he directed me to send it, with a letter of his writing, to a merchant of his acquaintance at the place; and then proposed my staying with him till an account came of the return.

Never was anything more honourable than the proceedings upon this procuration; for in less than seven months I received a large packet from the survivors of my trustees, the merchants, for whose account I went to sea, in which were the following particular letters and papers inclosed.

First, there was the account-current of the produce of my farm or plantation, from the year when their fathers had balanced with my old Portugal captain, being for six years; the balance appeared to be one thousand one hundred and seventy-four moidores in my favour.

Secondly, there was the account of four years more, while they kept the effects in their hands, before the government claimed the administration, as being the effects of a person not to be found, which they called civil death; and the balance of this, the value of the plantation increasing, amounted to nineteen thousand four hundred and forty-six crusadoes, being about three thousand two hundred and forty moidores.

Thirdly, there was the Prior of the Augustines' account, who had received the profits for above fourteen years; but not being able to account for what was disposed of by the hospital, very honestly declared he had eight hundred and seventy-two moidores not distributed, which he acknowledged to my account; as to the king's part, that refunded nothing.

There was also a letter from my partner congratulating me very affectionately upon my being alive, giving me an account how the estate was improved, and what it produced a year; with the particulars of the number of squares or acres it contained, how planted, how many slaves there were upon it: and making two-and-twenty crosses for

blessings, told me he had said so many *Ave Marias* to
thank the Blessed Virgin that I was alive; inviting me
very passionately to come over and take possession of my
own; and, in the meantime, to give him orders to whom
he should deliver my effects, if I did not come myself;
concluding with a hearty tender of his friendship, and that
of his family; and sent me, as a present, seven fine leopards'
skins, which he had, it seems, received from Africa, by
some other ship that he had sent thither, and which, it
seems, had made a better voyage than I. He sent me also
five chests of excellent sweetmeats, and a hundred pieces
of gold uncoined, not quite so large as moidores. By the
same fleet, my two merchant-trustees shipped me one
thousand two hundred chests of sugar, eight hundred rolls
of tobacco, and the rest of the whole account in gold.

I might well say now, indeed, that the latter end of Job
was better than the beginning. It is impossible to express
the flutterings of my very heart when I looked over these
letters, and especially when I found all my wealth about
me; for, as the Brazil ships come all in fleets, the same
ships which brought my letters brought my goods: and
the effects were safe in the river before the letters came
to my hand. In a word I turned pale, and grew sick; and
had not the old man run and fetched me a cordial, I
believe the sudden surprise of joy had overset nature, and
I had died upon the spot: nay, after that, I continued very
ill, and was so some hours, till a physician being sent for,
and something of the real cause of my illness being known,
he ordered me to let blood; after which I had relief, and grew
well: but I verily believe, if I had not been eased by the
vent given in that manner to the spirits, I should have died.

I was now master, all on a sudden, of above fifty thousand
pounds sterling in money, and had an estate, as I might
well call it, in the Brazils, of above a thousand pounds a
year, as sure as an estate of lands in England; and, in a
word, I was in a condition, which I scarce knew how to
understand, or how to compose myself for the enjoyment

of. The first thing I did was to recompense my original benefactor, my good old captain, who had been first charitable to me in my distress, kind to me in the beginning, and honest to me at the end. I showed him all that was sent me; I told him that, next to the providence of Heaven, which disposes of all things, it was owing to him; and that it now lay on me to reward him, which I would do a hundred-fold; so I first returned to him the hundred moidores I had received of him, then I sent for a notary and caused him to draw up a general release or discharge from the four hundred and seventy moidores, which he had acknowledged he owed me, in fullest and firmest manner possible. After which, I caused a procuration to be drawn, empowering him to be the receiver of the annual profits of my plantation; and appointing my partner to account him, and make the returns, by the usual fleets, to him in my name; and by a clause in the end, made a grant of one hundred moidores a year to him during his life, out of the effects, and fifty moidores a year to his son after him, for his life: and thus I requited my old man.

I had now to consider which way to steer my course next, and what to do with the estate that Providence had thus put into my hands; and indeed, I had more care upon my head now than I had in my silent state of life in the island, where I wanted nothing but what I had, and had nothing but what I wanted; whereas, I had now a great charge upon me, and my business was how to secure it. I had not a cave now to hide my money in, or a place where it might lie without lock or key, till it grew mouldy and tarnished before anybody would meddle with it; on the contrary, I knew not where to put it. My old patron, the captain, indeed, was honest, and that was the only refuge I had. In the next place, my interest in the Brazils seemed to summon me thither; but now I could not tell how to think of going thither till I had settled my affairs, and left my effects in some safe hands behind me. At first I thought of my old friend the widow, who

I knew was honest, and would be just to me; but then she was in years, and but poor, and, for aught I knew, might be in debt; so that, in a word, I had no way but to go back to England myself, and take my effects with me.

It was some months, however, before I resolved upon this; and therefore, as I had rewarded the old captain fully, and to his satisfaction, who had been my former benefactor, so I began to think of my poor widow, whose husband had been my first benefactor, and she, while it was in her power, my faithful steward and instructor. So, the first thing I did, I got a merchant in Lisbon to write to his correspondent in London not only to pay a bill, but to go find her out, and carry her in money a hundred pounds from me, and to talk with her, and comfort her in her poverty, by telling her she should, if I lived, have a further supply: at the same time, I sent my two sisters in the country a hundred pounds each, they being, though not in want, yet not in very good circumstances; one having been married and left a widow; and the other having a husband not so kind to her as he should be. But, among all my relations or acquaintances, I could not yet pitch upon one to whom I durst commit the gross of my stock, that I might go away to the Brazils, and leave things safe behind me; and this greatly perplexed me.

I had once a mind to have gone to the Brazils, and have settled myself there, for I was, as it were, naturalized to the place; but I had some little scruple in my mind about religion, which insensibly drew me back, of which I shall say more presently. However, it was not religion that kept me from going there for the present; and as I had made no scruple of being openly of the religion of the country all the while I was among them, so neither did I yet; only that, now and then, having of late thought more of it than formerly, when I began to think of living and dying among them, I began to regret my having professed myself a Papist, and thought it might not be the best religion to die with.

But, as I have said, this was not the main thing that kept me from going to the Brazils, but that really I did not know with whom to leave my effects behind me; so I resolved at last to go to England with them, where, if I arrived, I concluded I should make some acquaintance, or find some relations, that would be faithful to me; and, accordingly, I prepared to go to England with all my wealth.

In order to prepare things for my going home, I now (the Brazil fleet being just going away) resolved to give answers suitable to the just and faithful account of things I had from thence; and, first, to the Prior of St. Augustine, I wrote a letter full of thanks for his just dealings, and the offer of the eight hundred and seventy-two moidores which were undisposed of, which I desired might be given, five hundred to the monastery, and three hundred and seven-two to the poor, as the prior should direct; desiring the good padre's prayers for me, and the like. I wrote next a letter of thanks to my two trustees, with all the acknowledgment that so much justice and honesty called for: as for sending them any present, they were far above having any occasion of it. Lastly, I wrote to my partner, acknowledging his industry in the improving the plantation, and his integrity in increasing the stock of works; giving him instructions for his future government of my part, according to the powers I had left with my old patron, to whom I desired him to send whatever became due to me, till he should hear from me more particularly; assuring him that it was my intention not only to come to him, but to settle myself there for the remainder of my life. To this I added a very handsome present of some Italian silks for his wife and two daughters, for such the captain's son informed me he had: with two pieces of fine English broadcloth, the best I could get in Lisbon, five pieces of black baize, and some Flanders lace of a good value.

Having thus settled my affairs, sold my cargo, and turned all my effects into good bills of exchange, my next difficulty was which way to go to England. I had been accustomed enough to the sea, and yet I had a strange aversion to go to England by sea at that time; and though I could give no reason for it, yet the difficulty increased upon me so much, that though I had once shipped my baggage in order to go, yet I altered my mind, and that not once, but two or three times.

It is true I had been very unfortunate by sea, and that might be one of the reasons; but let no man slight the strong impulses of his own thoughts in cases of such moment; two of the ships which I had singled out to go in—I mean, more particularly singled out than any other—having put my things on board one of them, and in the other having agreed with the captain, I say two of these ships miscarried; viz., one was taken by the Algerines, and the other was cast away on the start, near Torbay, and all the people drowned, except three; so that in either of those vessels I had been made miserable, in which most, it was hard to say.

Having been thus harassed in my thoughts, my old pilot, to whom I communicated everything, pressed me earnestly not to go by sea, but either to go by land to the Groyne, and cross over the Bay of Biscay to Rochelle, from whence it was but an easy and safe journey by land to Paris, and so to Calais and Dover; or to go up to Madrid, and so all the way by land through France. In a word, I was so prepossessed against my going by sea at all, except from Calais to Dover, that I resolved to travel all the way by land; which, as I was not in haste, and did not value the charge, was by much the pleasanter way: and to make it more so, my old captain brought an English gentleman, the son of a merchant in Lisbon, who was willing to travel with me; after which we picked up two more English merchants also, and two young Portuguese gentlemen, the last going to Paris only: so that in all there were six of us, and five servants; the two merchants and the two Portuguese contenting themselves with one servant between two, to save the charge; and as for me, I got an English sailor to travel with me as a servant, besides my man Friday, who was too much a stranger to be capable of supplying the place of a servant upon the road.

In this manner I set out from Lisbon; and our company being very well mounted and armed, we made a little troop, whereof they did me the honour to call me captain, as well because I was the oldest man, as because I had two servants, and, indeed, was the origin of the whole journey.

As I have troubled you with none of my sea journeys, so I shall trouble you now with none of my land journeys; but some adventures that happened to us in this tedious and difficult journey I must not omit.

When we came to Madrid, we, being all of us strangers to Spain, were willing to stay some time to see the court of Spain, and what was worth observing; but, it being the latter part of the summer, we hastened away, and set out from Madrid about the middle of October; but when we came to the edge of Navarre, we were alarmed, at several towns on the way, with an account that so much snow was fallen on the French side of the mountains that several travellers were obliged to come back to Pampeluna, after having attempted at an extreme hazard to pass on.

When we came to Pampeluna itself, we found it so indeed; and to me, that had been always used to a hot climate, and to countries where I could scarce bear any clothes on, the cold was unsufferable; nor, indeed, was it more painful than it was surprising, to come but ten days before out of Old Castile, where the weather was not only warm, but very hot, and immediately to feel a wind from the Pyrenean Mountains so very keen, so severely cold, as to be intolerable, and to endanger benumbing and perishing of our fingers and toes.

Poor Friday was really frightened when he saw the mountains all covered with snow, and felt cold weather, which he had never seen or felt before in his life. To mend the matter, after we came to Pampeluna, it continued snowing with so much violence, and so long, that the people said winter was come before its time; and the roads, which were difficult before, were now quite impassable; in a word, the snow lay in some places too thick for us to travel, and being not hard frozen, as is the case in the northern countries, there was no going without being in danger of being buried alive every step. We stayed no less than twenty days at Pampeluna; when (seeing the winter coming on, and no likelihood of its being better, for it was the severest winter all over Europe that had been known in many years) I proposed that we should go away to Fontarabia, and there taking shipping for Bordeaux, which was a very little voyage. But, while I was considering this, there came in four French gentlemen, who, having been stopped on the French side of the passes, as we were on the Spanish, had found out a guide, who, traversing the country near the head of Languedoc, had brought them over the mountains by such ways that they were not much incommoded with the snow; for where they met with snow in any quantity, they said it was frozen hard enough to bear them and their horses. We sent for this guide, who told us he would undertake to carry us the same way, with no hazard from the snow, provided we were armed sufficiently to protect ourselves from wild beasts; for, he said, in these great snows, it was frequent for some wolves to show themselves at the foot of the mountains, being made ravenous for want of food, the ground being covered with snow. We told him we were well enough prepared for such creatures as they were, if he would insure us from a kind of two-legged wolves, which, we were told, we were in most danger from, especially on the French side of the mountains. He satisfied us that there was no danger of that kind in the way that we were to go; so we readily agreed to follow him, as did also twelve other gentlemen, with their servants, some French, some Spanish, who, as I said, had attempted to go, and were obliged to come back again.

Accordingly, we set out from Pampeluna with our guide on the 15th of November; and, indeed, I was surprised, when, instead of going forward, he came directly back with us on the same road that we came from Madrid, about twenty miles; when, having passed two rivers, and come into the plain country, we found ourselves in a warm climate again, where the country was pleasant, and no snow to be seen; but, on a sudden, turning to his left, he approached the mountains another way; and though it is true the hills and precipices looked dreadful, yet he made so many tours, such meanders, and led us by such winding ways, that we insensibly passed the height of the mountains without being much encumbered with the snow; and, all of a sudden, he showed us the pleasant and fruitful provinces of Languedoc and Gascony, all green and flourishing, though, indeed, they were at a great distance, and we had some rough way to pass still.

We were a little uneasy, however, when we found it snowed one whole day and a night so fast that we could not travel; but he bid us be easy; we should soon be past it all: we found, indeed, that we began to descend every day, and to come more north than before; and so, depending upon our guide, we went on.

It was about two hours before night, when, our guide being something before us, and not just in sight, out rushed three monstrous wolves, and after them a bear, from a hollow way adjoining to a thick wood; two of the wolves flew upon the guide, and, had he been far before us he would have been devoured before we could have helped him; one of them fastened upon his horse, and the other attacked the man with such violence that he had not time or presence of mind enough to draw his pistol, but hallooed and cried out to us most lustily. My man Friday being next me, I bade him ride up and see what was the matter. As soon as Friday came in sight of the man, he hallooed out as loud as the other, "Oh, master! Oh, master!" but, like a bold fellow, rode directly up to the man, and with his pistol shot the wolf that attacked him in the head.

It was happy for the poor man that it was my man Friday; for, having been used to such creatures in his country, he had no fear upon him, but went close up to him and shot him; whereas, any other of us would have fired at a farther distance, and have perhaps either missed the wolf, or endangered shooting the man.

But it was enough to have terrified a bolder man than I; and, indeed, it alarmed all our company, when, with the noise of Friday's pistol, we heard on both sides the most dismal howling of wolves; and the noise, redoubled by the echo of the mountains, that it was to us as if there had been a prodigious number of them; and perhaps there was not such a few as that we had no cause of apprehension; however, as Friday had killed this wolf, the other, that has fastened upon the horse, left him immediately, and fled, without doing him any damage, having happily fastened upon his head, where the bosses of the bridle had stuck in his teeth. But the man was most hurt; for the raging creature had bit him twice, once in the arm, and the other time a little above his knee; he was just, as it were, tumbling down by the disorder of his horse, when Friday came up and shot the wolf.

It is easy to suppose that at the noise of Friday's pistol we all mended our pace, and rode up as fast as the way, which was very difficult, would give us leave, to see what was the matter. As soon as we came clear of the trees, which blinded us before, we saw plainly what had been the case, and how Friday had disengaged the poor guide, though we did not presently discern what kind of creature it was he had killed.

But never was a fight managed so hardily, and in such a surprising manner, as that which followed between Friday and the bear, which gave us all, though at first we were surprised and afraid for him, the greatest diversion imaginable. As the bear is a heavy, clumsy creature, and does not gallop as the wolf does, which is swift and light, so he has two particular qualities, which generally are the rule of his actions; first, as to men, who are not his proper prey (he does not usually attempt them, except they first attack him, unless he be excessively hungry, which it is probable might now be the case, the ground being covered with snow), if you do not meddle with him, he will not meddle with you; but then you must take care to be very civil to him, and give him the road, for he is a very nice gentleman; he will not go a step out of his way for a prince; nay, if you are really afraid, your best way is to look another way and keep going on; for sometimes if you stop, and stand still, and look steadfastly at him, he takes it for an affront; but if you throw or toss anything at him, and it hits him, though it were but a bit of stick as big as your finger, he takes it for an affront, and sets all other business aside to pursue his revenge, and will have satisfaction in point of honour—that is his first quality; the next is, that if he be once affronted, he will never leave you, night or day, till he has had his revenge, but follow at a good round rate till he overtakes you.

My man Friday had delivered our guide, and when we came up to him, he was helping him off from his horse, for the man was both hurt and frightened, and indeed the last more than the first, when on a sudden we espied the bear come out of the wood, and a vast, monstrous one it was, the biggest by far that ever I saw. We were all a little surprised when we saw him; but when Friday saw him it was easy to see joy and courage in the fellow's countenance. "Oh, oh, oh," says Friday, three times, pointing to him; "oh, master! you give me te leave, me shakee te hand with him; me make you good laugh."

I was surprised to see the fellow so pleased. "You fool," said I, "he will eat you up." "Eatee me up! eatee me up!" says Friday, twice over again; "me eatee him up; me makee you good laugh; you all stay here, me show you good laugh." So down he sits, and gets his boots off in a moment, and puts on a pair of pumps (as we call the flat shoes they wear, and which he had in his pocket), gives my other servant his horse, and with his gun away he flies, swift like the wind.

The bear was walking softly on, and offered to meddle with nobody, till Friday coming pretty near, calls to him, as if the bear could understand him, "Hark ye, hark ye," says Friday, "me speakee with you." We followed at a distance, for now, being come down to the Gascony side of the mountains, we were entered a vast, great forest, where the country was plain and pretty open, though it had many trees in it scattered here and there. Friday, who had, as we say, the heels of the bear, came up with him quickly, and took up a great stone, and threw it at him, and hit him just on the head, but did him no more harm than if he had thrown it against a wall; but it answered Friday's end, for the rogue was so void of fear that he did it purely to make the bear follow him, and show us some laugh, as he called it. As soon as the bear felt the stone, and saw him, he turned about, and came after him, taking very long strides, and shuffling on at a strange rate, so as would have put a horse to a middling gallop; away ran Friday, taking his course as if he ran towards us for help; so we all resolved to fire at once upon the bear, and deliver my man; though I was angry at him heartily for bringing the bear back upon us, when he was going about his own business another way; especially I was angry that he had turned the bear upon us, and then run away; and I called out. "You dog!" said I, "is this your making us laugh? Come away, and take your horse, that we may shoot the creature." He heard me, and cried out, "No shoot, no shoot; stand still, you get much laugh"; and as the nimble creature ran two feet for the beast's one, he turned on a sudden on one side of us, and seeing a great oak tree fit for his purpose, he beckoned us to follow; and doubling his pace, he got nimbly up the tree, laying his gun down upon the ground at about five or six yards from the bottom of the tree. The bear soon came to the tree, and we followed at a distance; the first thing he did he stopped at the gun, smelled at it, but let it lie, and up he scrambles into the tree, climbing like a cat, though so monstrous heavy. I was amazed at the folly, as I thought it, of my man, and could not for my life see anything to laugh at yet, till seeing the bear get up the tree, we all rode near to him.

When we came to the tree, there was Friday got out to the small end of a large limb of the tree, and the bear got about half way to him. As soon as the bear got out to that part where the limb of the tree was weaker— "Ha!" says he to us, "now you see me teachee the bear dance"; so he began jumping and shaking the bough, at which the bear began to totter, but stood still, and began to look behind him, to see how he should get back; then, indeed, we did laugh heartily. But Friday had not done with him by a great deal; when seeing him stand still, he called out to him again, as if he had supposed the bear could speak English, "What, you no come farther? pray you, come farther"; so he left jumping and shaking the bough; and the bear, just as if he had understood what he said, did come a little farther; then he began jumping again, and the bear stopped again. We thought now was a good time to knock him on the head, and called to Friday to stand still, and we would shoot the bear; but he cried out earnestly, "Oh, pray! oh, pray! no shoot, me shoot by and then"; he would have said by and by. However, to shorten the story, Friday danced so much, and the bear stood so ticklish, that we had laughing enough indeed, but still could not imagine what the fellow would do; for first we thought he depended upon shaking the bear off; and we found the bear was too cunning for that too; for he would not go out far enough to be thrown down, but clung fast with great broad claws and feet, so that we could not imagine what would be the end of it, and what the jest would be at last. But Friday put us out of doubt quickly: for seeing the bear cling fast to the bough, and that he would not be persuaded to come any farther, "Well, well," says Friday, "you no come farther, me go; you no come to me, me come to you"; and upon this he went out to the smaller end of the bough, where it would bend with his weight, and gently let himself down by it, sliding down the bough till he came near enough to jump down on his feet, and away he ran to his gun, took it up, and stood still. "Well," said I to him, "Friday, what will you do now? Why don't you shoot him?"—"No shoot," says Friday, "no yet; me shoot now, me no kill; me stay, give you one more laugh"; and, indeed, so he did, as you will see presently; for when the bear saw his enemy gone, he came back from the bough where he stood, but did it very cautiously, looking behind him every step, and coming backward till he got into the body of the tree; then, with the same hinder end foremost, he came down the tree, grasping it with his claws, and moving one foot at a time, very leisurely. At this juncture, and just before he could set his hind feet upon the ground, Friday stepped up close to him, clapped the muzzle of his piece into his ears, and shot him dead as a stone. Then the rogue turned about to see if we did not laugh; and when he saw we were pleased, by our looks, he began to laugh very loud. "So we kill bear in my country," says Friday. "So you kill them?" says I; "why, you have no guns."—"No," says he, "no gun, but shoot great much long arrow." This was a good diversion to us; but we were still in a wild place, and our guide very much hurt, and what to do we hardly knew; the howling of wolves ran much in my head; and indeed, except the noise I once heard on the shore of Africa, of which I have said something already, I never heard anything that filled me with so much horror.

These things, and the approach of night, called us off, or else, as Friday would have had us, we should certainly have taken the skin of this monstrous creature off, which was worth saving; but we had near three leagues to go, and our guide hastened us; so we left him, and went forward on our journey.

The ground was still covered with snow, though not so deep and dangerous as on the mountains; and the ravenous creatures, as we heard afterwards, were come down into the forest and plain country, pressed by hunger, to seek for food, and had done a great deal of mischief in the villages, where they surprised the country people, killing a great many of their sheep and horses, and some people too. We had one dangerous place to pass, and our guide told us if there were more wolves in the country we should find them there; and this was a small plain surrounded with woods on every side, and a long narrow defile, or lane, which we were to pass to get through the wood, and then we should come to the village where we were to lodge. It was within half an hour of sunset when we entered the wood, and a little after sunset when we came into the plain; we met nothing in the first wood, except that in a little plain within the wood, which was not above two furlongs over, we saw five great wolves cross the road, full speed, one after another, as if they had been in chase of some prey, and had it in view; they took no notice of us, and were gone out of sight in a few moments. Upon this, our guide, who, by the way, was a faint-hearted fellow, bid us keep in a ready posture, for he believed there were more wolves a-coming. We kept our arms ready and our eyes about us; but we saw no more wolves till we came through that wood, which was near a half a league, and entered the plain. As soon as we came into the plain, we had occasion enough to look about us: the first object we met with was a dead horse; that is to say a poor horse which the wolves had killed, and at least a dozen of them at work, we could not say eating him, but picking his bones rather; for they had eaten up all the flesh before. We did not think fit to disturb them at their feast, neither did they take much notice of us. Friday would have let fly at them, but I would not suffer him by any means; for I found we were like to have more business upon our hands than we were aware of. We had not gone half over the plain, when we began to hear the wolves howl in the wood on our left in a frightful manner, and presently after we saw about a hundred coming on directly towards us, all in a body, and most of them in a line as regular as an army drawn up by experienced officers. I scarce knew in what manner to receive them, but found to draw ourselves in a close line was the only way; so we formed in a moment; but that we might not have too much interval, I ordered that only every other man should fire, and that the others, who had not fired, should stand ready to give them a second volley immediately, if they continued to advance upon us; and then that those who had fired at first should not pretend to load their fusils again, but stand ready, every one with a pistol, for we were all armed with a fusil and a pair of pistols each man; so we were, by this method, able to fire six volleys, half of us at a time; however, at present we had no necessity; for upon firing the first volley, the enemy made a full stop, being terrified as well with the noise as with the fire. Four of them being shot in the head, dropped; several others were wounded, and went bleeding off, as we could see by the snow. I found they stopped, but did not immediately retreat; whereupon, remembering that I had been told that the fiercest creatures were terrified at the voice of a man, I caused all the company to halloo as loud as we could; and I found the notion not altogether mistaken; for upon our shout they began to retire and turn about. I then ordered a second volley to be fired in their rear, which put them to the gallop, and away they went to the woods. This gave us leisure to charge our pieces again; and that we might lose no time, we kept going; but we had but little more than loaded our fusils, and put ourselves in readiness, when we heard a terrible noise in the same wood on our left, only that it was farther onward, the same way we were to go.

The night was coming on, and the light began to be dusky, which made it the worse on our side; but the noise increasing, we could easily perceive that it was the howling and yelling of those hellish creatures; and, on a sudden, we perceived two or three troops of wolves, one on our left, one behind us, and one in our front, so that we seemed to be surrounded with them; however, as they did not fall upon us, we kept our way forward, as fast as we could make our horses go, which, the way being very rough, was only a good hard trot. In this manner, we came in view of the entrance of a wood, through which we were to pass, at the farther side of the plain; but we were greatly surprised when, coming nearer the lane or pass, we saw a confused number of wolves standing just at the entrance. On a sudden, at another opening of the wood, we heard the noise of a gun, and looking that way, out rushed a horse, with a saddle and a bridle on him, flying like the wind, and sixteen or seventeen wolves after him full speed. Indeed, the horse had the advantage of them; but as we supposed that he could not hold it at that rate, we doubted not but they would get up with him at last: and no question but they did.

But here we had a most horrible sight; for, riding up to the entrance where the horse came out, we found the carcases of another horse and of two men, devoured by the ravenous creatures; and one of the men was no doubt the same whom we heard fire the gun, for there lay a gun just by him fired off; but as to the man, his head and upper part of his body were eaten up. This filled us with horror, and we knew not what course to take; but the creatures resolved us soon, for they gathered about us presently, in hopes of prey; and I verily believe there were three hundred of them. It happened, very much to our advantage, that at the entrance into the wood, but a little way from it, there lay some large timber trees, which had been cut down the summer before, and I suppose lay there for carriage. I drew my little troop in among those trees, and placing ourselves in a line behind one long tree, I advised them all to alight, and keeping that tree before us for a breastwork, to stand in a triangle, or three fronts, inclosing our horses in the centre. We did so, and it was well we did; for never was a more furious charge than the creatures made upon us in this place. They came on us with a growling kind of a noise, and mounted the piece of timber, which, as I said, was our breastwork, as if they were only rushing upon their prey; and this fury of theirs, it seems, was principally occasioned by their seeing our horses behind us, which was the prey they aimed at. I ordered our men to fire as before, every other man; and they took their aim so sure that indeed they killed several of the wolves at the first volley; but there was a necessity to keep a continual firing, for they came on like devils, those behind pushing on those before.

When we had fired a second volley of our fusils, we thought they stopped a little, and I hoped they would have gone off, but it was but a moment, for others came forward again; so we fired two volleys of our pistols; and I believe in these four firings we had killed seventeen or eighteen of them, and lamed twice as many, yet they came on again. I was loath to spend our last shot too hastily; so I called my servant—not my man Friday, for he was better employed, for, with the greatest dexterity imaginable, he had charged my fusil and his own while we were engaged —but, as I said, I called my other man, and giving him a horn of powder, I bade him lay a train all along the piece of timber and let it be a large train. He did so, and had but just time to get away, when the wolves came up to it, and some got upon it, when I, snapping an uncharged pistol close to the powder, set it on fire; those that were upon the timber were scorched with it, and six or seven of them fell, or rather jumped in among us with the force and fright of the fire: we dispatched these in an instant, and the rest were so frightened with the light, which the night—for it was now very dark—made more terrible, that they drew back a little; upon which I ordered our last pistols to be fired off in one volley, and after that we gave a shout; upon this the wolves turned tail, and we sallied immediately upon near twenty lame ones that we found struggling on the ground, and fell to cutting them with our swords, which answered our expectation, for the crying and howling they made was better understood by their fellows; so that they all fled and left us.

We had, first and last, killed about three-score of them, and had it been daylight we had killed many more. The field of battle being thus cleared, we made forward again, for we had still near a league to go. We heard the ravenous creatures howl and yell in the woods as we went, several times, and sometimes we fancied we saw some of them; but the snow dazzling our eyes, we were not certain. So in about an hour more we came to the town where we were to lodge, which we found in a terrible fright, and all in arms; for it seems that the night before the wolves and some bears had broke into the village and put them in such terror that they were obliged to keep guard night and day, but especially in the night, to preserve their cattle, and indeed their people.

The next morning our guide was so ill, and his limbs swelled so much with the rankling of his two wounds, that he could go no farther; so we were obliged to take a new guide here, and go to Toulouse, where we found a warm climate, a fruitful, pleasant country, and no snow, no wolves, nor anything like them; but when we told our story at Toulouse, they told us it was nothing but what was ordinary in the great forest at the foot of the mountains, especially when the snow lay on the ground; but they inquired much what kind of a guide we had got, who would venture to bring us that way in such a severe season, and told us it was surprising we were not all devoured. When we told them how we placed ourselves and the horses in the middle, they blamed us exceedingly and told us it was fifty to one but we had been all destroyed, for it was the sight of the horses which made the wolves so furious, seeing their prey, and that at other times they are really afraid of a gun; but being excessively hungry, and raging on that account, the eagerness to come at the horses had made them senseless of danger; and that if we had not, by the continued fire, and at last by the stratagem of the train of powder, mastered them, it had been great odds but that we had been torn to pieces; whereas, had we been content to have sat still on horseback, and fired as horsemen, they would not have taken the horses so much for their own, when men were on their backs, as otherwise; and, withal, they told us that at last, if we had stood all together, and left our horses, they would have been so eager to have devoured them, that we might have come off safe, especially having our firearms in our hands, and being so many in number. For my part, I was never so sensible of danger in my life; for, seeing above three hundred devils come roaring and open-mouthed to devour us, and having nothing to shelter us or retreat to, I gave myself over for lost; and, as it was, I believe I shall never care to cross those mountains again; I think I would much rather go a thousand leagues by sea, though I was sure to meet with a storm once a week.

I have nothing uncommon to take notice of in my passage through France—nothing but what other travellers have given an account of with much more advantage than I can. I travelled from Toulouse to Paris, and without any considerable stay came to Calais, and landed safe at Dover the 14th of January, after having a severe cold season to travel in.

I was now come to the end of my travels, and had in a little time all my new discovered estate safe about me, the bills of exchange which I brought with me having been very currently paid.

My principal guide and privy counsellor was my good ancient widow, who, in gratitude for the money I had sent her, thought no pains too much, nor care too great,

to employ for me; and I trusted her so entirely with everything, that I was perfectly easy as to the security of my
effects; and, indeed, I was very happy from the beginning,
and now to the end, in the unspotted integrity of this good
gentlewoman.

And now, having resolved to dispose of my plantation
in the Brazils, I wrote to my old friend at Lisbon, who,
having offered it to the two merchants, the survivors of
my trustees, who lived in the Brazils, they accepted the
offer, and remitted thirty-three thousand pieces of eight
to a correspondent of theirs at Lisbon to pay for it.

In return, I signed the instrument of sale in the form
which they sent from Lisbon, and sent it to my old man,
who sent me the bills of exchange for thirty-two thousand
eight hundred pieces of eight for the estate, reserving
the payment of one hundred moidores a year to him (the
old man) during his life, and fifty moidores afterwards
to his son for his life, which I had promised them, and which
the plantation was to make good as a rent-charge. And
thus I have given the first part of a life of fortune and
adventure—a life of Providence's chequer-work, and of
a variety which the world will seldom be able to show the
like of—beginning foolishly, but closing much more happily
than any part of it ever gave me leave so much as to hope for.

Any one who would think that in this state of com-
plicated good fortune I was past running any more hazards:
and so, indeed, I had been, if other circumstances had
concurred; but I was inured to a wandering life, and no
family, nor many relations; nor, however rich, had I contracted much acquaintance; and though I had sold my
estate in the Brazils, yet I could not keep that country
out of my head, and had a great mind to be upon the wing
again; especially, I could not resist the strong inclination
I had to see my island, and to know if the poor Spaniards
were in being there. My true friend, the widow, earnestly
dissuaded me from it, and so far prevailed with me that
for almost seven years she prevented my running abroad,

during which time I took my two nephews, the children of one of my brothers, into my care; the eldest, having something of his own, I bred up as a gentleman, and gave him a settlement of some addition to his estate after my decease. The other I placed with the captain of a ship; and, after five years, finding him a sensible, bold, enterprising young fellow, I put him into a good ship, and sent him to sea; and this young fellow afterwards drew me in, as old as I was, to farther adventures myself.

In the meantime, I in part settled myself here; for, first of all, I married, and that not either to my disadvantage or dissatisfaction, and had three children, two sons and one daughter; but my wife dying, and my nephew coming home with good success from a voyage to Spain, my inclination to go abroad, and his importunity, prevailed, and engaged me to go in his ship as a private trader to the East Indies; this was in the year 1694.

In this voyage I visited my new colony in the island; saw my successors, the Spaniards; had the whole story of their lives, and of the villains I left there; how at first they insulted the poor Spaniards; how they afterwards agreed, disagreed, united, separated, and how at last the Spaniards were obliged to use violence with them; how they were subjected to the Spaniards; how honestly the Spaniards used them—a history, if it were entered into, as full of variety and wonderful accidents as my own part; particularly, also, as to their battles with the Caribbeans, who landed several times upon the island, and as to the improvement they made upon the island itself—and how five of them made an attempt upon the mainland, and brought away eleven men and five women prisoners, by which, at my coming, I found about twenty young children on the island.

Here I stayed about twenty days—left them supplies of all necessary things, and particularly of arms, powder, shot, clothes, tools, and two workmen, which I brought from England with me—viz., a carpenter and a smith.

Besides this, I shared the lands into parts with them, reserved to myself the property of the whole, but gave them such parts respectively as they agreed on; and having settled all things with them and engaged them not to leave the place, I left them there.

From thence I touched at the Brazils, from whence I sent a bark, which I bought there, with more people to the island; and in it, besides other supplies, I sent seven women, being such as I found proper for service, or for wives to such as would take them. As to the Englishmen, I promised them to send them some women from England, with a good cargo of necessaries, if they would apply themselves to planting—which I afterwards could not perform. The fellows proved very honest and diligent after they were mastered, and had their properties set apart for them. I sent them also, from the Brazils, five cows, three of them being big with calf, some sheep, and hogs, which when I came again were considerably increased.

But all these things, with an account how three hundred Caribbees came and invaded them, and ruined their plantations, and how they fought with that whole number twice and were at first defeated, and one of them killed; but, at last, a storm destroying their enemies' canoes, they famished or destroyed almost all the rest, and renewed and recovered the possession of their plantation, and still lived upon the island—all these things, with some very surprising incidents in some new adventures of my own, for ten years more, I may perhaps give a further account of hereafter.

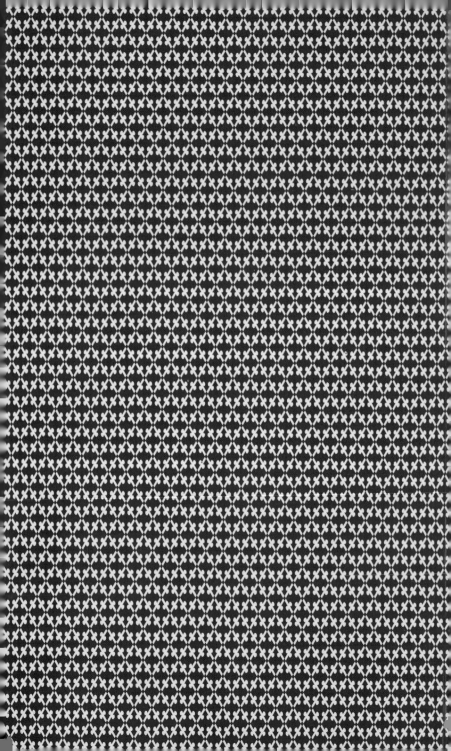